Patrick Kanouse

The nook™ Book

by Barnes & Noble

 800 East 96th Street, Indianapolis, Indiana 46240

ISBN-10: 0-7897-4119-9
ISBN-13: 978-0-7897-4119-6

The Library of Congress Cataloging-in-Publication data is on file.

Printed in the United States of America

Second Printing: March 2011

Trademarks

All terms mentioned in this book that are known to be trademarks or service marks have been appropriately capitalized. Que Publishing cannot attest to the accuracy of this information. Use of a term in this book should not be regarded as affecting the validity of any trademark or service mark.

Warning and Disclaimer

Every effort has been made to make this book as complete and as accurate as possible, but no warranty or fitness is implied. The information provided is on an "as is" basis. The author and the publisher shall have neither liability nor responsibility to any person or entity with respect to any loss or damages arising from the information contained in this book or from the use of the programs accompanying it.

Bulk Sales

Que Publishing offers excellent discounts on this book when ordered in quantity for bulk purchases or special sales. For more information, please contact

U.S. Corporate and Government Sales
1-800-382-3419
corpsales@pearsontechgroup.com

For sales outside of the U.S., please contact

International Sales
international@pearson.com

Associate Publisher
Greg Wiegand

Acquisitions Editor
Loretta Yates

Development Editor
Todd Brakke

Managing Editor
Kristy Hart

Project Editor
Betsy Harris

Copy Editor
Apostrophe Editing Services

Proofreader
Water Crest Publishing

Senior Indexer
Cheryl Lenser

Technical Editor
Todd Brakke

Publishing Coordinator
Cindy Teeters

Cover Designer
Anne Jones

Compositor
Nonie Ratcliff

Table of Contents

About the Author

Patrick Kanouse works as the structured authoring program manager for Pearson Education. Always a bookworm, he has gladly adopted ebook reading technologies, while still appreciating and valuing the printed book.

Patrick also teaches business technical report writing at IUPUI. Outside of teaching about writing, reading on his NOOKcolor, and writing about his NOOKcolor, he writes poetry, even publishing a PubIt book at BN.com that you can read on your NOOKcolor or NOOK. His website is patrickkanouse.com.

Patrick lives in Westfield, Indiana, with his wife and two Yorkies.

Dedication

This book is dedicated to my wife, Gina, who has always supported my every endeavor, even if it is immersed in some ancient history reading or volumes of poetry. Without her support, nothing that I attempt would be possible.

Acknowledgments

This book would not have been possible without Jim Cheshire's first edition, which was so well written that updating its content for this new edition was a minor task indeed. Thanks to Loretta Yates for asking me to revise and write this edition and to the efforts of the book team to make my words sound good: Todd Brakke, Betsy Harris, and San Dee Phillips.

I also appreciate the efforts of Angie Doyle, Mark Meyer, Jonathon Taylor, and John Herrin in assisting in testing the LendMe functions.

We Want to Hear from You!

As the reader of this book, *you* are our most important critic and commentator. We value your opinion and want to know what we're doing right, what we could do better, what areas you'd like to see us publish in, and any other words of wisdom you're willing to pass our way.

As an associate publisher for Que Publishing, I welcome your comments. You can email or write me directly to let me know what you did or didn't like about this book—as well as what we can do to make our books better.

Please note that I cannot help you with technical problems related to the topic of this book. We do have a User Services group, however, where I will forward specific technical questions related to the book.

When you write, please be sure to include this book's title and author as well as your name, email address, and phone number. I will carefully review your comments and share them with the author and editors who worked on the book.

Email: feedback@quepublishing.com

Mail: Greg Wiegand
          Associate Publisher
          Que Publishing
          800 East 96th Street
          Indianapolis, IN 46240 USA

Reader Services

Visit our website and register this book at quepublishing.com/register for convenient access to any updates, downloads, or errata that might be available for this book.

Introduction

Congratulations on your purchase of the NOOKcolor or NOOK, Barnes & Noble's (simply B&N from here on) ebook readers. The NOOKcolor, which debuted in November 2010, is a multitouch VividView color screen. The original NOOK, which first went on sale late in 2009, features an E Ink reading display that bears a remarkable resemblance to paper.

The NOOKcolor resembles a tablet like the iPad or Samsung Galaxy in many ways, but B&N has intentionally focused it as an ereading device without the full set of features to be found in a tablet. This focuses attention on the reading experience of books, newspapers, and magazines while keeping the price down. The NOOKcolor is an attempt to balance the features of the tablet with the immersive experience of reading. The NOOKcolor can hold approximately 6,000 books out-of-the-box. (The original NOOK can hold approximately 1,500 books.) In other words, if you read one book per week, your NOOKcolor can hold enough books for almost 116 years of reading, and if you add a microSD card to your NOOKcolor, you can easily hold enough books for many lifetimes!

> TIP: Many NOOKcolor owners refer to other NOOKcolor owners as NOOKies.

This book is intended to give you all the information you need to get the most out of your NOOKcolor and the associated supporting applications. You not only learn how to use your NOOKcolor and NOOK, but you also learn all the best places to get books and other content. After you've learned all the great resources available for books, you'll quickly find that you need a way to organize your ebooks, so you also learn how to do that using a free tool called Calibre.

By the time you finish this book, you'll be comfortable with all aspects of your NOOKcolor and NOOK. Following are some of the many things you can learn how to do in this book:

- ▶ Add your own pictures for use as a wallpaper or screensaver.
- ▶ Use the B&N's unique LendMe feature to lend and borrow books.
- ▶ Play music, audiobooks, podcasts, and more.
- ▶ Watch video.

▶ Read your ebooks on your iPhone, iPod Touch, iPad, computer, Android phone, or Blackberry.

▶ Get books (many free) from many sources on the Internet and load them onto your NOOKcolor and NOOK.

▶ Manage all your ebooks, and update author and title information if needed.

▶ Automatically download full-color covers for your books that display on your NOOKcolor and NOOK.

▶ Use your NOOKcolor and NOOK to browse the Web.

▶ Use your NOOKcolor to use enhanced features for children's and other books.

▶ Take advantage of special offers in B&N stores.

▶ Use highlights and bookmarks.

▶ Learn how to publish your books using B&N's PubIt feature.

▶ Install third-party applications on your NOOK to add functionality to it.

This book is divided into three parts:

▶ Part I, "NOOKcolor," focuses exclusively on using the NOOKcolor.

▶ Part II, "NOOK," focuses on using the NOOK and rooting it.

▶ Part III, "Beyond the NOOKs," focuses on using the NOOK-related apps, Calibre, and B&N's PubIt.

Mixed in with all this, you can find plenty of tips and tricks to help you get the most from your NOOKcolor and NOOK. You can also find a comprehensive list of questions and answers based on questions from actual NOOKcolor and NOOK owners.

NOTE: Writing this book presents a unique challenge. The E Ink original NOOK has some limitations with images. Although the images do appear, complex images or images with lots of information can be tedious to see. The NOOKcolor, however, presents images in a much better fashion, as do the related NOOK apps (excepting the Blackberry eReader app). Hence, for all aspects of the NOOKcolor and NOOK apps, the use of images will be more substantial than with the original NOOK chapters.

NOTE: Throughout this book you will encounter the terms *ebook* and *NOOKbook*. ebook will be used generically. NOOKbooks is what B&N calls its version of ebooks that it sells through B&N. These are still ebooks, and NOOKbook is more of a marketing piece, but the distinction is useful because only NOOKbooks sync between devices and support social features. Also, only NOOKbooks are visible in My NOOK Library on BN.com.

It's my hope that you don't have any questions about using your NOOK after reading this book, but if you do, please don't hesitate to send me email at NOOK@patrickkanouse.com. I'll gladly help if I can.

Thank you for buying *The NOOK Book*!

CHAPTER 1

Getting Started with Your NOOKcolor

Before we get into the details of using your NOOKcolor, let's take a look at some of the basics: gestures, setup, and basic navigation. With these basics in place, we'll then be able to discover all the other incredible things your NOOKcolor can do.

> NOTE: Barnes & Noble uses a lowercase *n* when it spells *NOOKcolor* and for the NOOKcolor's logo.

Understanding NOOKcolor Gestures

The NOOKcolor, excepting the Power button, Home button, and volume controls, is controlled by gestures:

- **Tap**: This is the most common gesture. Just press your finger to the screen and raise it. Usually you use this gesture with buttons and covers.

- **Press and Hold**: This is the same as the Tap gesture, but instead of raising your finger, you hold it to the screen for a couple of seconds. This often opens an additional menu from which to choose by a Tap, but you can encounter other results from a Press and Hold.

- **Swipe Left/Swipe Right**: The gesture, mostly, for turning pages. Like a Tap, touch your finger on the screen and quickly drag it to the left (or right) and lift your finger up.

- **Scroll**: Essentially the vertical version of the Swipe gesture. You can control the speed of the scroll by swiping up or down more rapidly. You can slow down or stop the scroll by Tapping the screen (to stop) or Pressing and Holding to slow the scroll.

- **Pinch and Zoom In/Pinch and Zoom Out**: This is a method for zooming in or out on pictures, PDFs, web pages, and so on. To zoom in or show part of the screen more closely, you place your index finger and thumb closely together on the screen (that is, pinch) and spread them apart. To zoom out or show more of the screen, you do the Pinch and Zoom In gesture in reverse—this is also called Unpinch.

Setting Up and Registering Your NOOKcolor

When you first turn on your NOOKcolor, you see a video that walks you through the basics of getting started, though you can tap Skip This Video. (You can see the video and some others related to using the NOOKcolor at http://www.barnesandnoble.com/nookcolor/support/).

The first step in getting started with your NOOKcolor is to set up and register it with Barnes & Noble (simply B&N from now on). First, you need to agree to the terms of service (see Figure 1.1). Then you see a screen to set your time zone. Choose your time zone and tap Next.

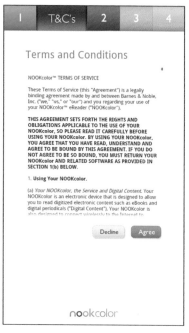

FIGURE 1.1   The Terms and Conditions screen appears when you start registering your NOOKcolor.

The next step is to set up the Wi-Fi access (see Figure 1.2). You can go to a B&N store, and your NOOKcolor will recognize its network and log on automatically. More likely, though, you are at home, so you need to set up the NOOKcolor to access your wireless network.

FIGURE 1.2   Pick your Wi-Fi network.

After you choose your time zone, your NOOKcolor searches for available networks. Choose your network. If it is password protected, you will be provided the opportunity to enter a password.

NOTE: Want Wi-Fi access on the go? The NOOKcolor and NOOK Wi-Fi need only a wireless network to access the Daily (articles from B&N), subscription content, and so on. Many wireless companies such as Verizon offer mobile Wi-Fi hotspots at reasonable prices. A mobile hotspot uses the 3G or 4G cellular network but treats it as a Wi-Fi connection, so you never need to be without wireless access.

Next you register your NOOKcolor. After signing on to a Wi-Fi network, you land on the Sign In screen. If you have an existing B&N account, enter your account information and tap Submit. If you don't have an account, you can create one by tapping Create an Account. Fill out the form and tap Submit (see Figure 1.3).

FIGURE 1.3   Create a B&N account if you do not already have one.

> NOTE: You can also set up a B&N account on your computer by visiting www.NOOKcolor.com/setup.

For more information on connecting your NOOKcolor to a Wi-Fi hotspot after your initial set up, **see** "Using Wi-Fi Hotspots," later in this chapter.

> TIP: There's a great walk-through video showing how to register your NOOKcolor at http://www.barnesandnoble.com/nookcolor/support/.

To register your NOOKcolor, you also need to provide a default credit card with a valid billing address to be associated with your B&N account. That said, you aren't required to register your NOOKcolor, but if you want to purchase ebooks from the B&N store, lend and borrow books using the LendMe feature, or use the special features available while in a B&N store, you need to register.

Using Wi-Fi Hotspots

Your NOOKcolor can connect to Wi-Fi networks other than the one you initially set up. B&N offers free Wi-Fi access in all B&N stores. If you take your NOOKcolor to a B&N store, it will automatically connect to the Wi-Fi hotspot in that store.

For more information on using your NOOKcolor in a B&N store, **see** Chapter 17, "Shopping and Visiting B&N on Your NOOK."

To connect your NOOKcolor to a Wi-Fi hotspot other than one in a B&N store, follow these steps:

1. Tap the Nav Arrow. (It's the up-point arrow just above the Home button.) This displays the Quick Nav Bar. You look at the Quick Nav Bar later, but for now tap Settings.

2. Tap Wireless on the touchscreen. If Wi-Fi is Off, tap Off to turn it On.

3. Tap the Wi-Fi hotspot you want to use. (Your NOOKcolor displays the SSID for all Wi-Fi hotspots in range.)

4. If required, enter the password for your Wi-Fi hotspot

5. Tap Connect.

Your NOOKcolor should now indicate that it is connected; you should see the Wi-Fi signal indicator in the Status Bar on the bottom right next to the battery indicator.

If your Wi-Fi hotspot isn't listed after you turn on Wi-Fi or is not in the list of Wireless Networks, tap Other Network. You can then enter the service set identifier (SSID), select the type of security (if the Wi-Fi is secured), and enter the password for your Wi-Fi hotspot if necessary. If you don't know this information, ask the person who set up the Wi-Fi network.

Your NOOKcolor can connect to a Wi-Fi hotspot that requires you to browse to a web page to authenticate yourself. For example, many hotel Wi-Fi hotspots require you to enter a room number or other information to connect. You can connect to a Wi-Fi hotspot that has this requirement by launching the web browser from the Quick Nav Bar after you've joined the Wi-Fi network.

Does My NOOKcolor's Battery Drain Faster with Wi-Fi Connected?

I tested my NOOKcolor's battery life using Wi-Fi hotspots. In my testing, the battery life was quite a bit shorter when using Wi-Fi than when not. However, Wi-Fi affects battery life only when your NOOKcolor is actually connected to a Wi-Fi hotspot. Simply having Wi-Fi turned on doesn't affect battery life.

You can significantly improve battery life by turning off Wi-Fi.

Disconnecting and Forgetting a Wi-Fi Hotspot

If you want to stop using a Wi-Fi hotspot, you have two options: disconnect or forget. Disconnect just prevents your NOOKcolor from connecting to that Wi-Fi hotspot. Forgetting the hotspot removes the information about the hotspot from your NOOKcolor. If you later want to reconnect to that hotspot, you will have to set it up all over again. To disconnect or forget a Wi-Fi hotspot, follow these steps:

1. Tap the Nav Arrow. This displays the Quick Nav Bar.

2. Tap Settings. This displays the Settings screen.

3. If Wi-Fi is turned off, turn it on.

4. Tap the Wi-Fi hotspot. This displays a pop-up window.

5. Tap Forget to disconnect from the Wi-Fi hotspot.

For more information on configuring the settings in your NOOKcolor (including turning off the Wi-Fi card), **see** "Your NOOKcolor's Settings" in Chapter 2, "Customizing and Configuring Your NOOKcolor."

Caring for Your NOOKcolor's Battery

Your NOOKcolor uses a high-tech battery called a lithium polymer battery. Unlike older rechargeable batteries, your NOOKcolor's battery doesn't suffer from a charge "memory." However, you should still follow some basic rules to maximize the life of your battery:

▶ Try to avoid fully discharging your battery. Recharge it when it gets down to about 20% or so. Although charging it repeatedly is not necessarily a bad thing, the battery seems to function optimally if you charge it only when it drops down toward that 20% area.

▶ To maximize battery life, turn off Wi-Fi and leave it off.

▶ Avoid high heat. Reading in sunlight is fine, but avoid storing your NOOKcolor near a heat source.

▶ If storing your NOOKcolor for a long period (a week or more), charge the battery to about 50% rather than giving it a full charge.

By following these steps, your NOOKcolor's battery should last years. If you do need to replace the battery, contact B&N Customer Service.

Charging Your NOOKcolor's Battery

You can charge your NOOKcolor's battery either by plugging your NOOKcolor into your computer's USB port or by plugging your NOOKcolor into a wall outlet using the supplied AC adapter. Plugging your NOOKcolor into a wall outlet charges the NOOKcolor more quickly.

> TIP: Just like any electronic device, your NOOKcolor is susceptible to power spikes and other electrical anomalies. If you want to ensure that your NOOKcolor is protected from electrical problems, plug it into a surge suppressor.

When You Are Not Reading

When you finish reading, you should let your NOOKcolor go to sleep instead of turning it off. You can force the NOOKcolor to sleep by pressing and quickly letting go of the Power button.

By leaving your NOOKcolor on with Wi-Fi on, it will occasionally download content from B&N such as subscription content and any books that you purchase from the B&N website. When you're ready to start reading again, simply press and release the power switch at the top of your NOOKcolor to wake it up. Alternatively, you can press the Home button.

Your NOOKcolor's Controls

Before you get into enjoying content on your NOOKcolor, let's go over the controls on your NOOKcolor (see Figure 1.4).

The Power Button

The Power button is the sole button on the top left side of the NOOKcolor. In addition to powering your NOOKcolor on and off, the Power button can wake your NOOKcolor when it's sleeping or put it to sleep when you finish reading.

To put your NOOKcolor to sleep or wake it using the Power button, press and release the Power button quickly. To turn off your NOOKcolor, press and hold the Power button for 5 seconds. To turn on your NOOKcolor again, press and release the Power button quickly.

Power button —

Volume controls

Micro SD Card
slot (on back)

Home button

FIGURE 1.4   Your NOOKcolor's controls.

The Home Button

The Home button is identified by the NOOKcolor logo (a lowercase n) and is located in the center of the black bar along at the bottom of the touchscreen display. Like the Power button, the Home button performs more than one function.

You can wake your NOOKcolor by pressing the Home button. If the touchscreen is already illuminated, tapping the Home button takes you to your NOOKcolor's Home screen.

The Volume Buttons

These two buttons at the top right of the NOOKcolor control the volume. If no videos, music, or other sounds is playing, the Volume buttons control the Notification volume (that is, when something new arrives such as subscription content). When video, music, or other sounds are playing, the Volume buttons control the sound of the media.

How Should I Clean My NOOKcolor's Touchscreen?

Your NOOKcolor's touchscreen is going to get dirty and covered in fingerprints. The best way to clean it is using a dry, microfiber cloth like the one you would use to clean eyeglasses. If you must use a cleaning fluid, spray it lightly on the cloth and then wipe the touchscreen. Use only cleaning sprays designed for cleaning LCD screens.

The Standard Touchscreen Menus

Because you interact with your NOOKcolor almost wholly by touch, it is a good idea to become oriented to the basic, consistent menus that you will see. The basics are covered here, but as you move along through the book, the details of each menu and its offerings will be provided.

The Home Screen

The Home screen is the default opening screen (assuming you are not reading a book) and the screen you end up on if you press the Home button. The Home screen has several features (see Figure 1.5).

FIGURE 1.5   The Home screen offers many ways to open ebooks.

▶ **The Daily Shelf**: The Daily is a row of cover icons just above the Nav Arrow. You can swipe left and right through the covers. These are recently downloaded items such as today's newspaper or books purchased. You can press and hold and then drag one of the icons into the area above the Daily to keep that content readily available. You can also tap the cover to open it.

▶ **Keep Reading**: This button at the top right displays the title of the latest item you were reading. Tapping it opens that book or magazine for reading.

▸ **More**: This button at the top displays a list of recently read items, divided up into general categories: Books, Periodicals, and Files. You can tap the title to open that content for reading.

▸ **Home Page**: This is the area above the Daily and below the Keep Reading and More buttons. This is an area for you to place frequently read items or items you quickly want to access. The Home Page actually is three pages. To switch from page to page, swipe right or left.

The Quick Nav Bar

You access the Quick Nav Bar by tapping the Nav Arrow. The Quick Nav Bar provides access to many features (see Figure 1.6):

▸ **Library**: Tapping this button takes you to your library where you can access books, documents, magazines, newspapers, and more.

▸ **Shop**: Tapping this button opens the B&N bookstore, from which you can purchase content and see recommendations.

▸ **Search**: Tapping this button searches your NOOKcolor for the text you enter.

▸ **Extras**: Tapping this button takes you to the NOOK apps installed on the device.

▸ **Web**: Tapping this button takes you to the web browser.

▸ **Settings**: Tapping this button takes you to the Settings screen.

FIGURE 1.6   The Quick Nav Bar is your friend.

The Status Bar

The bar at the bottom of the touchscreen provides a plethora, depending on what you've got active or enabled on your device, of informational items along with a couple of points of quick access (from left to right):

► **Wireless Networks**: If wireless networks are in the area you can connect to but you are not currently connected to (assuming you have Wi-Fi on), the Wireless icon with a question mark appears. Tapping it, opens up a screen for you to connect to one of those networks.

► **Pandora**: If you have Pandora on, tapping this button displays the current song playing. Tapping that takes you to the Pandora app.

► **Music Play**: If you have Music Player on, tapping this button displays the current song playing. Tapping that takes you to the Music Player app.

► **Notifications**: If you tap a blank part of this screen, a notification bubble pops up letting you know about any new downloads.

► **Reading Now**: Tapping this button opens the current content being read (functions like the Keep Reading button at the top of the Home screen).

► **Nav Arrow**: Tapping this open the Quick Nav Bar.

► **Wi-Fi**: If you see the Wi-Fi logo, the NOOKcolor is connected to a Wi-Fi hotspot.

► **Battery**: Provides a visual indication of the amount of charge remaining on the battery.

► **Time**: Provides the current time.

If you tap the area where the Wi-Fi logo and battery items are, a Quick Settings screen opens (see Figure 1.7). Here you can turn Wi-Fi on or off, mute all sounds, enable or disable automatic orientation of the screen depending on the orientation of your NOOKcolor, and adjust the brightness. (Tap Brightness and then adjust the slider by tapping and dragging.) For more information about the orientation setting, **see** the "Orientation" bullet in Chapter 2.

FIGURE 1.7   The Quick Settings screen provides quick access to several common settings.

Customizing and Configuring Your NOOKcolor

Your NOOKcolor has many features that enable you to easily customize it and make it your own. There are also many settings that control how your NOOKcolor operates. In this chapter, you examine how to customize and configure your NOOKcolor.

Using Custom Wallpaper

You can customize your NOOKcolor by using custom wallpaper images. Wallpaper appears on the Home pages when you are on the Home screen.

Choosing a Wallpaper

The easiest place to change your NOOKcolor's wallpaper is to go to the Home screen. Here's how:

1. Make sure your NOOKcolor is at the Home screen by pressing the Home button.

2. In an area of the Home page without a cover, press and hold. A pop-up menu appears (see Figure 2.1).

3. Tap Change Wallpaper.

4. Tap either Wallpaper or Photo Gallery (see Figure 2.2). Wallpaper are images provided by B&N or images you have loaded into the Wallpaper folder. Photo Gallery displays any photographs in JPG, PNG, or GIF formats you have placed on your NOOKcolor.

5. If you chose Wallpaper, choose the wallpaper you want, and you are taken back to the Home screen with that image as the wallpaper. If you chose Photo Gallery, choose the photo you want. An enlarged version of the photo appears with an orange outlined box and two buttons: Save and Discard.

FIGURE 2.1   This menu appears when you press and hold on a blank area of the Home page.

FIGURE 2.2   Make use of B&N provided image, add your own, or browse the Photo Gallery.

TIP: You can place images you want to use for wallpaper in the Wallpaper folder on your NOOKcolor. (Plug your NOOKcolor into your computer and navigate to that folder.) Because the Photo Gallery displays every JPG, GIF, and PNG file on your NOOKcolor, including cover images, the Photo Gallery list can quickly become lengthy.

6. The orange outlined box is for cropping the image to the size of the wallpaper (see Figure 2.3). Whatever is *inside* the orange outlined box will be used for the wallpaper. To move that box, press and hold and then drag it around to wherever you want it. Tap Save to make it the wallpaper and return to the Home screen, or tap Discard to exit to the Home screen.

FIGURE 2.3 Pick the area of the image you want to use for your Home screen.

Following is a beneficial alternative method while you are browsing your photos:

1. Tap the Nav Arrow.

2. Tap Extras.

3. Tap Gallery.

4. Tap the photo you want to make your wallpaper. This makes that photo appear on the screen.

5. Tap the photo and then tap Wallpaper in the menu options that appear at the bottom of the image.

6. The orange outlined box is for cropping the image to the size of the wallpaper. Whatever is *inside* the orange outlined box appears as the wallpaper. To move that box, press and hold and then drag it around to wherever you want it. Tap Save to make it the wallpaper and return to the Home screen, or tap Discard to exit to the photo.

Should You Use a Specific File Format for Images?

Your NOOKcolor supports JPEG, GIF, and PNG files. For images, using either JPEG or PNG is your best option. GIF isn't a good option for photographs, but if your image is a line art or text, GIF can work fine. If you're unsure, stick with JPEG.

One Step Further—Decals

If you want to take the ultimate step in customizing your NOOKcolor, a DecalGirl skin (www.decalgirl.com) is the perfect addition. DecalGirl skins are vinyl skins with adhesive backing that you can easily apply. Many skins also include matching NOOKcolor wallpaper that provides a truly unique look.

Your NOOKcolor's Settings

Your NOOKcolor offers configurable settings for controlling many of its features. Tap Settings on the Quick Nav Bar to access the Settings screen (see Figure 2.4).

Device Info Menu

The Device Info menu shown in Figure 2.5 displays battery charge, available storage on the NOOKcolor, microSD card storage, information about your NOOKcolor, legal information, and a way to deregister the device. For more information on adding a microSD card to your NOOKcolor, see "Adding and Using a microSD Card to Your NOOKcolor." This screen also displays your NOOKcolor's serial number along with your NOOKcolor's MAC address—the hardware address of the Wi-Fi modem.

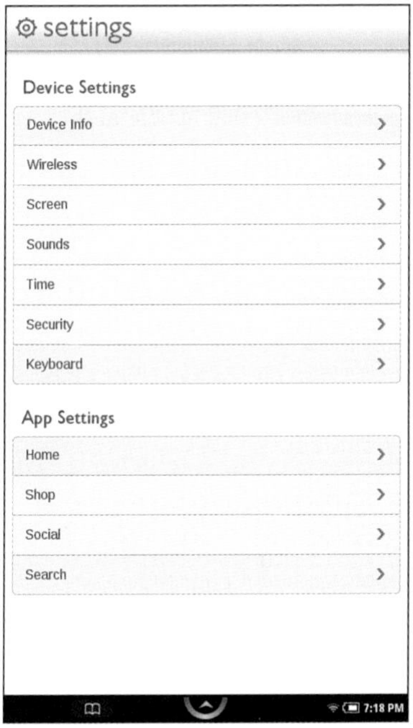

FIGURE 2.4   The Settings screen contains many options.

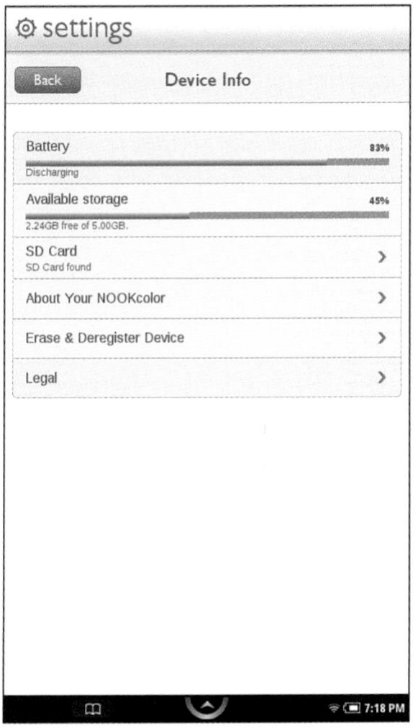

FIGURE 2.5   The Device Info menu.

If you tap About Your NOOKcolor, you see your profile information: owner name, account ID, and so on. Here you can see the software version (called *firmware*) currently installed on your NOOKcolor. B&N releases periodic updates to the NOOKcolor to improve performance and fix known issues. As long as your NOOKcolor has a connection to a Wi-Fi connection, your NOOKcolor can automatically download any updates that B&N releases.

Not all NOOKcolor owners receive new firmware updates at the same time. B&N rolls out new firmware over a period of about a week. If you want to manually update your NOOKcolor, you can visit www.barnesandnoble.com/NOOKcolor/support where B&N typically provides instructions for manually updating your NOOKcolor to the latest firmware.

If you tap Erase & Deregister, you will be warned that doing so removes all books and files, including sideloaded content, and deregistering the device. Then you have a button to do just that. You should not do this except for potentially severe problems with the NOOKcolor. More likely, you will use this if you are done with the NOOKcolor and want to give it to a friend.

> NOTE: Sideloaded content refers to all the ebooks from sources other than B&N and files you have placed on your NOOKcolor. The action of putting these files and ebooks on the NOOKcolor is called *sideloading*.

The Legal option provides more options to review the terms and conditions and such.

Wireless Menu

The Wireless menu provides options to turn the Wi-Fi on or off and to connect to Wi-Fi hotspots, which you have already done during the setup process in Chapter 1, "Getting Started with Your NOOKcolor," in the "Using Wi-Fi Hotspots" section.

Screen Menu

The Screen menu contains several options for configuring your NOOKcolor's display (see Figure 2.6).

- ▶ **Orientation**: This setting, on by default, enables switching from portrait to landscape mode automatically. Your NOOKcolor has an accelerometer in it that senses whether you hold the NOOKcolor upright or on its side. Much content can be viewed in either fashion (though not all). If you are reading or viewing content that can be in either, whenever you change from portrait to landscape or vice versa, the content adjusts its orientation as well.

FIGURE 2.6   The Screen menu.

NOTE: Some content, for example children's ebooks, are set up for either portrait or landscape mode but not both. Turning off automatic orientation does not
alter this. Therefore, if you have automatic orientation off, hold the NOOKcolor
in portrait mode, and open a children's ebook, that ebook appears in landscape
mode.

▶ **Brightness:** This setting controls the maximum brightness of the screen. To
   adjust the brightness, tap Brightness, and then drag your finger to adjust the
   slider (see Figure 2.7). When you are happy with the setting, tap OK to
   return to the menu.

▶ **Screen Timeout**: This controls the time interval after which your NOOKcolor
   puts itself to sleep. This timer is set to 2 minutes by default. To change the
   interval, tap Screen Timeout, and then tap the preferred time interval.

TIP: If you set the sleep timer to a time interval that is shorter than the
amount of time it takes you to read a page on the reading screen, your
NOOKcolor goes into sleep mode while you are reading. So be sure you set the
interval appropriately for your reading speed.

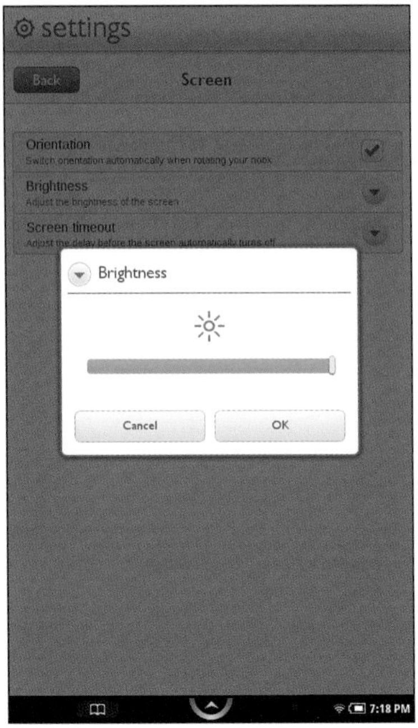

FIGURE 2.7   Adjusting the brightness of your screen lower at night makes for easier reading.

Sounds Menu

The Sounds menu contains several options for configuring your NOOKcolor's sound settings (see Figure 2.8).

▶ **Mute**: This setting turns off all sound. Even though it says "except for media," it mutes everything.

▶ **Media Volume**: This setting adjusts the volume for music, videos, and other media sound such as the reading segments of children's ebooks. To adjust the volume, tap Media Volume, and then drag your finger to adjust the slider. When you are happy with the setting, tap OK to return to the menu.

▶ **Notification Volume**: This setting adjust the volume for notifications such as disconnecting the NOOKcolor from your computer. To adjust the volume, tap Notification Volume, and then drag your finger to adjust the slider. When you are happy with the setting, tap OK to return to the menu.

FIGURE 2.8 The Sounds menu.

Time Menu

The Time menu contains several options for configuring your NOOKcolor's time settings (see Figure 2.9).

▸ **Use 24-Hour Format**: This enables you to choose between a 12-hour time format and a 24-hour time format.

▸ **Select Time Zone**: This setting enables you to select your current local time zone. Your NOOKcolor normally gets the current time using Wi-Fi access. However, if Wi-Fi service isn't available, it still displays the current time, provided you have configured your time zone. If you do not see the time zone you need here, tap Show All World Time Zones to see a longer list.

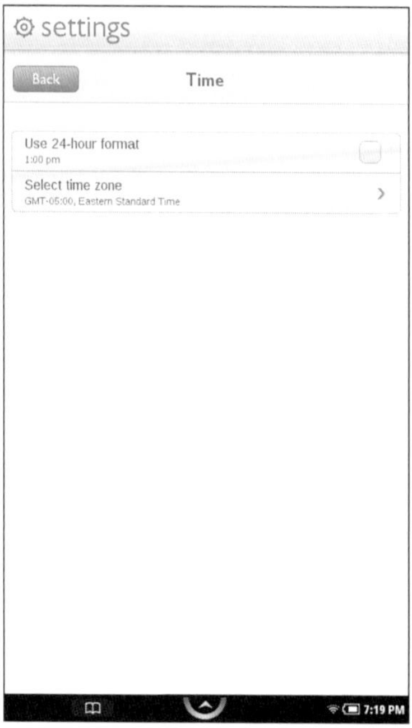

FIGURE 2.9   The Time menu.

Security Menu

The Security menu contains several options for configuring your NOOKcolor's security settings (see Figure 2.10).

▶ **Change Unlock Passcode**: This enables you to choose a four-digit passcode (or PIN) to lock your NOOKcolor when it goes to sleep or powers off (see Figure 2.11). Changing the passcode requires entering the soon-to-be-old passcode.

▶ **Require Passcode**: This setting enables the use of a passcode or not when the NOOKcolor powers on or is awoken from sleep. To gain access to the content on the NOOKcolor, a person must correctly enter the passcode.

FIGURE 2.10   The Security menu.

FIGURE 2.11   The passcode is a PIN for your NOOKcolor.

Keyboard Menu

The Keyboard menu contains several options for configuring your NOOKcolor's keyboard settings (see Figure 2.12).

▶ **Keyboard Sounds**: This enables you to set whether, when you type on the virtual keyboard, you hear click sounds every time you tap a key.

▶ **Auto-Capitalization**: This setting enables the NOOKcolor to auto-capitalize while typing. For example, if you type a period, for the next letter you type, the NOOKcolor capitalizes it. (If you don't want to capitalize that letter, tap the Shift key, which enables you to enter a lowercase letter.)

▶ **Quick Fixes**: This setting enables the NOOKcolor to correct common misspellings. For example, if you type "teh," the NOOKcolor automatically changes that to "the."

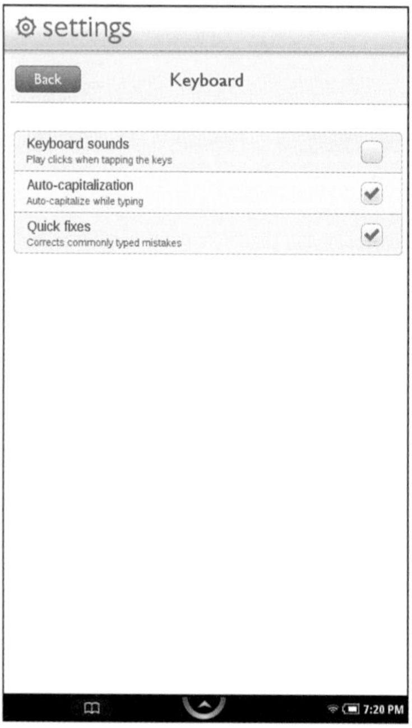

FIGURE 2.12   The Keyboard menu.

Home Menu

The Home menu contains several options for configuring your NOOKcolor's Home Screen settings.

▶ **Set Wallpaper**: This enables you to set the wallpaper. For more information about setting your wallpaper, **see** "Choosing a Wallpaper."

▶ **Clear Keep Reading List**: This setting enables you to clear the Keep Reading and More lists. The lists starts anew as you read content.

Shop Menu

The Shop menu contains several options for configuring your NOOKcolor's Shop settings (see Figure 2.13).

FIGURE 2.13   The Shop menu.

▶ **Require Password for Purchases**: This enables you to require a password entry for every purchase made through the B&N Bookstore on the NOOKcolor. Leaving this option disabled means that when you click Buy in the bookstore, you purchase it without having to enter the password.

▶ **Clear Shop Recent Searches**: This setting enables you to clear the Shop Searches. Whenever you search the B&N Bookstore on the NOOKcolor, it saves the recent searches. The searches are saved to make it easier to conduct searches. For example, you can search for ebooks related to Sherlock

Holmes but decide not to purchase now. When you go back to the B&N Bookstore on your NOOKcolor, you can type Sher, and Sherlock Holmes appears below the search text. You can then tap Sherlock Holmes and the search is performed.

Social Menu

The Social menu contains several options for configuring your NOOKcolor's Social settings (see Figure 2.14). Basically, you can link your Facebook and Twitter accounts and Google Contacts lists to this NOOKcolor, which enables you to share quotes and recommendations directly to your and your friends' Facebook walls and Twitter account.

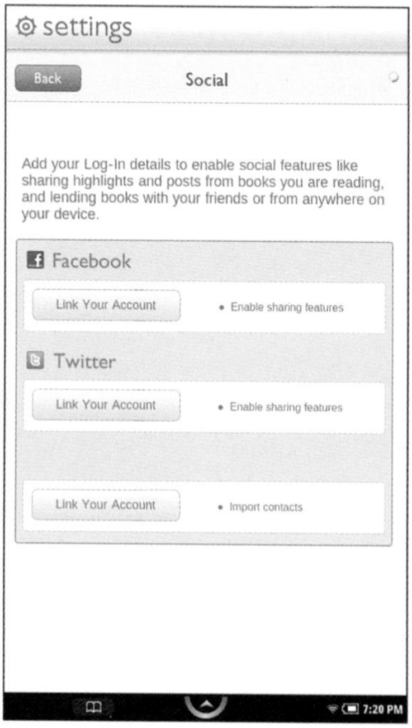

FIGURE 2.14   Connect your Facebook, Twitter, and Google Contacts with your NOOKcolor here.

▶ **Facebook**: This enables you to link your Facebook account to your NOOKcolor. If you have already linked your Facebook account, you can unlink it. To link it, tap Link Your Account. Then enter the required information and tap Log In (see Figure 2.15). For more information about Facebook with your NOOKcolor, **see** Chapter 8, "Using the Social Features of Your NOOKcolor."

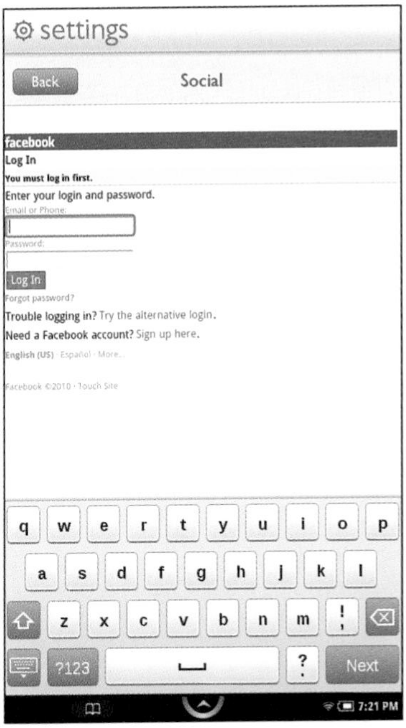

FIGURE 2.15   Link your Facebook account to your NOOKcolor.

▶ **Twitter**: This enables you to link your Twitter account to your NOOKcolor. If you have already linked your Twitter account, you can unlink it. To link it, tap Link Your Account. Then enter the required information and tap Sign In. Twitter asks you to allow this linking to occur. Tap Allow to do so (see Figure 2.16). For more information about Twitter with your NOOKcolor, **see** Chapter 8.

▶ **Google Contacts**: This enables you to link your Google Contacts list to this NOOKcolor. If you have already linked your Google Contacts list, you can unlink it. To link it, tap Link Your Account. Then enter the required information. If you want the NOOKcolor to remember this information should you come back to this screen, tap the Remember Me check box; then Tap Sign In. Google wants to know if you want to grant access to the NOOKcolor to do this linking. Tap Grant Access to do so (see Figure 2.17).

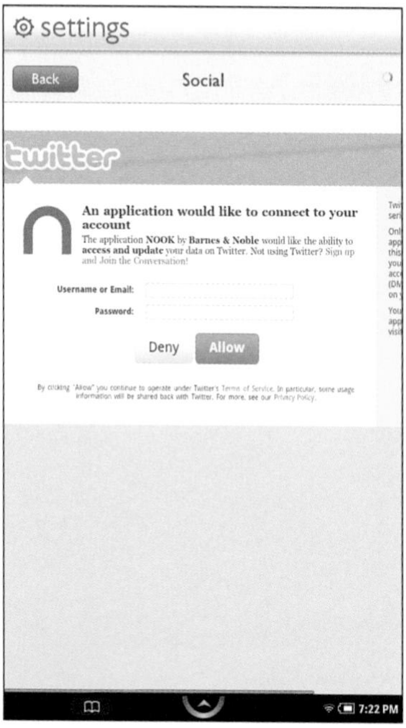

FIGURE 2.16   Link your Twitter account to your NOOKcolor.

Search Menu

The Search menu contains several options for configuring your NOOKcolor's Search setting (see Figure 2.18).

▶ **Searchable Items**: This enables you to adjust what searches are conducted on. When you tap Search from the Quick Nav Bar, you can search a variety of different categories. By default, Extras, Browser, Music, Library, and Shop are searched. You can turn off searching on Extras, Browser, and Music.

▶ **Clear Search Shortcuts**: This setting enables you to clear the list of recent searches. Whenever you search your NOOKcolor, it saves the recent searches. The searches are saved to make it easier to conduct searches.

FIGURE 2.17　Link your Google Contacts account to your NOOKcolor.

FIGURE 2.18   Adjust search functions on your NOOKcolor.

Adding and Using a microSD Card to Your NOOKcolor

Your NOOKcolor has approximately 8GB of built-in usable memory. That's enough memory for an enormous library of books. However, it might not be enough memory if you add pictures, music, videos, and audiobooks to your NOOKcolor. Therefore, your NOOKcolor's memory is expandable using a microSD card.

> TIP: A microSD card is not the same as an SD memory card like the kind typically used in digital cameras. A microSD card is approximately the size of your fingernail.

> NOTE: You will see both microSD and microSDHC. Your NOOKcolor can use either format—they are the same. The HC is used for microSD cards greater than 2GB in size.

Installing a microSD card in your NOOKcolor is easy—you don't even need to turn off your NOOKcolor.

1. Flip your NOOKcolor over so that the speaker is at the bottom. On the bottom right, flip up the metal plate (it's kept in place by a couple of small magnets) and pull it so that the small plastic connectors keeping the plate attached to the NOOKcolor are fully extended.

2. The microSD slot is the small opening. With the metal connectors of the microSD card facing the front of the NOOKcolor, slide the microSD card in, and push until it locks into place. The NOOKcolor automatically recognizes the card, and you hear a beep. Close the metal plate.

3. If the microSD card has not yet been formatted, a screen appears letting you know that formatting it will erase everything on the disk. Tap Format Now. Tap Format Now again to confirm.

On the Device Info screen (from the Quick Nav Bar, tap Setting, and then tap Device Info), tap SD Card (only available to tap if a microSD card is installed). This opens the SD Card screen. Here, you can see information related to the amount of free memory available on the microSD card.

If you tap Format SD Card, you can format the microSD card, which erases everything on the card. (This option is only available after tapping Unmount SD Card.) A confirmation screen to format and erase all data on the micro SD card appears. Tap Format to do so. Tap OK when done.

1. From the SD Card screen, tap Unmount SD Card (see Figure 2.19).

2. Flip your NOOKcolor over so that the speaker is at the bottom. On the bottom right, flip up the metal plate (it's kept in place by a couple of small magnets) and pull it so that the small plastic connectors keeping the plate attached to the NOOKcolor are fully extended.

3. With your finger, push the microSD card further into the slot. The microSD card partially pops out, letting you get a grip on it to pull it out completely. Close the metal plate.

When you connect your NOOKcolor to your computer, you now see your microSD card in addition to your NOOKcolor's built-in memory. (It is the drive called NO NAME.)

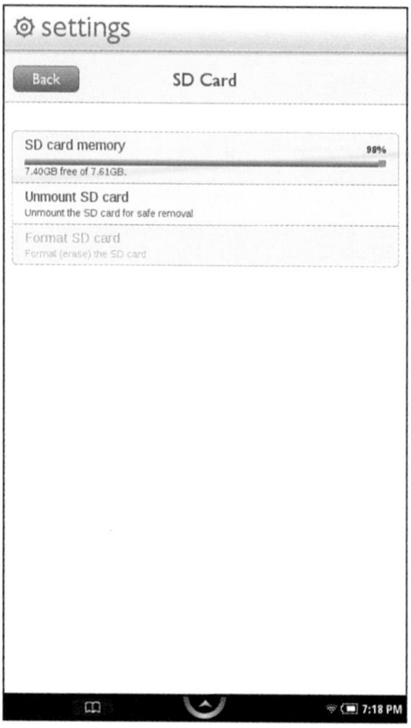

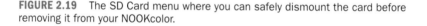

⚙ settings

Back   SD Card

SD card memory   99%
7.40GB free of 7.61GB.

Unmount SD card
Unmount the SD card for safe removal

Format SD card
Format (erase) the SD card

⌓   ⌄   📶 🔋 7:18 PM

FIGURE 2.19   The SD Card menu where you can safely dismount the card before removing it from your NOOKcolor.

NOTE: You can add a microSD card that already has items loaded on it, but the NOOKcolor folder structure is necessary, so it is easiest to install a blank microSD card into the NOOKcolor and then plug the NOOKcolor into your computer and load files into the appropriate categories (documents, videos, and so on).

Now that you have a microSD card installed, how do you access those files? From the Quick Nav Bar, tap Library and then tap My Files. You see two options near the top that you do not see if you do not have a microSD card installed: My NOOKcolor and Memory Card. By default, you are looking at the My NOOKcolor files. Tap Memory Card to switch to seeing the files on the microSD card. (Tap My NOOKcolor to go back to the NOOKcolor files.) You can then tap the folders and such just as if you were working with the My Files category. (For basic instructions in interacting with these files, **see** "Reading Microsoft Office and Other Documents on Your NOOKcolor" in Chapter 3.)

CHAPTER 3

Reading on Your NOOKcolor and Beyond

Although your NOOKcolor has many unique features and capabilities, its primary purpose is for reading ebooks and other content. One of the benefits of owning a NOOKcolor is that you can carry a complete library with you everywhere you go. If you don't happen to have your NOOKcolor with you, you can also read your ebooks on your PC, Mac, iPhone, iPad, iPod touch, Android phone, and Blackberry.

Various forms of content are available to read on Your NOOKcolor—NOOKbooks and other EPUB files, along with PDFs; Microsoft Word, Excel, and PowerPoint files; and plain text files. Appendix A, "Understanding ebook Formats," explains more about the details of ebook formats. You are probably already familiar with Microsoft documents, though you can use either the DOC or DOCX formats (and the corresponding XLS or XLSX and PPT or PPTX formats) used in all versions of Word.

Browsing Your Library

The two main places for content on your NOOKcolor are Home screen and Library.

The Home Screen

The Home screen includes the Daily Shelf, covers you have placed on the Home pages, and other ways to access your content. (**See** the section "The Home Screen" in Chapter 1, "Getting Started with Your NOOKcolor," for a complete review of the options.)

The Daily Shelf shows the most recent downloads on the left with less recent downloads on the right. Swipe left or right to see more of the Daily Shelf.

To open an ebook, magazine, or newspaper from the Home screen, tap the cover. The ebook, magazine, or newspaper opens to the last page that you were on when you closed it. However, NOOKkids books always open from the beginning.

> TIP: On an open space of the Home page, double-tap to have the book, magazine, and newspaper icons align in a grid format. Alternatively, press and hold on a blank area of the screen, and then tap Clean Up This Panel to achieve the same result.

The Home screen has three Home pages. (You can see which page you are on at the top, just beneath the Keep Reading bar by the three dots—the white one is the Home page you are on). You can add icons to the Home pages (not the Daily Shelf) by tapping and dragging a cover from the Daily Shelf. In the Library, you can press and hold a cover and then tap Add to Home from the menu that appears.

> NOTE: You can only add content purchased from B&N to the Home screen.

To remove an item from a Home page, press and hold the cover. Tap Remove from Home from the menu that appears.

To place an item on a different Home page, press and drag the cover over to the far right or left edge of the screen. The cover will slide to the next page. Release the cover.

> NOTE: If you have difficulty moving the last cover from a Home page to another, the best way to do that is to drag the cover down to the Daily Shelf, swipe to the Home page you want it on, and then drag it from the Daily Shelf to the Home page.

Finally, you can remove an item from the Daily Shelf by pressing and holding the cover. Tap Remove from Home from the menu that appears.

The Library

The Library contains all the content you've purchased from B&N and the content you have sideloaded (see Figure 3.1). This includes not only ebooks you've purchased, but also magazine and newspaper subscriptions, sample books, videos, music, Microsoft documents, PDFs, ebooks purchased from other sources, and free books downloaded from B&N and other sites.

To go to the Library, tap Library on the Quick Nav Bar. When at the Library, a set of buttons to choose from are always available:

▶ **Books**: Tapping this displays the full list of ebooks on your NOOKcolor, whether from B&N or other sources.

▶ **Magazines**: Tapping this displays the full list of magazines on your NOOKcolor, whether from B&N or other sources.

▶ **Newspapers**: Tapping this displays the full list of newspapers on your NOOKcolor, whether from B&N or other sources.

▶ **My Shelves**: Tapping this displays the shelves you have created and one default shelf: Archived.

▶ **My Files**: Tapping this displays the folders on your NOOKcolor and microSD card if installed.

▶ **LendMe**: Tapping this displays available ebooks from your library to lend, what ebooks you have borrowed, and what ebooks you have lent. For more information on the LendMe feature, **see** Chapter 4, "Lending and Borrowing Books with LendMe on Your NOOKcolor."

FIGURE 3.1   The Library where all your books and content are stored.

NOTE: For more information on using My NOOK Library on bn.com, **see** Chapter 22, "Using My NOOK Library."

If you purchase a book using the Shop on your NOOKcolor, that book is automatically downloaded to your NOOKcolor within a few minutes. If you purchase an ebook from B&N using your computer, the ebook is added to My NOOK Library on bn.com, but it isn't downloaded to your NOOKcolor automatically—though the cover appears. You can tell it was *not* downloaded because a green Download icon appears on the bottom of the cover. Tap the cover to download the NOOKbook.

CAUTION: If you plan to be away from Wi-Fi hotspots, you should make sure that the items that appear in My NOOK Library have actually been downloaded to your NOOKcolor.

So many options exist here, so work your way through each button and the myriad actions you can take in interacting with the Library.

Books

This is the default location after you tap Library from the Quick Nav Bar, unless you have tapped Newspapers or one of the other buttons, and then tapping Library from the Quick Nav Bar takes you to the last button you were on (see Figure 3.2). Note that all files placed in the microSD card's My Files\Books folder are shown here along with all NOOKbooks and documents in the NOOKcolor's My Files\Books folder or NOOKcolor's Digital Editions folder.

At the top of the screen, you have the Sort and View buttons. Tapping the Sort button enables you sort your ebooks by Title, Author, or Most Recent, which means either read or added (refer to Figure 3.2). The View by default is Grid view. Scroll up or down to view the library. The Grid view option is a series of nine squares (see Figure 3.3). Below that, you have Shelf view (you swipe left or right to view the entire shelf), Large List view, and Small List view. You can work with various Sorts and Views. For example, if you have 10 novels by Donna Leon and you sort by Author and view by Shelf view, all of Donna Leon's books appear on a shelf. Large List view shows a medium size cover, the full title, and the author. Small list view does the same, but with a small cover.

In general, sorting by title and using Shelf view is impractical (it's essentially a Large List view) because most titles are different. Table 3.1 shows some useful combinations.

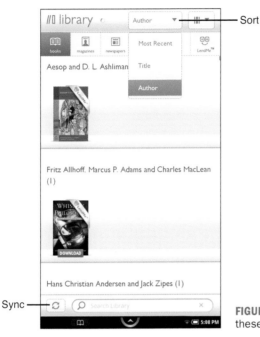

Sort

FIGURE 3.2 Sort your library by one of these choices.

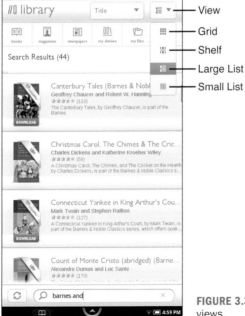

View

Grid

Shelf

Large List

Small List

FIGURE 3.3 View your library in one of these views.

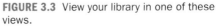

TABLE 3.1   Recommended Sort and View Combinations

Sort	View	Comments
Most Recent	Shelf	Shows the ebooks in Today, Yesterday, and date shelves
Author	Shelf	Shows the ebooks in shelves by author
Title	Grid	Shows the ebooks with large covers in a scrollable grid format
Title	Large/Small List	Shows the ebooks with covers and author information in a scrollable list format

From the Books part of the Library, you can interact with your ebooks in two ways. First, you can just tap the cover to open the ebook. Second, if you tap and hold the cover, a pop-up menu appears (see Figure 3.4) with several options:

FIGURE 3.4   The pop-up menu that appears after pressing and holding a cover.

> ▶ **Read**: This option is only available if you have downloaded the NOOKbook. Tapping this option opens the ebook for reading.

> ▶ **Download**: This option is only available if you have not yet downloaded the NOOKbook. Tapping this option downloads the NOOKbook assuming you have a Wi-Fi connection enabled.

▶ **View Details**: Tapping this option opens a screen with several options (see Figure 3.5). If it is a NOOKbook, you see the star rating from B&N. Tapping the Read button opens the ebook for reading. (Alternatively, if you have not downloaded the NOOKbook yet, you can tap Download to download the NOOKbook.)

Tap LendMe to see the LendMe screen. For more information on the LendMe feature, **see** Chapter 4.

Tap Recommend It to see the Recommend screen. For more information on the Recommend feature, **see** Chapter 8, "Using the Social Features of Your NOOKcolor."

The Overview tab provides text describing the ebook.

The More Like This tab provides cover images to NOOKbooks that B&N's computers think are like the particular book you are viewing. Tapping one of those covers opens a View Details screen for that NOOKbook.

If the NOOKbook is a sample or borrowed (for more information related to shopping and sampling NOOKbooks, **see** Chapter 9, "Shopping and Visiting B&N on Your NOOKcolor." You can tap Read Sample (or just Read for borrowed NOOKbooks) to read the sample or tap the Price button and then tap Confirm to purchase the NOOKbook.

▶ **Recommend**: Just like Recommend It from the View Details screen, you can recommend an ebook. For more information on the Recommend feature, **see** Chapter 8.

▶ **Add to Home**: This option lets you add it to the Home page with a single tap.

▶ **Add to Shelf**: This option lets you add it to a shelf. An Add to Shelf screen appears. You can tap an existing shelf to add that ebook to that shelf. Alternatively, you can tap Add to a New Shelf. The Create New Shelf screen appears. Type in the shelf name and tap Save. The shelf is created and that ebook is added to that shelf. You can add ebooks to multiple shelves.

▶ **Remove from Shelf**: This option lets you remove the ebook from a shelf. If you tap Remove from Shelf, the Select Self screen appears and displays all the shelves this ebook is in. Tap the shelf you want to remove this ebook from.

▶ **Archive**: This option lets you archive a NOOKbook. This removes it from ready access, though it does not remove it from your My NOOK Library at B&N. If the NOOKbook is already archived, this option reads Unarchive. Tapping it unarchives the NOOKbook.

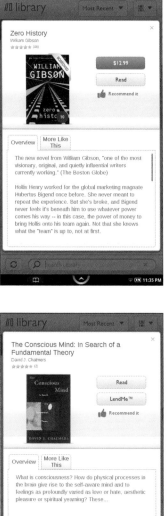

A Borrowed Book's
View Details screen

Standard View
Details screen

FIGURE 3.5   The View Details screen.

TIP: You can manage your ebook library (including archiving and unarchiving items) using My NOOK Library at bn.com. My NOOK Library is covered in detail in Chapter 22.

▶ **LendMe**: As in the View Details screen, you can lend a NOOKbook from this menu. For more information on the LendMe feature, **see** Chapter 4.

Books, magazines, and newspapers purchased from B&N often have notices on the cover regarding them:

▶ **New**: This is a recent NOOKbook you have purchased and not yet downloaded.

▶ **LendMe**: This NOOKbook can be lent to a friend.

▶ **Borrowed**: You have borrowed this NOOKbook from a friend. The number of days left (out of 14) is in a small, gray circle at the bottom right of the cover.

▶ **Lent**: You have lent this NOOKbook to a friend. The number of days left (out of 14) is in a small, gray circle at the bottom right of the cover.

▶ **Sample**: This is only a portion of the NOOKbook to give you a chance to review before you buy.

▶ **Download**: The NOOKbook is not yet downloaded. Tap the cover to download it.

Magazines

This is where B&N places all your magazines (as opposed to newspapers) that you purchase from B&N (see Figure 3.6). Also, if you placed any files in either the NOOKcolors Magazines folder or in the microSD card's My Files\Magazines folder, those documents are shown here as well. You have the same options here as you do with the Books section.

Newspapers

This is where B&N places all your newspapers (as opposed to magazines) that you purchase from B&N (see Figure 3.7). Also, if you have placed any files in either the NOOKcolors Newspapers folder or in the microSD card's My Files\Newspapers folder, those documents are shown here as well. You have the same options here as you do with the Books section.

FIGURE 3.6   The Magazines screen.

FIGURE 3.7   The Newspapers screen.

My Shelves

The NOOKcolor enables you to organize your ebooks into categories, or shelves, that you can name (see Figure 3.8). If you have a lot of ebooks and you want to categorize them beyond just author name, title, and most recent, this is how you can do it.

FIGURE 3.8   The My Shelves view.

My Shelves shows you any existing shelves. (Two exist by default: Favorites and Archived.) To add a shelf, tap Create New Shelf. The Create New Shelf screen appears. Type the name of the shelf and tap Save.

You can also edit existing shelves by tapping Edit next to the shelf you want to edit (see Figure 3.9). Here you can do several things. A listing of titles appears. To add titles to this shelf, tap the check box next to the title so that a check mark appears. Tap Save to add those titles to the shelf. Tapping Remove, instead, removes those titles from the shelf. Tap Rename to rename the shelf.

My Files

My Files lets you access files on the NOOKcolor internal memory or on the microSD card. The view defaults to the files on your NOOKcolor. Tap Memory Card, which appears only if a microSD card is installed, to access the files there.

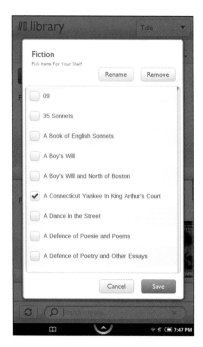

FIGURE 3.9   Edit existing shelves.

The folder structure on the NOOKcolor and on the microSD card is straightforward, as shown in Figure 3.10. You can view either the folders and files with small or large folder icons by tapping the View icon. Books, Magazines, and Newspapers have already been covered because they appear in the appropriate locations in the Library.

> NOTE: Adobe Digital Editions (ADE) ebooks also appear in the Books section of the Library. For more information about ADE ebooks, see Appendix A.

Interacting with documents, music, and videos is covered in the appropriate sections throughout this book.

LendMe

For more information on the LendMe feature, **see** Chapter 4.

The Sync button forces a sync with My NOOK Library, downloading any new content, and so on. You can also tap the Search Library box to search your library for particular books and such.

FIGURE 3.10   Two views of the My Shelves screen.

How Can I Delete Sideloaded Content Because There Isn't a Menu Option for Removing It?

Sideloaded content—ebooks and documents not purchased from BN.com— must be deleted by connecting your NOOKcolor to your computer and removing the content. The easiest way to manage your sideloaded content is to use Calibre, a free ebook management application. Calibre is covered in Chapter 21, "Managing Your ebooks with Calibre."

Reading NOOKbooks on Your NOOKcolor

If you open a NOOKbook or sideloaded EPUB file for the first time, after you select it, you are taken to the starting point that the publisher has chosen for that item. This might or might not be the first page. For example, some ebooks open on the first page of Chapter 1. Other ebooks open on the cover or title page. The publisher of the book decides which page is visible when you first open an ebook.

NOTE: You can expect in early 2011 to begin seeing cookbooks with embedded video. How do you make cute chocolate curls or cut up a chicken? Tap to see.

If you are opening a NOOKbook that you have read on the NOOKcolor before in any of the NOOK apps, NOOKstudy, or original NOOK, you are taken to the last location you were reading. If you open a sideloaded EPUB file you have read on the NOOKcolor before, it opens to the last page you were on in the NOOKcolor. In other words, non-B&N content does not sync across applications.

As you're reading, swipe right across the page to go to the previous page or swipe left across the page to go to the next page.

Of course, there's more to reading books than just reading, right? Figure 3.11 shows the reading screen and the Reading Tools available. To see the Reading Tools, quickly tap the reading screen.

Following are features of the Reading Tools:

- ▶ **Bookmark**: Tap this to add a bookmark. Chapter 5, "Using Highlights, Bookmarks, and Annotations," covers using bookmarks in detail.

- ▶ **Scroll Bar**: Drag this to quickly slide through the book.

- ▶ **Flag**: Appears only for B&N purchased content. Tap this to access some options not on the Reading Tools bar. **See** Chapter 8 for more details.

▶ **Reading Tools Bar**: This bar has five buttons: Content, Search, Share, Text, and Brightness. You see each of these buttons in action in the following sections.

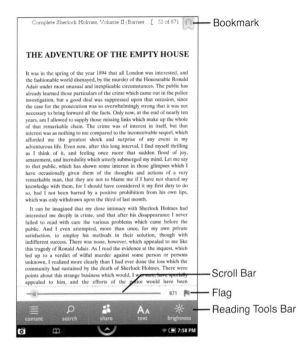

FIGURE 3.11   The reading interface.

To exit the Reading Tools, tap anywhere on the reading screen without those tools appearing.

Finally, while reading, you can press and hold on a word. The Text Selection Toolbar appears (see Figure 3.12). If you want to select more than that single word, drag the selection highlight to the end of the block of text you want to select. For the Highlight, Note, and Look Up button, **see** Chapter 5. For the Share button, **see** Chapter 8. Looking up words is discussed in the "Looking Up Words" section of this chapter.

Changing the Text Font and Text Size

Your NOOKcolor enables you to easily change the text font and text size while reading. To change the font or the text size, tap the reading screen, and then tap Text on the Reading Tools bar (see Figure 3.13).

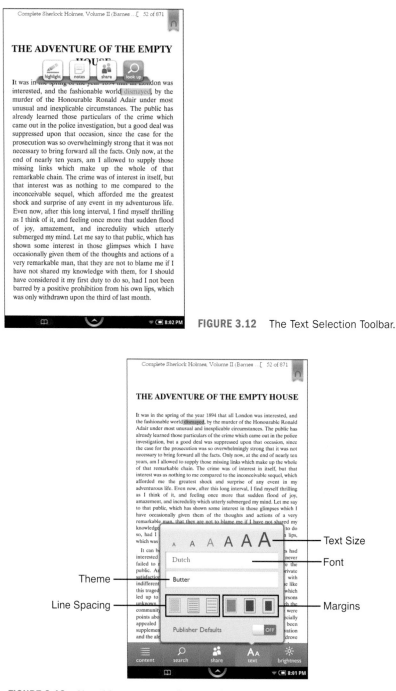

FIGURE 3.12   The Text Selection Toolbar.

FIGURE 3.13   Use this screen to adjust the font size among other things.

Your NOOKcolor supports six text sizes, represented by the A. The current text size A is colored teal. Tap the A for the size you want. You can see the text size adjust behind the text menu. Adjust the text size to whichever size you want.

To change the text font, tap the Font selection, which enlarges and shows a check mark next to the current font. You have six fonts to choose from, and you can see a representation of them in the Font selection. (Scroll to see all the fonts.) You can see the font change.

- ▶ You cannot change the text font if the publisher created the content with a specific font embedded in it.

- ▶ You cannot change the text font for PDF files. If the creator of the PDF file embedded a particular font, your NOOKcolor uses that font. Otherwise, it uses the default font.

- ▶ Some ebooks consist of pages scanned as images, usually as PDF files. You cannot change the text font for these ebooks.

> NOTE: Tapping Publisher Defaults to On changes all settings on this screen to the options chosen by the Publisher for all content that you read. You can toggle that back to Off at anytime.

Changing the Color Theme, Line Spacing, Margins, and Brightness

Your NOOKcolor enables you to change the color scheme, space between lines, and margins while reading. To change these, tap the reading screen, and then tap Text on the Reading Tools bar.

Tap the Theme box to change the color settings for the background and text. You have six options ranging from Normal (black on white) to Night (white on black). Tap your choice. The reading screen changes to reflect that, so choose any you like.

> TIP: With Butter, the background screen is not so white. However, if you read at night with no ambient light, you might prefer the Night or Gray option.

The Line Spacing options are similar to using single-space or double-space. The current selection is in a teal color, and you have three options. Tap the option you want. The reading screen adjusts.

The Margin options determine the amount of white space on the right and left sides of the text. The current selection is in a teal color, and you have three options. Tap the option you want. The reading screen adjusts.

To adjust the Brightness of the screen, tap Brightness. You see the familiar scrollbar that you can tap and drag to the desired brightness.

Looking Up Words

One of the most convenient features of your NOOKcolor is to quickly look up the definitions of words you don't know. If you're reading a book and encounter a word you don't know or are curious about, press and hold on that word until the Text Selection toolbar appears. Tap Look Up. A window appears with a dictionary entry (see Figure 3.14). You can also tap Wikipedia or Google. Tapping either takes you to the browser, opens up the corresponding website, and enters that word as the search criteria. (Tap the Keep Reading link Status bar to return quickly to your book.)

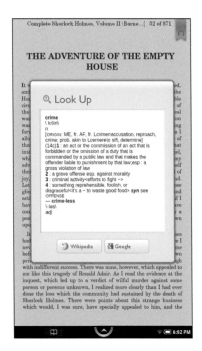

FIGURE 3.14   Your dictionary goes wherever your NOOKcolor goes.

> NOTE: Looking up words is not supported for certain types of ebooks:
>
> ▶ Magazines
>
> ▶ ADE PDFs and PDFs
>
> ▶ NOOKbooks for Kids

To search your ebook, tap the Search button, and then type the text you want to search. A keyboard and text entry box appear. Type your search words and tap Search. If it finds your word, the word is highlighted in yellow (see Figure 3.15). You can then tap either the left or right keys to go to and highlight the next appearance of that word. Tap the X to exit search mode. If you want to search for a different word or phrase, tap in the box that contains your original search term.

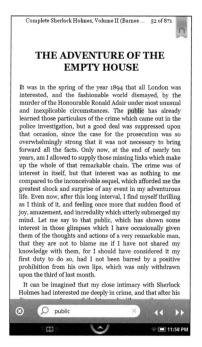

FIGURE 3.15   Searching your ebook is easy.

> TIP: Typing lots of uppercase letters? Tap the Shift key twice. (It has a white highlight around the key.) This enables you to enter only uppercase letters. Tap the Shift key again to release the caps lock.

Reading Magazines on Your NOOKcolor

In addition to books, B&N provides magazine subscriptions for your NOOKcolor. B&N automatically delivers subscription content to your NOOKcolor if a Wi-Fi connection is available. For more information on subscribing to content on your NOOKcolor, **see** Chapter 9.

B&N recognizes that many magazines are more image intensive than ebooks, and the NOOKcolor takes full advantage of that to display a rich reading environment for magazines. Often, magazines are read in landscape mode (see Figure 3.16), though portrait mode works as well.

FIGURE 3.16   Reading magazines is best in landscape view.

NOTE: Some magazines function more like newspapers (for example, *The New York Review of Books*), so if you encounter a magazine like that, use the "Reading Newspapers on Your NOOKcolor" section for more appropriate instructions.

CAUTION: Some magazines (for example, *The New Yorker*) work only on the original NOOK. These will probably be updated in the near future to also work on the NOOKcolor.

When you open a magazine, you can use pinch and zoom techniques to narrow in on pages. If you tap the page, you see the Thumbnail view at the bottom of the page (see

Figure 3.17). This is a thumbnail of each page that you can scroll through. Tap the thumbnail to go to that page.

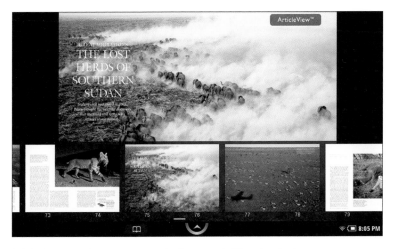

FIGURE 3.17   Scroll through a magazine's pages in Thumbnail view.

Pinching and zooming and dragging can be tedious for reading articles, and this is where the Article View comes in handy. When you see that button, tap Article View, and a secondary reading window opens on top of the magazine (see Figure 3.18). This is the text of the article (with an opening image) that you can scroll through to read more easily. Tap the X to close Article View. The good news is that your NOOKcolor remembers where you were in the article, so if you tap Article View again for that article, it takes you to where you last stopped reading. You can also swipe left and right to navigate from article to article.

While in Article View, if you tap the screen in the article, a Reading Tools bar appears (see Figure 3.19). This is slightly more limited than for ebooks, containing only Content, Text, and Brightness controls.

The Content option provides a table of contents for the magazine with brief descriptions of each article (see Figure 3.20). The Text and Brightness options are identical, excepting the Publisher Default option, as the Text and Brightness options for ebooks.

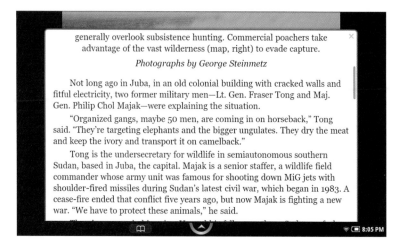

generally overlook subsistence hunting. Commercial poachers take
advantage of the vast wilderness (map, right) to evade capture.

Photographs by George Steinmetz

Not long ago in Juba, in an old colonial building with cracked walls and
fitful electricity, two former military men—Lt. Gen. Fraser Tong and Maj.
Gen. Philip Chol Majak—were explaining the situation.

"Organized gangs, maybe 50 men, are coming in on horseback," Tong
said. "They're targeting elephants and the bigger ungulates. They dry the meat
and keep the ivory and transport it on camelback."

Tong is the undersecretary for wildlife in semiautonomous southern
Sudan, based in Juba, the capital. Majak is a senior staffer, a wildlife field
commander whose army unit was famous for shooting down MiG jets with
shoulder-fired missiles during Sudan's latest civil war, which began in 1983. A
cease-fire ended that conflict five years ago, but now Majak is fighting a new
war. "We have to protect these animals," he said.

FIGURE 3.18   Reading an article.

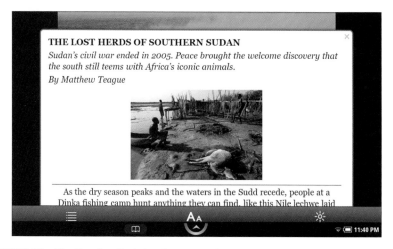

THE LOST HERDS OF SOUTHERN SUDAN

*Sudan's civil war ended in 2005. Peace brought the welcome discovery that
the south still teems with Africa's iconic animals.*

By Matthew Teague

As the dry season peaks and the waters in the Sudd recede, people at a
Dinka fishing camp hunt anything they can find, like this Nile lechwe laid

FIGURE 3.19   The Reading Tools bar in a magazine.

FIGURE 3.20   The contents of a magazine.

Reading Newspapers on Your NOOKcolor

In addition to books, B&N provides newspaper subscriptions for your NOOKcolor. B&N automatically delivers subscription content to your NOOKcolor if a Wi-Fi connection is available.

For more information on subscribing to content on your NOOKcolor, **see** Chapter 9.

Unlike books, newspaper content isn't presented in a linear format. Content is often presented as article headlines followed by a small synopsis of each article (see Figure 3.21). To read the specific article, tap the headline for that article. After an article is open, use swipe left and right gestures to navigate between pages just as you do when reading a book.

Tapping the screen displays the Reading Tools, which are the same as the ebook Read Tools (see Figure 3.22).

FIGURE 3.21   Reading a newspaper.

Tap to go to the front page of the newspaper.

Tap to go to the previous article.

Tap to go to the next article.

Reading Tools Bar

FIGURE 3.22   The Reading Tools bar is the same for ebooks and newspapers.

Many newspapers set their contents to go from section to section. Tap the Content button and tap the section (scroll if you need to) to go to that section (see Figure 3.23), where you can see a list of articles.

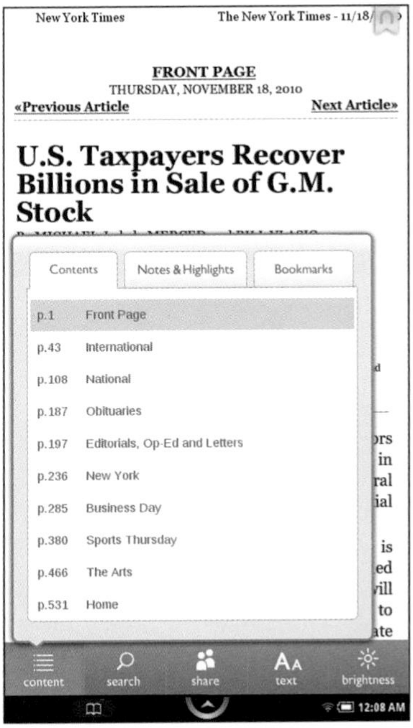

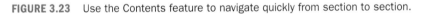

FIGURE 3.23   Use the Contents feature to navigate quickly from section to section.

Newspaper content often contains links that make navigating the content easier. For example, when reading *The New York Times*, you can move to the next or previous articles (as available) by tapping Previous Article or Next Article.

For more information on subscription content, including when your NOOKcolor automatically deletes subscription content, **see** Chapter 9.

Reading NOOKbooks for Kids on Your NOOKcolor

One of the exciting things about the NOOKcolor are the NOOKbooks for Kids; many of them (and growing) feature Read to Me. If you are shopping at BN.com, you will see two formats for children's books: NOOK kids read to me and NOOK kids. NOOK kids read to me has the enhanced Read to Me experience. The regular NOOK kids book lacks that feature, though it functions in every other way as a NOOKbook for Kids. If you are shopping from your NOOKcolor, there is not explicit indication whether the Read to Me feature is available for that NOOKbook; thus, I recommend shopping from your computer.

> NOTE: At bn.com, interactive content on NOOKbooks for Kids is also highlighted. (See the example in the book *Jamberry*.) However, at the time of this writing, the interactive NOOKbooks for Kids are unavailable.

NOOKbooks for Kids function differently than other content you read (or listen to) on the NOOKcolor. The books open in landscape mode. The first page you are presented with has at least a Read by Myself button, though it can also have a Read to Me button (see Figure 3.24).

FIGURE 3.24   Tap Read to Me to have your NOOKcolor read to you.

Read to Me opens the next page of the book, and you hear a voice reading the title (and not a mechanical voice). Each time you swipe to the next page, the voice reads the text on that page.

Read by Myself opens the next page of the book, but no voice begins reading. Instead, you can choose to have segments of the text read to you while you're reading if you want.

Picking either choice does not limit you to that choice again when you next open the book or return to the cover page.

NOOKbooks for Kids features a Thumbnail view much like magazines (see Figure 3.25). Tap the upward pointing arrow to display the thumbnails. You can then scroll through these and tap the thumbnail you want to advance directly to that page. If you chose Read to Me, after that page opens, the reading begins. Tap the downward pointing arrow to hide the thumbnails.

FIGURE 3.25   NOOKbook for Kids' Thumbnail view.

If you tap a block of text, the text displays in a whitish balloon for easier reading. In addition, you see a right-pointing yellow arrow. Tapping that arrow reads to you that particular bit of text in that balloon. This works whether you chose Read to Me or Read by Myself earlier and does not alter what happens on the next page. In other words, if you chose Read by Myself, choosing to have a balloon of text read to you does not then activate Read to Me for the rest of the NOOKbook for Kids.

> NOTE: NOOKbooks for Kids are *not* available to read on any device other than the NOOKcolor.

Reading Microsoft Office and Other Documents on Your NOOKcolor

Beyond the NOOKbooks, magazines, ebooks from other sources, and newspapers you can read, on your NOOKcolor you can also read Microsoft Office documents, HTML files, and PDFs.

Reading Microsoft Office Documents

Your NOOKcolor has Quickoffice installed, which is an application running on your NOOKcolor that can open and read Microsoft Office documents.

> NOTE: You cannot *edit* the content of Office documents on your NOOKcolor.

A great thing about this is you don't have to worry about which version of Word or Excel you have, you can open them up so long as they are valid Office documents. Have Word 2010 DOCX files? You can open these as easily as you open Word 2003 DOC files. No worries either between Mac or PC.

To open an Office document, tap Library from the Quick Nav Bar and tap My Files. You can then navigate to the location on either the NOOKcolor or microSD card where your Office document is located. (Generally, these are in the My Files\Documents folder.)

You see a listing of files. You have two options at this point. Tapping the File icon opens the file. Pressing and holding the File icon displays a menu with Read, View Details, and Add to Shelf options, which are familiar options previously described in the chapter.

The different types of Office documents have some similar and some different options available when you open them, so now look at them individually.

Word

After the Word document opens, the Status bar adds two icons: Return and Reading Tools (see Figure 3.26). Tap the Return icon to undo the most recent action. (For example, if you tap it immediately after opening the document, you return to the folder from which you opened it.)

Tap the Reading Tools icon to see a list of options:

- ▶ **Search**: Searches for words or phrases in the document.

- ▶ **Page View**: Displays individual pages versus continually flowing text. This option is available only when you are in Reflow view.

- ▶ **Reflow View**: Displays the text in continually flowing text. This option is available only when you are in Page view.

- ▶ **Go to Page**: Tap this and type the page number you want to go directly to. This option is available only when you are in Page view.

▶ **Properties**: Displays some basic information about the document.

▶ **About**: Shows information about Quickoffice.

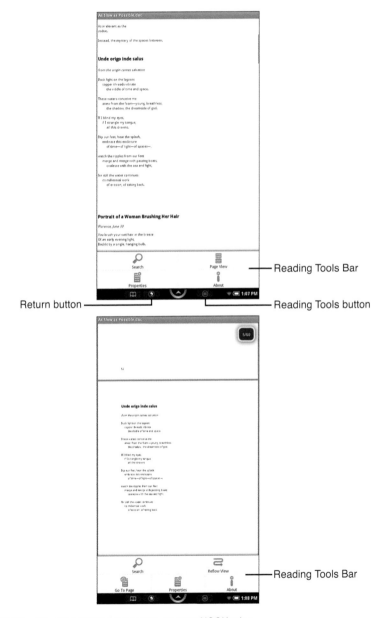

FIGURE 3.26   Reading Word documents on your NOOKcolor.

While reading Word documents in either Page or Reflow view, you can use pinch and zoom to zoom in and out of the document. If you tap the reading screen, two zoom control buttons appear at the bottom of the page.

Excel

After the Excel document opens, the Status bar adds two icons: Return and Reading Tools. Tap the Return icon to undo the most recent action. (For example, if you tap it immediately after opening the document, you return to the folder from which you opened it.)

Tap the Reading Tools icon to see a list of options (see Figure 3.27):

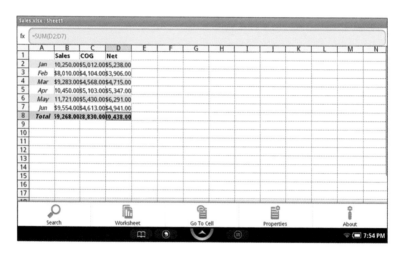

FIGURE 3.27   View Excel spreadsheets on your NOOKcolor.

▶ **Search**: Searches for words or phrases in the document.

▶ **Worksheet**: Opens a menu that enables you to move from worksheet to worksheet.

▶ **Go to Cell**: Opens a text entry screen. Type the cell (for example, D1) that you want to go to. The cell is then selected.

▶ **Properties**: Displays some basic information about the document.

▶ **About**: Shows information about Quickoffice.

While reading Excel documents, you can use pinch and zoom to zoom in and out of the document. If you tap the reading screen, two zoom control buttons appear at the bottom of the page.

The FX row at the top shows the formula or text in the selected cell. You cannot modify it, but you at least can see what is going into that cell.

PowerPoint

After the PowerPoint document opens, the Status bar adds two icons: Return and Reading Tools. Tap the Return icon to undo the most recent action. (For example, if you tap it immediately after opening the document, you return to the folder from which you opened it.)

Tap the Reading Tools icon to see a list of options (see Figure 3.28):

▶ **Go to Slide**: Tap this and type the slide number you want to go directly to. This option is available only when you are in Page view.

▶ **Start Slideshow**: Start the slideshow. During the slideshow, which advances automatically through the slides, if you tap the screen, a slide control bar appears. Use this to pause or restart the slideshow or advance to the beginning or end slides or back and forth to the next slide. The Reading Tool icon also shows a Stop Slideshow button.

▶ **Properties**: Displays some basic information about the document.

▶ **About**: Shows information about Quickoffice.

FIGURE 3.28 Watch PowerPoint presentations on your NOOKcolor.

While reading PowerPoint documents, you can use pinch and zoom to zoom in and out of the document. If you tap the reading screen, two zoom control buttons appear at the bottom of the page. Advancing through the slides is either done by either swiping (in portrait mode) or scrolling (in landscape mode).

Reading HTML Files

After you tap to open an HTML file, the HTML file is opened in the web browser. For more information about using the web browser, **see** Chapter 7, "Using NOOKextras and Surfing the Web" for more information.

Reading PDFs

This section is specifically about PDFs outside of Adobe Digital Editions PDFs (ADE PDFs). ADE PDFs operate like regular ebooks.

Similar to Office documents, when a PDF opens, the Return and Reading Tools icons appear on the Status bar.

Tap the Reading Tools icon to see a list of options (see Figure 3.29):

FIGURE 3.29   Reading a PDF document.

- ▶ **Fit Page**: Tap this to have the page of the PDF fit within the entire screen. This works in either portrait or landscape mode.

- ▶ **Fit Width**: Shows the PDF page to fit the width of that page. (In general, this means that you get a closer view of the page, particularly in landscape mode.)

▶ **Go To Page**: Tap this and type the page number you want to go directly to.

▶ **Properties**: Displays some basic information about the document.

▶ **About**: Shows information about Quickoffice.

While reading PDF documents, you can use pinch and zoom to zoom in and out of the document. If you tap the reading screen, two zoom control buttons appear at the bottom of the page (see Figure 3.30).

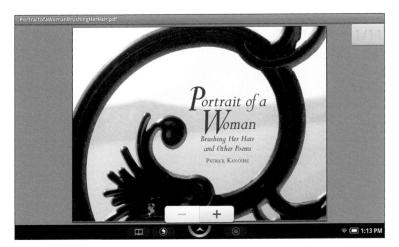

FIGURE 3.30   The Zoom controls for a PDF document.

CHAPTER 4

Lending and Borrowing Books with LendMe on Your NOOKcolor

To keep readers from sharing ebooks with all their friends, publishers usually protect ebooks with digital rights management (DRM), which ties an ebook to an individual, and unless that individual can prove that he is an authorized reader, the ebook will not open.

DRM is one of the reasons some people don't like ebooks. After all, when readers find a good read, they like to pass it on to friends and family. The number of people with whom you can share a physical book is fairly limited, but because ebooks are digital copies of a book, they can literally be shared with millions of people quite easily via email, Facebook, and any number of other methods.

One of the unique features that B&N added to your NOOKcolor is the ability to lend some NOOKbooks to other readers using the LendMe feature. Although there are some restrictions when lending and borrowing books, the LendMe feature is a step in the right direction.

Lending Books with LendMe

To lend a book to someone, the book must support LendMe. Not all books do. If a book does support lending, you see the LendMe logo on the book's page on bn.com, as shown in Figure 4.1. You also see the LendMe logo banner on the top-right corner of the cover on the NOOKcolor and in the NOOK apps.

LendMe™   This NOOKbook is Lendable How it works

FIGURE 4.1 The LendMe logo appears on a book's page at bn.com if the book is lendable.

> NOTE: When shopping for ebooks on your NOOKcolor, the LendMe logo appears as a banner on the top-right cover of the cover, just like the covers on your NOOKcolor.

The NOOKcolor has many methods for lending books to your friends.

Lending from Your Library

If you are at the Home screen or in your library:

1. Press and hold the cover and then tap LendMe. The LendMe screen appears (see Figure 4.2).

FIGURE 4.2   Tap With Contacts or On Facebook to pick a friend to lend to.

2. Tap With Contacts or On Facebook. Either option gives you a similar screen (see Figure 4.3). The primary difference is the *method* the lend offer is communicated. If you choose With Contacts, the person is sent an email. If you choose On Facebook, the offer is posted on the person's wall (see Figure 4.4).

3. Select a contact, or select Add Contact to add someone not currently in your contact list. Tap Next.

FIGURE 4.3   Select one of your Facebook friends.

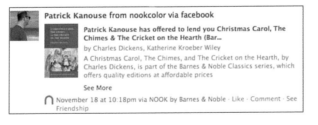

FIGURE 4.4   The loan offer appears on your friend's wall.

TIP: You can filter the Contacts list by tapping the Filter By option and choosing either All Contacts, Barnes & Noble, or Google. You can also type in the Search field to narrow the list by name.

TIP: Typed the name and selected the contact but you cannot move on to the next step? Tap the Hide Keyboard button. Now you can tap Next.

If you use the On Facebook option, tap Select Friend to see a list of your Facebook friends. Type in the Search field to narrow your search, select your friend, and tap Done.

4. Type a message to send with the lend invitation. (The message is optional.)

5. Tap Send or Post.

Your NOOKcolor sends the offer and lets you know when it is successfully sent. The cover banner LendMe changes to Lent. Also, if you visit My NOOK Library, you can see details about when the offer was sent, who is borrowing it, and when it will be back to your library (see Figure 4.5).

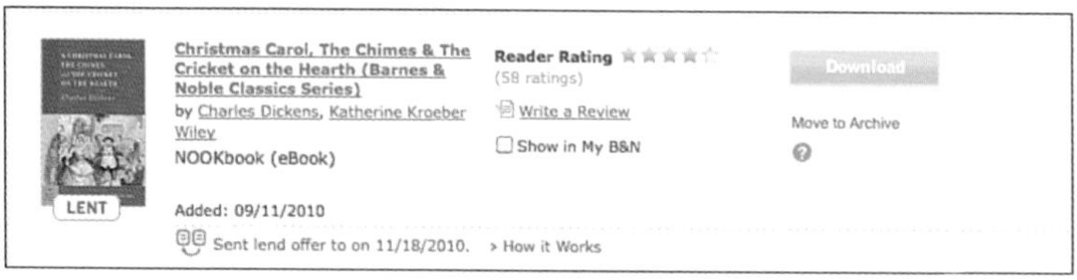

FIGURE 4.5   The loan status on My NOOK Library.

NOTE: If you press and hold a cover and tap View Details, you have a LendMe option there as well. Tap LendMe and then follow the previous steps.

Lending from LendMe in the Library

If you tap Library from the Quick Nav Bar, you see LendMe as an option. Tap LendMe. The screen shows a series of shelves. Swipe left or right to move back and forth among the covers on the shelf. The three shelves are Borrowed, Books Available for Lending, and Lent to Others. You can also tap the large red banner at the top that takes you to the LendMe app (**see** the section "Using the LendMe NOOKextra" for more information about the LendMe app). To lend books, follow the steps in the section "Lending from Your Library."

Rules for Lending

Choose carefully when lending a book because after you lend a NOOKbook, you can never lend that particular NOOKbook to anyone again. However, a NOOKbook is considered to be on loan only if your friend accepts the LendMe offer. If your friend rejects the offer or if she allows the offer to expire without accepting it, you can lend the NOOKbook again after it's returned to your library.

FIGURE 4.6 The LendMe screen.

I Want to Lend a NOOKbook to One of My Friends. Does My Friend Have to Own a NOOKcolor for Me to Lend Her a NOOKbook?

No. Your friend can read a NOOKbook you've lent to her using the NOOK apps, or original NOOK. However, your friend cannot read the book unless the email address you used to send the LendMe offer is associated with her B&N account.

The person to whom you've loaned the NOOKbook has 7 days to accept the loan offer. If she doesn't accept within 7 days, the book is returned to your library. The loan offer can also be rejected, in which case the book is returned to your library immediately.

A NOOKbook is loaned for 14 days, and while it is on loan, Lent appears on the cover and you cannot read the book. When you loan a book, you also loan your DRM rights to the book. Only one person can possess the DRM rights to a book at any one time, so you need to wait until the book is returned to your library before you can read the book again.

CAUTION: There is no way to cancel a LendMe offer.

Borrowing Books

When a friend lends you a book, you receive a notification of the offer (see Figure 4.7). You have 7 days to either accept the offer or reject it. You can accept or reject the loan offer from your NOOKcolor, original NOOK, or any of the NOOK apps.

FIGURE 4.7   Versions of the same offer on different NOOK devices: NOOK for iPad, NOOK for iPhone, NOOK for PC app, My NOOK Library, and NOOKcolor.

If you accept a loan offer from your NOOKcolor, that book is also available for the loan period in NOOK apps or original NOOK, and vice versa.

You can determine how much time is left on your loan period by looking at the cover. You see a number in the bottom right that indicates the number of days left. If you press and hold the cover and tap View Details, the price of the NOOKbook appears. You can tap the price to purchase the NOOKbook.

Using the LendMe NOOKextra

You need to understand that the LendMe NOOKextra or LendMe app is related but separate from the LendMe program. The key difference is that to use the LendMe app, your friend must also have a NOOKcolor.

If you have a circle of friends with NOOKcolors, you can see what NOOKbooks they have available to lend and make a request. Here's how you do this:

1. From the Quick Nav Bar, tap Extras. Then tap LendMe. Alternatively, from the Library, tap LendMe and then tap the Borrow Books from Friends with the LendMe App button. The LendMe NOOKextra app opens.

FIGURE 4.8   The LendMe NOOKextra app.

2. From the View menu, tap either Friends or Books depending on how you want to view what's available.

3. If you are viewing by friend, tap the friend's name for which you want to see available NOOKbooks. Tap Request to ask to borrow this NOOKbook. Alternatively if you are viewing by available books to borrow, tap the book and then tap Request to borrow this NOOKbook.

4. Type a message and tap Send. The request is sent. They see a request like that shown in Figure 4.9.

FIGURE 4.9   A friend is requesting to borrow a book.

Additionally on this screen, you have the familiar search functionality. The Refresh button updates the books available for borrowing in case someone else has borrowed it or the lender removes it from eligibility. Speaking of that, if you tap the Settings button, you can choose to show certain NOOKbooks to your friends (see Figure 4.10). If you want to hide a NOOKbook from lending, tap Show. The slider changes to Hide. You can change this back by tapping Hide.

> NOTE: You must be connected to a Wi-Fi hotspot to refresh the available books or alter the LendMe visibility. If you are not connected to a hotspot, tapping either button opens a Network Settings screen for you to choose a hotspot, if available.

FIGURE 4.10   Hide books from your friends so they cannot borrow it.

Why would you want to hide a book from lending? You may be reading it at this moment and don't want to decline a request, or you may have a friend you know wants to borrow the book. Because the book can only be lent once, you want to remove it from view so that others cannot request it and you, again, have to decline.

CHAPTER 5

Using Highlights, Bookmarks, and Annotations

Take a look at one of your favorite books, and you can likely find notes in the margins and perhaps dog-eared pages. Jotting down notes about passages that impact you or marking pages you want to come back to visit later is how you make books a personalized possession. Fortunately, you don't have to forgo these things when it comes to ebooks, because your NOOKcolor lets you easily highlight passages and add bookmarks and notes to pages.

> NOTE: Your NOOKcolor, original NOOK, NOOK apps, Barnes & Noble eReader for the Mac and Blackberry, and NOOKstudy all support adding highlights and notes. However, notes and highlights entered in the eReader software or on the original NOOK are not shared with other devices. On the NOOKcolor, NOOK apps, and NOOKstudy, if you add a note or highlight on one device, that note or highlight is available on another device—except for the original NOOK and Barnes & Noble eReader app.

Using Highlights, Notes, and Bookmarks on Your NOOKcolor

When you think of highlighting something in a book, you typically think of using a yellow highlighter marker to draw attention to portions of the text. Highlighting on your NOOKcolor is similar to that…but with a highlighter that has multiple colors all in one.

> TIP: Highlighting and notes are not supported for magazine content. You can add only highlights and notes in ebooks that support them. Caveat: Magazines that are more like newspapers (for example, *The New York Review of Books*) do support highlighting and notes.

A note in an ebook is simply a highlighted area with a message attached. Therefore, the steps necessary to add, view, edit, and delete notes are the same as the steps for using highlights.

Adding a Highlight or a Note

To highlight text or add a note in an ebook, follow these steps:

1. Press and hold a word. The word appears in a bubble, and that is your signal to raise your finger. The word is highlighted and the Text Selection toolbar appears.

2. If you want to highlight only that word, move to step 3. If you want to highlight a block of text, notice the highlighted word is bounded by two blue bars. Press, hold, and drag one of the blue bars to the location you want to end the highlight (see Figure 5.1).

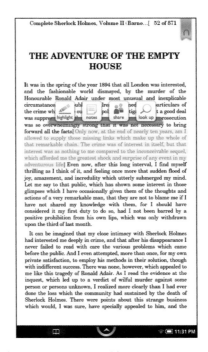

FIGURE 5.1   Highlight the text you want to add a note to.

> NOTE: The initial word highlighted must always be the first or last word in the highlight.

3. Tap Highlight to just add a highlight. Tap Note if you want to add a note. If you chose the former, the text is highlighted. If you chose the latter, the Edit Note screen appears (see Figure 5.2).

FIGURE 5.2   Enter your note.

4. Type your note and tap Post.

5. The highlight is added and a Note icon appears next in the margin (see Figure 5.3).

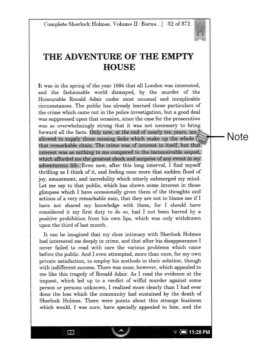

FIGURE 5.3   Your note is added.

Viewing, Editing, and Deleting Highlights and Notes

The simplest way to edit a note is to tap the highlighted text. A pop-up menu appears (see Figure 5.4), giving you several options:

- ▶ **View Note**: Tap this to view the note. This appears only if a note is attached to that highlight. After you are in the note, you can tap Edit to edit the note.

- ▶ **Edit Note**: Tap this to edit the text of the note. This appears only if a note is attached to that highlight.

- ▶ **Add Note**: Tap this to add a note to highlighted text. An Add Note screen appears. Type in your note and tap Post. This appears only if no note is attached to that highlight.

- ▶ **Remove Note**: Tap this to remove the note. The highlight will remain. This appears only if a note is attached to that highlight.

- ▶ **Remove Highlight**: Tap this to delete both the note and highlight.

▶ **Change Color**: Tap the color you want to change the color of the highlight for that particular one. You can use all three colors for highlights in the same ebook.

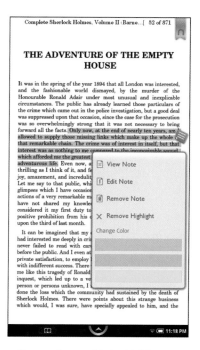

FIGURE 5.4   Your options after you have added a highlight and note.

> TIP: You can view the note text by tapping the Note icon on the page. From there, you can then tap Edit to edit the text of the note.

To navigate or jump to notes throughout an ebook, from the Reading Tools toolbar (tap the screen), tap Content. Then tap Notes & Highlights. You see a listing of the notes in the ebook (scroll if you need to see more) as shown in Figure 5.5. You see the text that was highlighted, the page number of the note, and the date and time it was last edited. Tap the particular note you want to jump to. The contents screen disappears, and you are taken to the page with the highlight or note you tapped.

A couple of other notes about this screen's contents. Two other options exist: Clear All and Notes & Highlights On/Off. If you tap Clear All, you delete all notes and highlights in the ebook. If you turn Notes & Highlights to Off, you turn off the visibility of the highlights, though the Note icon stays in the margin. You can turn Notes & Highlights back to On to have the highlights reappear.

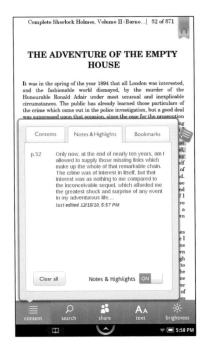

FIGURE 5.5   Jump to a specific note.

Using Bookmarks

Bookmarks enable you to easily return to a particular page. Unlike notes, bookmarks do not have any text associated with them. Bookmarks work in all your ebooks, magazines, and newspapers. Bookmarks are not supported in subscription content.

For ebooks and newspapers (and magazines that read like newspapers), to add a bookmark on the page you're reading, tap the reading screen, and then tap the icon that looks like a bookmark in the top right corner. It drops down a bit and changes to blue. Tap it again to remove the bookmark.

For magazines, to add a bookmark on the page you're reading, you must be in portrait view. Tap the reading screen and then tap the + icon in the top-right corner (see Figure 5.6). It folds down. (Think of flipping the corner of a page in a book.) Tap it again to remove the bookmark. You cannot add bookmarks or remove individual bookmarks in landscape view.

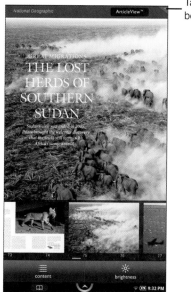

Tap to add bookmark.

FIGURE 5.6   Bookmarks in magazines.

To return to a bookmark, from the Reading Tools toolbar, tap Content and then tap Bookmarks. A list of pages containing bookmarks appears (see Figure 5.7). Tap the bookmark you want to go to; your NOOKcolor immediately takes you to that page.

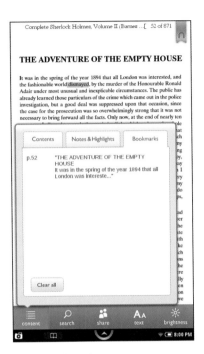

FIGURE 5.7 Jump to a specific bookmark.

To remove a bookmark, tap Clear All to remove all bookmarks in that ebook, magazine, or newspaper.

CHAPTER 6

Playing Music, Audiobooks, Podcasts, and Videos

For those of you who love to read, almost nothing stirs up as much nostalgia as the thought of listening to some nice music while reading a good book and maybe sipping a nice glass of wine. Your NOOKcolor can't make wine, but it can provide the other two ingredients to this nostalgic scene.

> NOTE: You can also listen to music via the online radio service, Pandora. To learn more about using Pandora, **see** Chapter 7's section "Playing Music with Pandora on Your NOOKcolor."

Adding Audio Files to Your NOOKcolor

The Music folder on your NOOKcolor is used specifically for audio files (whether on the NOOKcolor itself or on the microSD card). When you add audio files to this folder, your NOOKcolor recognizes the files and enables you to play the audio using its built-in audio player.

> NOTE: Your NOOKcolor supports the following audio file types: MP3, AAC, MID, MIDI, M4A, WAV, and AMR. The best options are MP3 and AAC given their ubiquitous presence.

Playing Audio on Your NOOKcolor

To play audio on your NOOKcolor, you first need to copy the MP3 files to its memory or to a microSD card in your NOOKcolor. Audio files should be copied into the Music folder (My Files\Music). If your microSD card does not have a Music folder, create one before copying audio files to it.

TIP: If you haven't done so already, first load your music into a music player on your desktop or laptop (iTunes, Media Player, and so on). Doing so enables you to set album and artist name, and so on, which affects how easy it is to navigate your music in the Music Player on your NOOKcolor.

After you copy your audio files to the Music folder, you can play them using the music player on your NOOKcolor.

Using the Music Player

The Music Player on your NOOKcolor is a basic music player. So if you're expecting an iPod on your NOOKcolor, you'll be disappointed. However, for playing background music while reading and for listening to audiobooks and podcasts, your NOOKcolor's Music Player is a great feature.

To launch the music player, from the Quick Nav Bar, tap Extras and then tap Music. The Music Player has two views for you to interact with your music: Browse and Now Playing (see Figure 6.1). If Browse appears in the top-right corner, you are in Now Playing view and vice versa.

FIGURE 6.1 Browse view in Music Player.

NOTE: Now Playing view is only available when a piece of music has been selected to play.

TIP: The speakers on your NOOKcolor are mono and don't produce great sound. You'll hear better audio if you use headphones or ear buds plugged into the mini-jack at the top of your NOOKcolor.

The following buttons are available just above the typical music control buttons in the Music Player in Browse view from left to right:

▶ **List**: Displays your music is alphabetical order (by name of the file). You can scroll through this list. Additionally, a small, fast Scroll icon appears on the right as you begin to scroll (see Figure 6.2). You can use this to scroll faster by pressing and dragging it up and down. You can use the Resort buttons on the left to drag a specific track up or down in the order. This last action permanently alters the order in this screen. Tap a track to begin playing.

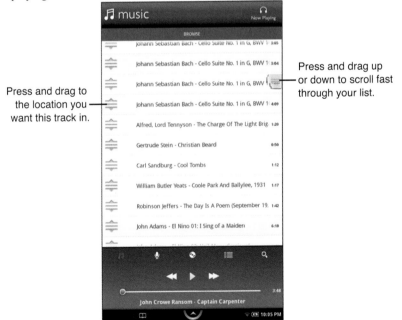

FIGURE 6.2   Viewing your music in a list.

▶ **Artist**: Displays your music according to artist. Tapping the artist name shows the albums associated with that artist. Tapping the album takes you to a List as in the previous bullet but only with that album. Tap a track to begin playing, and you go to the Now Playing view with the music playing.

▶ **CD**: Displays your music according to albums. Tapping the album takes you to a List as in the previous bullet but only with that album. Tap a track to begin playing, and you go to the Now Playing view with the music playing.

▶ **Browse**: Displays your music by most recently added.

▶ **Search**: Tapping this lets you search for artist, album, and so on. Tapping a track starts playing the track and takes you to Now Playing view. Tapping an album or artist takes you to the appropriate Album or Artist screen in Browse view.

You also have your typical music player controls:

▶ **Location in Track/Total Track Time**: Informational items only. The time listed on the left shows the time location within the track. The time on the right shows the total track time.

▶ **Play/Pause**: If the Music Player is playing audio, tapping this button pauses the audio. Otherwise, it resumes playing the audio.

▶ **Previous/Next Track**: Tapping this button takes you either to the previous or next track.

▶ **Scrubber**: The scrubber enables you to change the position in the current audio file quickly. Drag your finger on the scrubber to change the position. When you lift your finger from the touchscreen, the track plays from that location.

The following buttons (see Figure 6.3) above the typical music control buttons are available in the Music Player in Now Playing view:

TIP: If the button color is red, that feature is activated (that is, in use). If the button color is white, that particular feature is not active.

▶ **Shuffle**: Toggles shuffle mode on or off. Each time shuffle is toggled on, a new random order is created for the currently playing tracks.

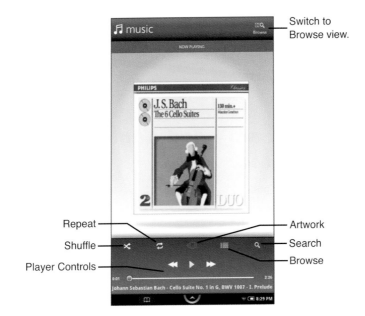

FIGURE 6.3 Now Playing view in Music Player.

▶ **Repeat**: Tapping once colors the button red, but the repeat is not activated. Tap again. A 1 appears in the center of the button. Repeat is now on. Note that it repeats the track endlessly…not just once.

▶ **Artwork**: The artwork for the track being played. (If none is available, a large music icon appears.)

▶ **Browse**: Displays your music by name. Additionally, a small, fast Scroll icon appears on the right as you begin to scroll. You can use this to scroll faster by pressing and dragging it up and down. You can use the Resort buttons on the left to drag a specific track up or down in the order. This last action permanently alters the order in this screen.

▶ **Search**: Tapping this lets you search for artist, album, and so on. Tapping a track starts playing the track and takes you to Now Playing view. Tapping an album or artist takes you to the appropriate Album or Artist screen in Browse view.

You also have your typical music player controls as indicated earlier.

While playing audio, you can tap the X button in the audio player to close the audio player interface. Your audio continues playing, but you can interact with other menus on your NOOKcolor. To stop the audio from playing, tap the Pause button prior to closing the audio player.

> TIP: Don't want to mess with opening up the Music Player, and such? From the Quick Nav Bar, tap Library, tap My Files, navigate to the Music folder, find the track you want to play, and tap that file. The Music Player opens and begins playing that track.

Playing Podcasts and Audiobooks on Your NOOKcolor

In addition to listening to music, you can also use the audio player on your NOOKcolor to play podcasts and audiobooks.

Podcasts

Podcasts are audio programs released on a regular schedule. You can subscribe to a podcast using any number of software applications, and when a new episode is released, it's automatically downloaded to your computer.

Podcasts are available that cover just about every topic of interest that you can think of. For example, podcasts can help you use your computer or help you take better pictures. Some podcasts deliver the news daily or weekly and some podcasts cover entertainment gossip. Other podcasts enable you to listen to your favorite radio shows on demand whenever you want.

If you own an iPhone, iPad, or iPod, you almost certainly already have iTunes on your computer. iTunes lets you easily subscribe to podcasts. You can search or browse for podcasts in the iTunes store. If you own a Microsoft Zune, you can subscribe to podcasts using the Zune Marketplace. If you don't already have an application that you can use to subscribe to podcasts, you can download Juice, a free podcast receiver that makes finding and subscribing to podcasts easy. Juice is available from http://juicereceiver.sourceforge.net.

When you subscribe to a podcast, each time you launch your podcast application (whether that's iTunes, Zune, Juice, or some other application), it checks for new episodes. If it finds a new episode, it downloads it automatically to your computer. You can then copy that episode to your NOOKcolor. You need to check the documentation and options for the software you use to determine where it stores podcasts it downloads.

> TIP: Be sure that you subscribe to podcasts in MP3 format. Some podcasts offer an MP3 version and versions in other formats. Only MP3 podcasts work on your NOOKcolor.

Podcasts should be copied to the Music folder on your NOOKcolor. The podcast will be available when you start the Music Player on your NOOKcolor.

Audiobooks

Audiobooks are recordings of someone reading a book out loud. They are the digital version of books on tape. The most popular source of audiobooks is Audible.com, but your NOOKcolor is not compatible with Audible audiobooks. However, you can enjoy plenty of sources of MP3 audiobooks on your NOOKcolor.

Following are sources of MP3 audiobooks you can use on your NOOKcolor:

▶ **Audiobooks.org**: Free audiobook versions of some classic books. There aren't many books here, but the ones they offer are of good quality.

▶ **Simply Audiobooks (www.simplyaudiobooks.com/downloads)**: For a few dollars per month, you can download as many audiobooks as you want. Simply Audiobooks offers both MP3 and WMA audiobooks, so be sure you choose the MP3 versions for your NOOKcolor.

▶ **B&N Audiobooks (www.barnesandnoble.com/subjects/audio)**: B&N offers a wide assortment of audiobooks. If you're a B&N member, you can get some great deals for your NOOKcolor.

▶ **Google Product Search**: Google Product Search (www.google.com/prdhp) is an excellent way to locate MP3 audiobooks. Simply search for "mp3 audiobook," and you can find a vast assortment from many merchants.

After you download an audiobook, copy it to the Music folder on your NOOKcolor. You can then play it by selecting the file from the Media Player playlist.

> TIP: You can listen to most MP3 tracks in your music player. Check out the Teaching Company's (www.teach12.com) courses, many of which are available as audio downloads. As noted, always choose the MP3 version of files.

Playing Video Files on Your NOOKcolor

No similar video player exists for videos as for music; however, watching videos on your NOOKcolor is easy. The ideal video format is MP4, though 3gp, 3g2, m4v, and OGG also work. You may want to have QuickTime Pro or another bit of software available to convert video to the MP4 format (assuming it is not DRM protected).

NOTE: Although the B&N website says that only MP4 is supported, the user manual included on the NOOKcolor indicates that the other formats are supported. The user manual is *more* correct because the NOOKcolor does support those formats.

I have had trouble getting some video to play—a blank screen with a Back button shows and that's it. I had the most success, by far, taking my Flip camera videos and converting them among the various formats and getting them to play with sound. (Though, I had more trouble with the OGG format than any.) DRM protected videos are even more troublesome. If you have a video that you can copy, rip it to your computer using MP4. That's your best bet. I expect improved video support capabilities will be available with future firmware updates.

To play a video on your NOOKcolor, you first need to copy the files to its memory or to a microSD card in your NOOKcolor. The files should be copied into the Videos folder (My Files\Videos). If your microSD card does not have a Videos folder, create one before copying audio files to it.

To play a video on your NOOKcolor, from the Quick Nav Bar, tap Library and then the My Files tab. Open the My Files folder in the list, navigate to the Videos folder, find the video you want to play, and tap the video (see Figure 6.4). The video opens with controls familiar to videos and a Back button. (Tapping this takes you back to the Videos folder.)

TIP: Have a TiVo? I do (actually, more than one). You can transfer the TV shows from TiVo to your laptop and then place these (in MP4 format) onto your NOOKcolor—TV wherever you go!

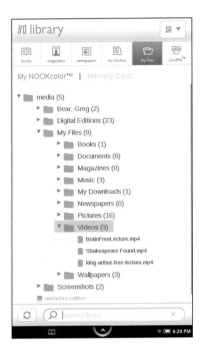

FIGURE 6.4   Navigate to the Videos folder and tap a video to play it.

CHAPTER 7

Using NOOKextras and Surfing the Web

The NOOKcolor includes a markedly improved web browser experience over the original NOOK's browser. Also, B&N added NOOKextras, which include games, the Music Player you learned about in Chapter 6, "Playing Music, Audiobooks, Podcasts, and Videos," and other items.

Using NOOKextras

NOOKextras are, for lack of a better term, apps. If you have an iPhone, iPad, or Android phone, you are familiar with these downloadable programs you can add to those devices. Well, a NOOKextra is an app created specifically for the NOOKcolor.

> NOTE: Though it is an Android-based device, you cannot download and use apps from the Android marketplace. That is...unless you root your NOOKcolor. Rooting means a legal form of hacking, and rooting your NOOKcolor is easy. See Chapter 10, "Rooting Your NOOKcolor," for how.

In the first part of 2011, B&N plans to open a NOOKextras store, where you can download and purchase additional apps. This is a curated store, which means that B&N will review and authorize the apps like Apple does for iPhone and iPad apps and unlike the Android marketplace.

You can get NOOKextras by tapping Extras from the Quick Nav Bar. B&N preloaded several NOOKextras to your NOOKcolor (see Figure 7.1).

▶ **Chess**: Tap this to play some chess.

▶ **Contacts**: Tap this to see the list of your contacts, both B&N and Google (if you linked your Google contacts).

▶ **Crossword**: Tap this to play a crossword puzzle from *The New York Sun*.

▶ **Gallery**: Tap this to open up an app to view images on the NOOKcolor.

▶ **LendMe**: Tap this to open the LendMe app (see Chapter 4, "Lending and Borrowing Books with LendMe on Your NOOKcolor," for more details about lending and borrowing NOOKbooks.

▶ **Music**: Tap this to open the Music Player (see Chapter 6 for more details about using the Music Player.

▶ **Pandora**: Tap this to open the Pandora application and listen to music.

▶ **Sudoku**: Tap this to play a game of Soduko.

FIGURE 7.1   The NOOKextras on your NOOKcolor.

Playing Chess on Your NOOKcolor

Feel like playing a game of chess? Well, your opponent is just a tap away. When you tap Chess in NOOKextras, the game opens with the board displayed (see Figure 7.2). Tap Settings to set your color (Brown, Black, or Random). Brown moves first. In settings you can also set the difficulty (Easy, Normal, or Hard). Finally, you can also set the amount of time allowed to win. On this latter setting, you can set it so that only you or the NOOKcolor or both have a designated amount of time to win the game.

FIGURE 7.2 Take on the NOOKcolor in a game of chess.

> NOTE: The time allowed is used up only when it is that player's turn. In other words, if you give yourself 5 minutes to win the game, your clock counts down only when it's your turn to move.

The game is straightforward to use. After starting the game, press and hold the piece you want to move, and drag to the spot you want it. The game does not let you make an illegal move. (It say "Wrong move!") If you mess up, you can tap Undo to go back to the previous positions.

If you tap Pause Game, you pause the game and can resume simply by tapping Resume Game. Also, if you leave the game to go read an ebook or magazine, you can return to the game by going to the Quick Nav Bar, tapping Extras, and tapping Chess.

Tap Resign to, well, you know…admit defeat.

Using Contacts on Your NOOKcolor

If you linked your Google Contacts during the set up phase discussed in the Chapter 2 "Social Menu" section, you see them here (if you haven't already attempted to share quotes yet). Tap Contacts to open the Contacts app.

Here, you can filter your contacts by All, Barnes & Noble, and Google (see Figure 7.3). By default, all are shown. The Barnes & Noble set are contacts stored only on your NOOKcolor. Google contacts are all your Google contacts (assuming you chose to link your Google account to your NOOKcolor and use Google Contacts).

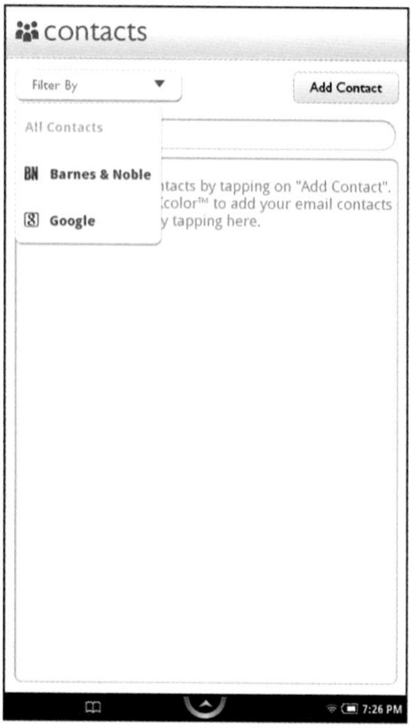

FIGURE 7.3   Filter your contacts to narrow your list.

> TIP: Until I bought my NOOKcolor, I did not use Google Contacts. But then I realized I didn't want to add a hundred contacts manually, so I went to where I kept my contacts (in this case, Mac's Address Book) and exported the contacts. I then imported them into Google Contacts (under Google Contacts' More Actions menu). I did it one time to get that.

> NOTE: If you linked Google to your NOOKcolor, you cannot edit the Google Contacts' information on the NOOKcolor.

Use the Search Contacts box to search for a specific person, or you can scroll through your list.

If you want to add a B&N contact, tap Add Contact (see Figure 7.4). Fill in the First and Last Names, and add an email address. You can add more email addresses for that contact by tapping Add New Email. Tap Done when you have entered in all the information.

If you need to later edit that contact, find it in your Contacts, tap the name, and then tap Edit. Adjust as necessary and tap Done.

FIGURE 7.4 Adding a contact is easy.

Playing Crossword on Your NOOKcolor

The NOOKcolor features a crossword puzzle game featuring crosswords from *The New York Sun*. To play, from the Quick Nav Bar, tap Extras and then tap Crossword (see Figure 7.5). Tap Game and tap your difficulty level. A new puzzle appears. You can interact in several ways with the puzzle and enter your answers (or delete your mistakes).

You can tap any of the white cells in the puzzle. It highlights the word. The darker green cell is where any letter you type appears. Tap the cell again, and it switches to either the across or the down word.

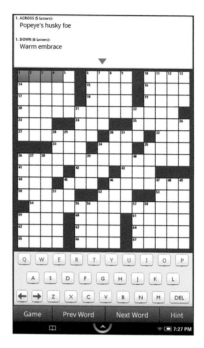

FIGURE 7.5 Play a crossword game to pass the time.

The clues to the puzzles are at the top of the screen. If you tap that area, it expands and you can scroll through either the Across or Down list. Tap the clue to highlight the word in the crossword puzzle.

You can also navigate from word to word by tapping either the Prev Word or Next Word buttons at the bottom of the screen. This particular option cycles through the words depending on your current selection.

Tapping the particular word in the crossword is the easiest to move from word to word.

To enter your answer, tap the letters as appropriate. Tapping one letter enters that letter in the cell and then moves to the next cell for you to enter the letter. Tap DEL to delete the letter. Use the arrow keys to move from letter to letter in the word.

If you get stuck, you can tap Hint and it enters the letter for the currently selected cell.

NOTE: At this time, there seems to be no way to check your puzzle's answers.

Using the Gallery on Your NOOKcolor

Gallery is a photo gallery on your NOOKcolor that displays JPG, GIF, PNG, or BMP images.

NOTE: The Gallery app in its current incarnation is not very useful for this reason: Gallery collects every JPG, GIF, PNG, or BMP on your NOOKcolor and microSD card and displays them here—every single one. If you have numerous images for covers not from NOOKbooks, when you open Gallery, you can see all of them.

Start Gallery by tapping Extras from the Quick Nav Bar. Then tap Gallery. Your photos appear (see Figure 7.6). You can choose to look at them in either Picture or Grid view. If you are in Picture view, in the top-right corner, you see an option called Grid and vice versa. Tap this to switch to the other view. You can do most of your interaction with images in Picture view. Grid view is useful for quickly navigating your photos.

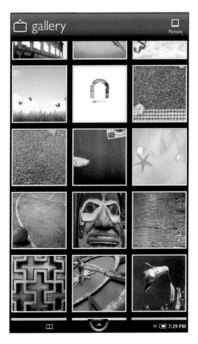

FIGURE 7.6   The gallery of images on your NOOKcolor.

When you find a photo you want to see in Picture view, tap it. The image appears all alone on the screen then. You can still move between images in Picture view by swiping right or left. You can also use pinch and zoom techniques to zoom in and out.

Tap the image to display the Photo Tools bar (see Figure 7.7). You have six options here:

FIGURE 7.7 Use the Photo Tools bar to manipulate your images.

▶ **Slideshow**: Tap this option to start a slideshow. The screen shows only the image, and after a pause the next image appears. To see the order of the images, take a look at them in Grid view before starting the slideshow.

To exit the slideshow, tap the Home button.

▶ **Wallpaper**: Tap this option to set this images as your Home screen image.

After you tap Wallpaper, a version of the photo appears with an orange outlined box and two buttons: Save and Discard. The orange outlined box is for cropping the image to the size of the wallpaper. Whatever is *inside* the orange outlined box will be used for the wallpaper. To move that box, press and hold, and then drag it around to wherever you want it. Tap Save to make it the wallpaper, and return to Gallery, or tap Discard to exit back to Gallery.

▶ **Crop**: Tap this option crop the image to remove portions of it that you do not want. When you tap Crop, the photo appears with an orange outlined box and two buttons: Save and Discard. Like making wallpaper, whatever is on the inside of the orange box is retained. With crop, however, you can tap the orange outline and drag it smaller or larger. Tap Save to make it the wallpaper and return to Gallery, or tap Discard to exit back to Gallery.

FIGURE 7.8   Adjust the orange box to crop out what you don't want in the image.

▶ **Left/Right**: These two buttons rotate the image either clockwise or counter-clockwise. Use this if an image appears on its side and you want it right-side up.

▶ **Delete**: Tap this to delete the image from your NOOKcolor.

Playing Music with Pandora on Your NOOKcolor

On the original NOOK, one of the earliest hacks to it was to add a Pandora music player. Pandora is a web-delivered streaming music service, for free (Pandora.com). You create stations based on artists or types of music, and Pandora plays music from that artist or type of music and similar types of music—think of stations as playlists.

You can create multiple stations. As you're listening to music, you can give it a thumbs up or down to indicate how well the selection matches your expectations to that station. Pandora uses this to refine the music it picks.

If you listen to Pandora on your NOOKcolor, you can leave the app to read, surf the Internet, or do other things while Pandora continues to play.

> NOTE: You must be connected to a Wi-Fi hotspot and the Internet to listen to Pandora.

A couple of things to note about Pandora: Because it is free and the licenses it has signed with music distribution companies, you can skip a song that you don't like (by tapping the Next Song button or tapping thumbs down *while* the song is playing). However, you are limited to 6 skips per station per hour and a total of 12 skips per day across all stations.

The first time you start Pandora on your NOOKcolor, you can either enter existing account information and tap Login or register for a new account by tapping Register for Free (see Figure 7.9). If the latter, fill out the Create New Account information, and tap Register for Free.

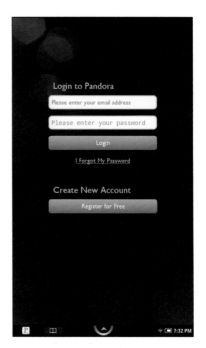

FIGURE 7.9   Setting up Pandora for the first time.

If you have an existing account, when you log in, the NOOKcolor Pandora app grabs all your stations.

After the Pandora app starts, to add a station follow these steps:

1. Tap Add Station. The Add Station screen appears.

2. In the Artist, Song, or Composer field, type in what you are looking for. Tap Done.

3. Depending on your search, you may see many results or just a few. Tap the one that best meets your needs. Pandora switches to play mode and adds the station so that you can access it any time by tapping My Stations.

Tap My Stations to see a list of your stations (see Figure 7.10). Tap the station you want to listen to. Tap Edit and then the hyphen in a Circle icon at the left to delete that station.

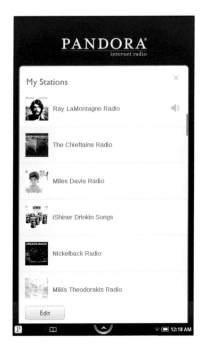

FIGURE 7.10   Your Pandora stations.

While listening to music, you can use the thumbs up or down icons, bookmark a song or artist, pause playing, or tap skip to next song (see Figure 7.11).

FIGURE 7.11   The Pandora music player.

NOTE: If you are not viewing the Pandora application (that is, you're reading a book while Pandora is playing songs), you can always tap the Pandora Notification icon to see what is playing. If you tap the Notification icon, the Pandora app opens.

Playing Sudoku on Your NOOKcolor

Sudoku is a wildly popular puzzle game, and the original NOOK had a Sudoku game (with release 1.3). You can continue to enjoy the pleasures of Sudoku on your NOOKcolor. To play Sudoku, from the Quick Nav Bar, tap Extras, and then tap Sudoku.

When you first start Sudoku, tap New Game (see Figure 7.12). Then tap which game difficulty you want. (If you have previously started a game and left it, you can either resume the existing game or tap New Game to start a new game).

NOTE: The difficulty of Sudoku is measured by the number of prefilled numbers you are provided.

FIGURE 7.12 Play Sudoku to keep your mind sharp.

A puzzle appears and you can begin play. You have two primary options for entering numbers: Pen and Notes. Notes enables you enter the possible numbers you think might fill that cell without committing to that number (see Figure 7.13). Pen enters that number as your choice. (You can easily overwrite it by choosing another or tapping Undo or Clear Cell.)

TIP: If the number appears in red in the cell, that number is already used in that row and cannot be used again.

Use the number pad to enter the numbers in either Pen or Notes mode. Undo cancels out your last action and redo reverts that back. For example, if you enter 3 in a cell and then enter 4, tapping Undo takes that cell back to 3. Tapping Redo returns it to 4. Tap Clear Cell to remove any numbers from the cell.

Tap Pause Game to stop the timer. You can then resume playing by tapping Resume Game or the arrow button in the center of the puzzle screen.

Tapping Quit Game quits that particular game, so you can play a new one.

If you leave the game to go read or surf the Internet, the game automatically pauses.

FIGURE 7.13   Use notes to help solve the puzzle as if you were writing it on paper.

Browsing the Web with Your NOOKcolor

The NOOKcolor comes with a full-featured web browser (see Figure 7.14). Right now, it does not support Flash, though it is widely expected that a future update will provide Flash support. Flash is a platform created by Adobe that allows for animation and interactivity and is used frequently on websites.

To start the browser, from the Quick Nav Bar, tap Web.

If you are familiar with the web browser on the original NOOK, forget what you knew. The NOOKcolor browser is by far a better browser experience. The original NOOK's browser displayed the page on the E Ink and you navigated with the small touchscreen. This was tedious at best. The browser on the NOOKcolor displays the whole page in color, allows you to tap links to navigate, and lets you pinch and zoom to specific locations on the web page.

NOTE: To access web pages, you must be connected to a Wi-Fi hotspot.

FIGURE 7.14   The NOOKcolor's web browser.

An Overview of Browsing on Your NOOKcolor

Browsing the web on your NOOKcolor is easy. From the Quick Nav Bar, tap Web to open the browser. The browser opens to the home page or last page you were on.

At the top, you see a typical looking web browser interface:

- ▶ **Back Button**: Tap to go back to the previous web page.

- ▶ **Address Bar**: Tap to enter a new web address or search the web. Tapping gives you the keyboard, and you can either enter a specific web address, or you can type a search term. As you type, a series of tappable links appears below the bar. This displays previously searched terms and websites. You can continue typing and tap Go, which performs a Google search.

- ▶ **Stop Button**: Tap to stop the current page loading.

- ▶ **Bookmarks**: Tap to access bookmarks, most visited sites, and your history. For more information about the Bookmarks options, **see** "Using the Bookmarks Screen."

- ▶ **Options**: Tap to access additional options, settings, and so on. For more information about the Options, **see** "Using the Browser Options."

> NOTE: You can view web pages in either portrait or landscape mode.

When you are at a web page, press and hold, and then drag to maneuver the page. You can zoom into an area of the page by either tapping twice quickly on that area of the screen or tapping once and then using the plus button at the bottom of the screen.

To zoom back out, tap twice on an area of the screen, or tap once and then use the minus button at the bottom of the screen.

> NOTE: To do a lot of the functions in the web browser, you have to wait for the page to load completely.

Tap a link to go to that link if it is a regular hyperlink (for example, going to another web page). Some links download items to your NOOKcolor. For example, if you press and hold on an image, you can get a menu to save or view the image (see Figure 7.15). However, if you are at Project Gutenberg go to the download section for a specific book and tap the EPUB link, the file downloads to your NOOKcolor (see Figure 7.16). These downloads go to the My Files\My Downloads folder.

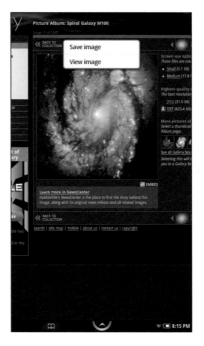

FIGURE 7.15   Some links offer you an opportunity to save or view the file.

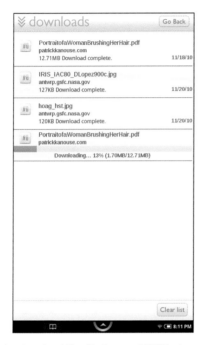

FIGURE 7.16   Some links download the file to your NOOKcolor.

If you press and hold a hyperlink (see Figure 7.17), a menu appears with these options:

▶ **Open**: Opens the link. This is the same at tapping the link.

▶ **Open in New Window**: Opens the link in a new window, thus leaving your existing window in place.

▶ **Bookmark Link**: Adds a bookmark to the link you are pressing.

▶ **Copy Link URL**: Copies the link to the Clipboard.

> NOTE: In the browser, copying text or links is allowed in a couple of places. However, I have yet to find a place where I can paste the said text.

FIGURE 7.17   Your options after you press and hold a hyperlink.

If you press and hold in a nonlink area of the web page, a menu appears with these options (see Figure 7.18):

- ▶ **Find on Page**: Tap this to search for specific text on this page. The keyboard appears. Type in what you want to search for. Tap Search. The keyboard drops away and the number of occurrences found on the page is shown. If more than one appearance is on the page, use the back and forward buttons to highlight the word.

- ▶ **Select Text**: Tap this to select text on the page. After you tap Select Text, press at the starting point of the text you want to select, and drag to the ending of the text. Lift your finger, and you receive a note that the text has been copied to the Clipboard.

> NOTE: Because it is a web page, sometimes when selecting text, you grab a couple of columns, and so on. It's imperfect and, given that I have yet to find the place to paste the text, I'm not sure of the point as yet.

▶ **Page Info**: Tap this to see some information related to the page.

▶ **Settings**: Tap this to access the browser settings. For more information about the Options, **see** "Using the Browser Options."

▶ **Downloads**: Tap this to see any downloads you have made from the NOOKcolor to the My Downloads folder.

▶ **Bookmark This Page**: Tap this to add this page to your bookmarks.

FIGURE 7.18 Your options after you press and hold a nonhyperlink area on a web page.

Using the Bookmarks Screen

The Bookmarks screen, shown in Figure 7.19, enables you to add bookmarks, modify existing ones, and other options. The screen opens with three tabs: Bookmarks, Most Visited, and History.

To get to the Bookmarks screen, tap the Bookmarks button. The Bookmarks screen opens at the Bookmarks tab. The bookmarks are thumbnails of the web pages. The top-left thumbnail, with Add overlaid on it, is actually not yet a bookmark. You can make this a bookmark by tapping it. The Add Bookmark window appears. You can adjust the name of the bookmark and location. (I recommend leaving this as is.) Tap OK to make it a bookmark.

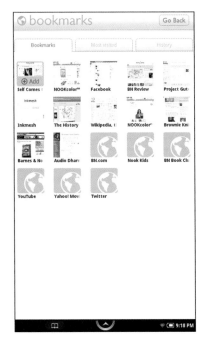

FIGURE 7.19   The Bookmarks screen.

The other thumbnails are your bookmarks. Tap the thumbnail to open that web page. If you press and hold the thumbnail, a pop-up menu provides these options (see Figure 7.20):

- ▶ **Open**: Opens the link. This is the same at tapping the link.

- ▶ **Open in New Window**: Opens the link in a new window, thus leaving your existing window in place.

- ▶ **Edit Bookmark**: Opens the Edit Bookmark window. Here you can adjust the name and location (that is, the hyperlink address) of the bookmark.

- ▶ **Copy Link URL**: Copies the link to the clipboard.

- ▶ **Delete Bookmark**: Deletes the bookmark. You will be asked to confirm that you want to delete it.

- ▶ **Set as Homepage**: Sets this bookmark as your home page.

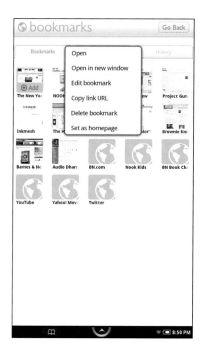

FIGURE 7.20   Additional options on the Bookmarks screen.

The Most Visited tab lists the web pages you have visited the, well, most often. A star appears to the right of the link. Gold means that it is a bookmark. Gray means that it is not a bookmark.

You can tap a link to go to that web page. If you press and hold the link, you see a set of options similar to the preceding list of options with one exception: Delete Bookmark is replaced by Remove from History. Tapping this removes the web page from your history.

> **NOTE:** You might think that tapping Remove from History would remove the link from the History tab on the Bookmarks screen. Although logical, you would be incorrect to think this. On the Most Visited tab, the Remove from History option is better labeled Remove from Most Visited.

The History tab lists the web pages you have visited. A star appears to the right of the link. Gold means that it is a bookmark. Gray means that it is not a bookmark. Scrolling down to the bottom of the list provides options for sites visited Yesterday, 5 Days Ago, and 1 Month Ago. Tapping one of those reveals more sites.

You can tap a link to go to that web page. If you press and hold the link, you see a set of options similar to the previous list of options. Tapping Remove from History removes the web page from the history.

On the screen, you can also tap Clear History to wipe out the entire history at once.

Using the Browser Options

As mentioned previously, tap the Options button to access browser settings and other options (see Figure 7.21). The following appears in the drop-down menu:

- ▶ **New Window**: Tap this to open a new window and leave the current window in place.

- ▶ **Bookmarks**: Tap this to open the Bookmarks screen. For more information about the Bookmarks options, **see** "Using the Bookmarks Screen."

- ▶ **Windows**: Tap this to see all the windows currently open. Tap the window you want to go to. Tap the X button to close that window.

- ▶ **Refresh**: Tap this to refresh the page, which is particularly useful if the page receives periodic updates.

- ▶ **Forward**: If you have tapped the Back button, tap Forward to go back to the previous page.

- ▶ **More Options**: Provides many items already covered, except for Settings.

Many settings about the web browser are available. Most of them are self-explanatory, but a few are covered in detail here.

Tap Text Size to adjust how large the text appears on web pages. Consider this the same as adjusting the text size in ebooks. You have several options: Tiny, Small, Normal, Large, and Huge.

Tap Default Zoom to set how the browser opens pages initially. You have three options: Far, Medium, and Close. Far shows more of the web page than the other two, which means that you have to zoom in more to get close. Close starts in very close, usually requiring more pressing and dragging to maneuver around the page.

> TIP: I think Medium is the best setting. If you use Far, when you double-tap quickly a part of the page, the page zooms in quickly equivalent to the Close setting size. Medium seems to strike the right balance between easy visibility without being too close.

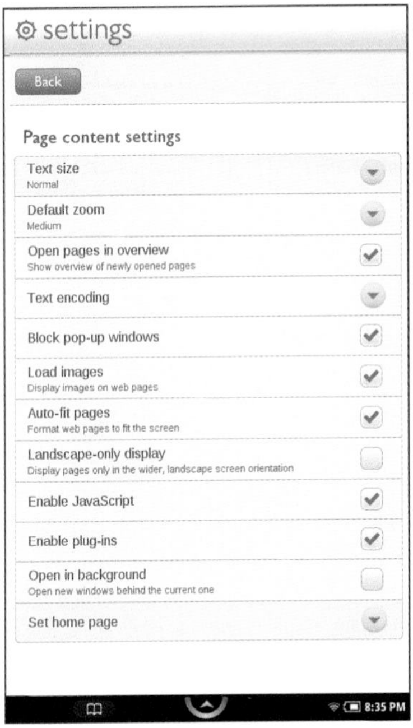

FIGURE 7.21   The browser's Options screen.

The Open Pages in Overview setting determines how newly opened pages first appear. If this setting is turned on, the web page appears in the browser showing the page in a zoomed out view (though not equivalent to the Far setting in Default Zoom).

With the Open in Background setting off, when you choose to open a link in a new window, that new window is what you see. With this setting on, that new window is hidden until you choose it by tapping Options and then tapping Windows.

You can use the Set Homepage option here to set the current web page as the home page.

The NOOKcolor's web browser is, as you have learned, feature rich. As an anecdote about how you can make use of this browser, I share a recent experience. I was about to attend a meeting (via a phone conference). The agenda was in my email, but just as I needed it, my computer decided that it needed to shut down suddenly. Rather than waiting for the slow rebooting and start up, I opened my NOOKcolor's web browser, signed onto my email, tapped the attachment, and downloaded the file (a Word document) to My Downloads. I then opened the file with Quickoffice. I was using the agenda as the meeting was starting while my computer was still booting up.

CHAPTER 8

Using the Social Features of Your NOOKcolor

As I'm sure you know, Facebook and Twitter are big deals these days—everyone is sharing everything. The NOOKcolor makes this sharing even easier. You can share your reading status, share quotes, and rate and recommend books. You can share to specific contacts, on BN.com, Facebook, and Twitter. Because many of these options overlap and at the same time are scattered across the interface, this chapter focuses on Facebook sharing.

> NOTE: Although the locations for the sharing features are scattered, they make sense in their location. Basically, B&N provides many locations for the sharing features to make it easy to share.

> NOTE: For LendMe coverage, **see** Chapter 4, "Lending and Borrowing Books with LendMe on Your NOOKcolor."
>
> Using Facebook and Twitter features requires that you link your Facebook and Twitter accounts to your NOOKcolor. **See** Chapter 2's "Social Menu" section for linking your accounts.

> NOTE: The social features work only for NOOKbooks and newspapers purchased from B&N. Only magazines purchased from B&N that function like newspapers (for example, *The New York Review of Books*) enable the social features.

You can access the Facebook social features by pressing and holding a cover image and tapping Recommend, tapping Recommend It on the View Details screen, tapping Share from the Reading Tools toolbar, or tapping Share from the Text Selection toolbar. Now deal with each of these contexts in turn.

Using Recommend from the Cover Menu or View Details Screen

Pressing and holding a cover either on the Home screen or in the Library displays a menu. Tap Recommend to see your recommend options (see Figure 8.1). Tap Facebook to see the Facebook Recommendation screen (see Figure 8.2)—if you are not currently connected to a Wi-Fi hotspot, the Network Setting screen appears for you to connect to one. Alternatively, you can press and hold a cover, tap View Details, and then tap Recommend It.

To post to your Facebook wall:

1. Tap Post to My Wall.

2. Type your message that will appear. As you type, you see the number of available characters (max of 420) go down, giving you an indication of how much space you have left.

3. Tap Post. Your NOOKcolor sends the recommendation to your wall.

FIGURE 8.1   Where do you want to recommend this NOOKbook?

FIGURE 8.2   Use this screen to post a recommendation to your wall.

If you want to post to a friend's wall, tap Post to a Friend's Wall (see Figure 8.3) and then tap Select Friend. You can search for a name. To select a friend, tap the button on the right of the name. You can select however many friends you want. Tap Done. Type your message and then tap Post. Your NOOKcolor sends the recommendation to your friend's or friends' walls.

> TIP: When you go to select friends, if you use the search box to narrow the list down, you may find that you now have a way to leave the screen. Actually, it's just hidden. Tap the hide keyboard key to get to the Done button.

FIGURE 8.3   Use this screen to post a recommendation to a friend's wall.

Using Share from the Reading Tools Toolbar

While reading a NOOKbook or newspaper, you can tap the Share button on the Reading Tools toolbar. You have three options: Recommend, Rate and Review, and Post Reading Status (see Figure 8.4).

▶ **Recommend**: This functions exactly as the previous section, "Using Recommend from the Cover Menu or View Details Screen," functions.

▶ **Rate and Review**: Tapping this allows you to rate and review the book on BN.com, which appears on the B&N book's specific web page. You must provide both a rating and either a headline or review before you can post. After you tap Post, the information is sent to BN.com.

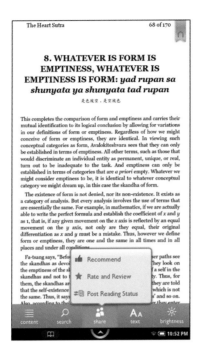

FIGURE 8.4   Tap the Share button to access the social features for NOOKbooks.

▶ **Post Reading Status**: This option enables you to post how far along you are in reading this NOOKbook to Facebook. A brief headline indicating how far you are into the NOOKbook and its title is followed by the synopsis of the NOOKbook as found on BN.com.

After tapping Share and tapping Post Reading Status, tap the check box for Facebook or Twitter (or both) and then tap Post. The update is sent.

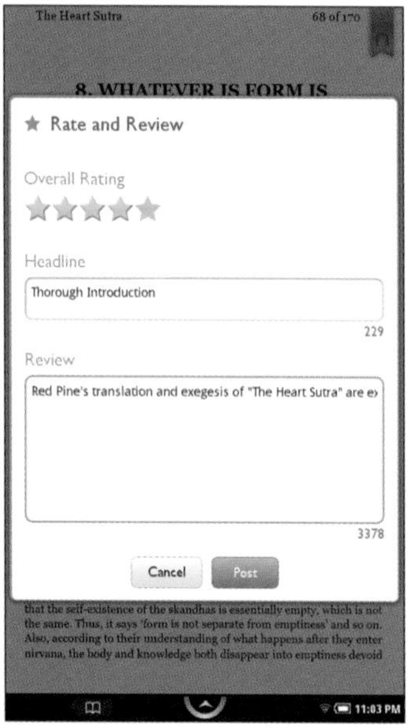

FIGURE 8.5 Rating and reviewing a NOOKbook posts that rating and review on BN.com.

FIGURE 8.6 Sharing the reading status posts how far you are into that NOOKbook on Facebook and Twitter.

Using Share from the Text Selection Toolbar

Use this share function when you have a quote you want others to see:

1. Press and hold the word you want to start the quote.

2. When the Text Selection toolbar appears, finish highlighting the quote by dragging the ending blue bar to where you want.

3. Tap Share.

4. Tap Facebook (see Figure 8.7).

FIGURE 8.7   Sharing a quote.

5. Tap either Post to My Wall or Post to a Friend's Wall.

   For Post to My Wall, type a message and tap Post.

   For Post to a Friend's Wall, tap Select Friend. Select your friend or friends. Type your message. Tap Post.

The appropriate wall or walls are updated.

Using the Flag Reading Tools Bar

Remember the flag on the Reading Tools bar in the reading screen (that flag off to the right of the scroll bar). When you finish reading a NOOKbook, tap it to get access to more social functions. When you tap the flag, the We Hope You Enjoyed It screen appears (see Figure 8.8). You can rate and review it for BN.com, lend it to a friend (if it is a LendMe book), or recommend it to friends via your Contacts, Facebook, or Twitter.

FIGURE 8.8   What the Flag offers.

Also, if you click one of the covers in the Customers Who Bought This Also Bought section, the NOOKstore version Details screen appears so that you can buy your next NOOKbook, download a sample, or add it to your wishlist.

So What About Twitter and Contacts?

NOOKcolor's support for Twitter and Contacts functions identically to Facebook, except that you share with specific contacts via email or your Twitter feed (see Figure 8.9). Twitter has a more limited character count, however.

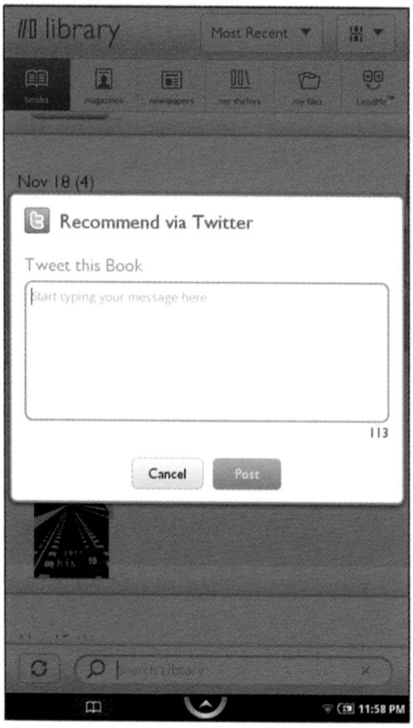

FIGURE 8.9   Sharing a recommendation via Twitter.

TIP: If you have a WordPress blog, check out the NOOKcolor widget at http://wordpress.org/extend/plugins/nook-color-widget/. This widget displays the cover of book you are reading.

CHAPTER 9

Shopping and Visiting B&N on Your NOOKcolor

One of the greatest features of your NOOKcolor is the capability to sample and buy content from B&N directly from the device. As long as you have a Wi-Fi connection, you can get new content for your NOOKcolor no matter where you are. However, you can also use the B&N website to sample and purchase content for your NOOKcolor.

> NOTE: Only customers with billing addresses in the Unites States, Canada, or a U.S. territory can order content from the B&N eBookstore. Citizens of U.S. territories are unable to preorder items.

Shopping on Your NOOKcolor

To shop on your NOOKcolor, from the Quick Nav Bar, tap Shop. Your NOOKcolor displays the NOOKstore Home screen (see Figure 9.1).

Navigating the NOOKstore

The NOOKstore is divided into three parts. The top half features several constituent categories that you navigate by swiping left or right. The categories follow:

- ▶ B&N Recommends
- ▶ Expand Your Mind and Your Horizons
- ▶ Explore History's Most Interesting Figures
- ▶ Edward's Picks
- ▶ Calling All History Buffs
- ▶ Stay in Step with the World
- ▶ Sessalee's Picks
- ▶ Fall into This Season's Biggest Blockbusters

FIGURE 9.1   The opening of the NOOKstore.

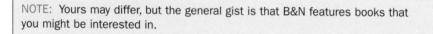

NOTE: Yours may differ, but the general gist is that B&N features books that you might be interested in.

If you are interested in an ebook, tap the cover to see the Details screen.

The bottom half is mostly dominated by categories based on your buying patterns, Picked Just for You, along with fast selling items, bargains, and new releases. Similarly, tap the cover to see the Details screen.

The bottom has a Browse button and a Search box. Type into the search box keywords, authors, titles—what have you. A list of titles appears. You can tap the cover to see the Details screen and tap the price to purchase the ebook (followed by a Confirm button). You can sort the list by Top Matches, Best Selling, Title, Price, and Release Date. Also, you can view them in one of three ways, similar to the Library view options: Grid, Large Cover List, and Small Cover List.

Browsing the NOOKstore

Tap the Browse button to see a variety of ways you can stroll through the available content (see Figure 9.2). The section is self-explanatory, so a lot of details here explaining the categories isn't necessary.

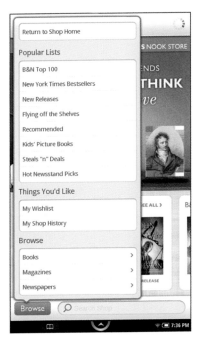

FIGURE 9.2 Browsing the NOOKstore.

The Popular Lists categories take you to specific lists of books. You can view in Grid, Large Cover List, and Small Cover List views. Additionally, tap the cover to see the Details screen, or tap the price to buy.

The Browse section functions like a narrowing list. Tap Books and you can see a host of sections. Tap a section to narrow this further. And this may run several more deep. You'll recognize your view options.

In the Things You'd Like section, the My Shop History brings up things you have sampled, looked up, and bought. The My Wishlist option shows your wishlist. Please note, that this wishlist is *not* the same as your BN.com wishlist. At this time, the two are separate.

> TIP: Myself? I dislike managing multiple wishlists. So I use the NOOKcolor's browser to add to my B&N wishlist via the BN.com website. I use the Shop feature for its ease of use.

Sampling and Buying Content

After you locate and select an item you're interested in, if you tap the cover to get to the Details screen (see Figure 9.3), you see an overview page that describes the item and shows the rating of the item from other B&N readers. In addition, you see the following options:

- ▶ **Add to Wishlist**: Adds the item to your NOOKcolor's wishlist.

- ▶ **Recommend It**: Gives you the opportunity to recommend the title. **See** Chapter 8, "Using the Social Features of Your NOOKcolor," for more information.

- ▶ **Overview**: The default view displayed when you select an item.

- ▶ **Customer Reviews**: Displays reviews from other B&N customers. The number of reviews presented is likely to be smaller than the number of ratings.

- ▶ **Editorial Reviews**: Displays editorial reviews for the item. This view often shows details from the publisher along with critic reviews of the item. It can span multiple pages.

- ▶ **More Like This**: Displays similar titles that you might be interested in. Tap the cover to jump to that ebook's Details screen.

If you like what you see, you can download a sample to your NOOKcolor by tapping Free Sample. (Sampling is valid only with NOOKbooks.) Samples typically consist of the first chapter of an ebook. However, it's up to the publisher to decide what to provide as a sample. In some cases, samples might contain just a few pages. In other cases, samples consist primarily of front matter, such as the title page, table of contents, dedication, and so on. One sample I downloaded contained nine pages of front matter and two pages of actual manuscript—hardly enough to get a feel for the book.

> NOTE: Samples never expire. You can keep a sample for as long as you'd like.

FIGURE 9.3   The Details screen in the NOOKstore.

If you decide to buy a book after reading the sample, simply go to the Details screen by tapping the cover (you can do this in the NOOKstore, on your Home screen, or in the Library) or tapping Buy Now in the reading screen of the sample. Because samples and full NOOKbooks are completely separate products, a purchased book will not open at the point where the sample ended. You need to manually navigate to the point where you stopped reading the sample.

> NOTE: If a B&N gift card is associated with your account, the cost for items purchased from the B&N NOOKstore are applied against that gift card. If there is not enough credit left on the card, B&N charges the remaining balance to your credit card on file.

If you want to remove a sample from your NOOKcolor, you need to visit My NOOK Library at bn.com from your computer. There is currently no way to remove a sample from your NOOKcolor without using your computer to do so. If you delete a sample unintentionally, you can download it again.

For more information on using My NOOK Library, **see** Chapter 22, "Using My NOOK Library."

> ### Is It Possible to Accidentally Purchase a Book You Have Already Purchased from B&N's eBookstore?
>
> Your NOOKcolor will not even present the option of purchasing a book you already own. If you select a book in the NOOKstore that you already own, you are shown an option to download or read the book, depending upon whether the book is already on your NOOKcolor. However, you will not be shown an option to buy the book. It will read Purchased.
>
> Some classic titles are released by multiple publishers. Two books of the same title from two different publishers are not considered the same title, so in these cases, you can purchase the same book twice.

Subscription content also enables sampling prior to purchasing, but it works a bit differently than it does with NOOKbooks. When you subscribe to a newspaper or magazine, you are given a 14-day free trial (see Figure 9.4). If you cancel your subscription within that 14-day period, you will not be charged. If you cancel after the 14-day trial period, you will be refunded a prorated amount based on when you cancel.

FIGURE 9.4   The trial period for a magazine.

> NOTE: You can buy the current issue by tapping Buy Current Issue without subscribing.

You can use a trial subscription only once for any particular item. For example, if you subscribe to *The Wall Street Journal* and cancel your subscription within the 14-day trial period, you will be charged beginning immediately if you were to subscribe to *The Wall Street Journal* again because you have already taken advantage of a trial subscription.

> NOTE: Subscriptions can be canceled only using My NOOK Library at bn.com. You cannot cancel a subscription using your NOOKcolor.

Your NOOKcolor automatically downloads subscription content when it's available. In addition to seeing the new content in My B&N Library, you'll also receive notifications in The Daily for any new subscription content your NOOKcolor downloads.

> NOTE: You cannot sample NOOKbooks for Kids that have Read to Me functionality.

Shopping on Your Computer

It's often easier and more convenient to shop for ebooks from your computer. Any books you purchase on your computer are added to My NOOK Library and are available for reading on your NOOKcolor.

To shop for NOOKbooks, magazines, and newspapers on your computer, browse to bn.com/ebooks. You can get samples of ebooks, subscribe to periodicals, and purchase books from the NOOKstore.

When you purchase, subscribe to a periodical, or choose to sample a NOOKbook from the online NOOKbook Store, the content is automatically added to your My NOOK Library. You can read the item on your NOOKcolor or NOOK by opening connecting to Wi-Fi or Fast and Free Wireless. On your NOOK, you may need to tap Check for New B&N Content in B&N Library.

One of the great features of using the B&N website for browsing NOOKbooks is that you can see which other formats are available. For example, if an MP3 audiobook is available for a title you're browsing, a link to the audiobook is there, so you can download it if you want.

When shopping for NOOKbooks for kids, look for the "NOOK kids read to me" statement in Format section. These NOOKbooks have the Read to Me feature enabled. If the format for a NOOKbook for kids is simply NOOKbook, you will not have the Read to Me option for that NOOKbook for kids.

While shopping for NOOKbooks, if you see that no NOOKbook is available for an in print book, on the product page for the print book, you see a link titled "Tell the publisher you want this in NOOKbook format." Click that link and you receive a message: "Thank you. We've notified the publisher that you'd like the book in ebook format." No guarantees, but at least the publisher will hear about it.

Whether you choose to shop from your NOOK or your computer, B&N provides plenty of great content for your NOOK at the NOOKbook Store. However, there are also plenty of other sources for great ebooks for your NOOKcolor and NOOK. Some of those sources you can find in Appendix B, "Sources for ebooks Other than B&N," which you can then sideload to your NOOKcolor or NOOK.

Using Your NOOKcolor in a B&N Store

As mentioned earlier, B&N stores have a Wi-Fi hotspot so your NOOKcolor can access free Wi-Fi while in the store (see Figure 9.5). B&N uses this hotspot to offer you special promotions called More in Store while in the store. Your NOOKcolor automatically connects to a B&N hotspot when in the store, but you do need to ensure that Wi-Fi is turned on. (It's on by default.)

After your NOOKcolor connects to the B&N hotspot, from the Quick Nav Bar, tap Shop.

In the top half of the NOOKstore, you see More in Store (see Figure 9.6). Generally, these offerings consist of several articles B&N feels might be interesting. Tap Read Free Content to see what's available. You are likely to find some interesting and others that don't interest you at all. If you'd like to get a sneak preview of what's available before you drive down to your local B&N, you can browse to http://www.barnesandnoble.com/=NOOK/moreinstore/ and see a list of all the More in Store offerings.

> NOTE: You need to be connected to the B&N hotspot to download and read the More in Store offerings.

FIGURE 9.5 The NOOKcolor found the BN Wi-Fi hotspot.

FIGURE 9.6 The NOOKstore page that appears when you are in a B&N store.

When you're connected to a B&N hotspot in a B&N store, you have the ability to read any NOOKbook in the B&N store for up to an hour. Find a NOOKbook you'd like to read, tap the cover, the Details screen opens (see Figure 9.7). Tap the Read in Store button. The book opens. Read for up to an hour (see Figure 9.8).

> NOTE: Bookmarks, annotations, and highlights are not supported for Read in Store content.

If you read a bit of a book in the store, exit out of the book you were reading, get up for a cup of coffee, and decide you want to keep reading, at top the NOOKstore, tap the Recently Read in Store link. Tap the cover to see the Details screen.

FIGURE 9.7 Tap the Read in Store button to enjoy something to read on your NOOKcolor while drinking a coffee.

FIGURE 9.8   The details for reading this book in store.

If you want to see what is available for reading in the store, go back to the main NOOKstore page, and swipe left in the top half until you get to the Read in Store page (see Figure 9.9). Tap Browse Read in Store eBooks.

There's no doubt that B&N has a unique opportunity because of its brick-and-mortar presence. No other ebook reader has the capability of being paired with a retail outlet, and there's every indication that B&N intends to beef up this feature in the future. It's certainly one of the more unique capabilities of the NOOKcolor, and NOOKcolor owners should be excited about what More in Store might offer in the future.

FIGURE 9.9 Browse for books to read in store.

NOTE: If you had the original NOOK, you know that you could show it to get a free cookie, coffee, smoothie, percentage off something, and more in the store. Currently, you can't get freebies or discounts with the NOOKcolor.

CHAPTER 10

Rooting Your NOOKcolor

At the beginning this book, I mentioned that B&N used Google's Android operating system in your NOOKcolor. Choosing Android makes business sense because it's an open-source operating system, and B&N didn't have to pay a small fortune to use it. However, the most exciting thing about Android for you is that it lets you easily root the NOOKcolor and add new features.

The idea of rooting your NOOKcolor may seem daunting or way too technical. However, I can assure you that rooting the NOOKcolor to get basic Android Market apps installed is super easy, only requiring a bit of prep work and a few steps. This minimal effort (it can be done inside a half hour) is well worth the benefits because you are turning your NOOKcolor into a tablet (albeit without a microphone or camera).

NOTE: To complete the steps in this chapter, you must have at least a 128 MB microSD card.

NOTE: Rooting is another term for hacking, though without the illicit connotation of hacking.

An Introduction to Rooting Your NOOKcolor

B&N locked down Android on your NOOKcolor to prevent you from accessing some of Android's capabilities. However, by following a process called *rooting* your NOOKcolor, you can open up these capabilities to make your NOOKcolor more powerful and useful.

NOTE: In the Android OS, *root* is the superuser who has access to everything in the OS. By rooting your NOOKcolor, you can become the superuser on your NOOKcolor.

Following are just a few of the things you can do after you root your NOOKcolor:

▶ Install eReader for Andriod.

> NOTE: If for nothing else, this may be the single most significant reason to root your NOOKcolor. If you have a bunch of secure eReader books you purchased from Fictionwise (and now cannot read on your NOOKcolor), by rooting your NOOKcolor you gain access to those ebooks.

▶ Add additional games.

▶ Use alternative browsers, PDF readers, and media players.

▶ Add calculator and note-taking apps.

▶ Access the Android Market.

These are just a few examples of the power unleashed by rooting your NOOKcolor.

> **Is It Risky to Root My NOOKcolor?**
>
> You root your NOOKcolor using a process called *softrooting*, which involves installing a special software update for your NOOKcolor. Therefore, rooting your NOOKcolor is no more risky than installing a software update, and it's a completely reversible process.
>
> **With that said, rooting your NOOKcolor is not sanctioned by B&N and doing so voids your warranty. Rooting is one of those things you must do at your own risk, but, in my opinion, the benefits far outweigh the downfalls.**

How to Root Your NOOKcolor

The experts on rooting your NOOKcolor all hang out at nookdevs.com. Everything you need to know about rooting your NOOKcolor, installing applications, and hacking the NOOKcolor in general is available on this site. All the files required to root your NOOKcolor are freely downloadable from nookdevs.

There are a few prerequisites you should consider before venturing down the path of rooting your NOOKcolor. First and foremost, you obviously need to have a registered NOOKcolor.

CAUTION: If you do not register your NOOKcolor with B&N prior to rooting, you will not be able to buy books from the NOOKcolor's NOOKbookstore.

Second, you need a 128 MB or higher microSD card. Any existing data on this card will be completely erased, so make sure you have it backed up. Third, you need a computer that can read that microSD card. Fourth, you need a working Wi-Fi connection for your NOOKcolor. Finally, you need to have a Google account (also called a Gmail account). You can get one from http://mail.google.com/mail/signup. You do not need to use it ever again, though you do need it for this process.

After you decide to experience the new functionality of your NOOKcolor by rooting it, the steps required are quite easy:

1. Upgrade your NOOKcolor to version 1.1.0.

2. Create a disk image on a microSD card.

3. Install the microSD card disk image on your NOOKcolor.

4. Enter some information into a couple of applications.

5. Install any additional applications you want on your NOOKcolor.

Now look at each of these steps in detail.

TIP: The steps I walk you through are documented at http://nookdevs.com/ NookColor_Rooting. However, there are a few points of possible confusion on that page, so although you can use it as a reference, follow my steps here for a successful rooting experience.

Upgrading to NOOKcolor 1.1.0

Technically, you can root your NOOKcolor with either the 1.0.0, 1.0.1, or 1.1.0 upgrade to the NOOKcolor firmware. If, after you have rooted your NOOKcolor with version 1.0.0 firmware and then it upgrades to the version 1.0.1 firmware, you will need to re-root your NOOKcolor. Because there is no real good reason not to upgrade to the 1.1.0 version, go ahead and do so. To find out which version of the NOOKcolor firmware is currently installed on your NOOKcolor, from the Quick Nav Bar, tap Settings, Device Info, About Your NOOKcolor.

Create a Disk Image

In this step, you create a bootable disk on the microSD card. To do this, you need to download the `auto-rooter-3.0.0.zip` file from http://www.mediafire.com/?46vb5569wm35kp6. Unzip the file and place the `auto-rooter-3.0.0.img` file somewhere easily accessible.

> NOTE: If you choose *not* to update your NOOKcolor's firmware to 1.1.0, download the appropriate `auto-rooter-2.12.15.img.zip` file for your firmware version. All the other steps that follow are the same.

The next step is to download software that will allow you to create an image on a microSD card. For Linux and Mac instructions for creating a disk image, see http://nookdevs.com/NookColor_Rooting. If you are on a PC, from that same website, follow these steps:

1. Plug in a microSD card to your PC.

> CAUTION: Following these steps will completely erase the microSD card, so make sure you back it up to another drive.

2. Download the `win32diskimager-RELEASE-0.1-r15-win32.zip` file from https://wiki.kubuntu.org/Win32DiskImager. Unzip the file on your computer. Double-click the file `win32diskimager.exe` file, which starts the program.

3. Browse to the `auto-rooter-3.0.0.img` file and select it.

4. For Device, choose the drive letter of the microSD card.

5. Click Write. The disk image will be created. When it finishes, click Exit. The microSD card is now ready to root your NOOKcolor.

Rooting Your NOOKcolor

> CAUTION: Before you proceed any farther, make sure that your NOOKcolor has at least a 50% battery charge. You don't want your NOOKcolor to shut down during an update because it can cause problems.

Now we are going to actually do the rooting process, which is strikingly easy. Follow these steps:

1. Unplug your NOOKcolor from the computer and power it off.

2. Insert the microSD card you created a disk image on in the previous section into your NOOKcolor.

3. Plug the USB cable into your computer and your NOOKcolor. The NOOKcolor will begin the booting process. Be patient through this.

4. Windows will probably complain about missing drivers after the NOOKcolor has rebooted. Don't worry about it and just cancel the warnings.

5. Remove the microSD card.

Finishing Rooting Your NOOKcolor

You have only a few more steps to complete before you can begin to download Android Market apps and expand your NOOKcolor into a tablet.

After the NOOKcolor has rebooted in the previous section, follow these steps:

1. If your screen is locked, unlock it.

2. Skip the Sign In steps at the Android Welcome screen.

3. You are asked to Enable Location Services. Do so.

4. Connect to a Wi-Fi network.

5. From the Quick Nav Bar, tap Extras. You see quite a few new items here (see Figure 10.1). Tap YouTube. (If YouTube fails to launch, don't worry and move on to the next step.)

6. You now see two new options on either side of the Nav arrow: Return and Menu (see Figure 10.2). Tap the Menu button (the one *right* of the Up arrow). Another set of options appears.

7. Tap My Channel. Tap Add Account and enter your Gmail username and password, which also function as your YouTube username and password. Tap Sign In.

8. Exit YouTube by tapping the Home button.

9. From the Quick Nav Bar, tap Extra, and tap Gmail.

FIGURE 10.1   The initial rooted NOOKcolor Extras screen.

FIGURE 10.2   The Return and Menu options in the rooted NOOKcolor.

10. Tap Menu and tap Accounts. Tap Add Account. Tap the Google logo and then Next. Tap Sign In and enter your username and password and Sign In. The Gmail app will attempt to sync. If it fails, that is okay.

11. From the Quick Nav Bar, tap Extras, and then tap Market. Accept the terms of service.

12. From the Quick Nav Bar, tap Extra, and then tap NookColor Tools. Make sure the Allow Non-Market Apps checkbox is filled in.

That's it! You have successfully rooted your NOOKcolor!

Installing Applications on Your Rooted NOOKcolor

Now that you have your NOOKcolor rooted, you want to install applications, right? Well, it is super easy (I'll use the NOOK for Android by B&N app as an example):

1. From the Quick Nav Bar, tap Extras, and then tap Market. You can search the market for apps, browse by category, and view downloads (see Figure 10.3). Tap the Search icon and type NOOK and tap the magnifying glass button. A list of downloads appears (see Figure 10.4).

FIGURE 10.3   The Android Market front page.

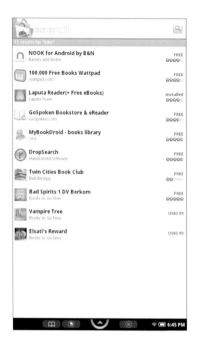

FIGURE 10.4   The search results page in the Android Market.

2. Tap the NOOK for Android by B&N app line. Tap Install and then tap OK (see Figure 10.5). You will be informed that it is downloading. Tap the Menu option and tap Downloads to watch the progress.

3. When it is finished downloading and installed, tap the NOOK for Android by B&N app line. Tap Open.

4. Enter your B&N account information (the one associated with your NOOKbooks). Tap Register. Your app is synced up with your B&N account. You can now read your NOOKbooks on your NOOKcolor (I know this sounds a bit odd, but the point is now you know how to install apps and the process is the same for others.

Simple, right? And that's how installing other apps works. Check out the eReader app, which you can sync up to your Fictionwise account.

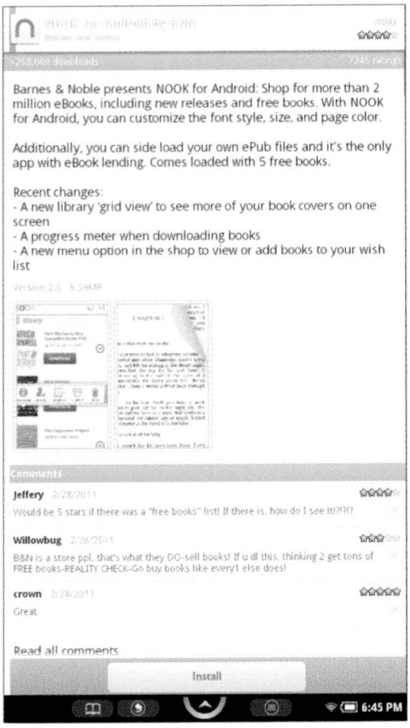

FIGURE 10.5   The Install NOOK for Android by B&N app page.

A Few Things to Note

Now that you have rooted your NOOKcolor, you should keep a few things in mind:

▶ The NOOKcolor does not have a GPS, camera, or microphone, so apps that use those features will not work (for example, you cannot make calls with the Skype app).

▶ Many of the references in the apps and market refer to your phone. This is quite natural because Android is widely deployed on phones. This terminology will change over time as more Android tablets (for example, the Samsung Galaxy) reach the market.

▶ The Return and Menu options change from app to app. The Menu options in particular provide access to settings, viewing options, and so on.

▶ After you have installed apps, they appear in the Extras area only after a while, though you can make them appear right away by powering off and then powering on your NOOKcolor.

▶ Whenever you press the Home button, you are presented with two options asking you to complete the action using Home and Softkeys. Most of the time, tap Home. For more information about Softkeys, see the following section.

▶ nookdevs.com keeps a list of known app issues, whether working or not. You can see the list here: http://nookdevs.com/NookColor_working_apps. This does not mean you cannot install other apps, but you may run into some oddities here and there.

What Is Softkeys?

You by now have seen the option to use Softkeys, but what is Softkeys? Basically, Softkeys is an app that provides some buttons that are normally on phones that are not available on other devices. I personally haven't found much use for Softkeys, though it does have a nice function. If you tap the Softkeys icon, a set of buttons appears on the top and bottom of the NOOKcolor screen. The top shows the most recent apps you have opened. Tapping one of those opens that app.

Problems with YouTube

Sometimes the YouTube app simply refuses to start. There is, fortunately, a simple way to resolve the problem. Download the Titanium Backup app from the Android Market (the free version). Once that is installed, open it and tap OK to get through the warnings. Tap Backup/Restore and scroll down to YouTube. Tap YouTube and then tap Wipe Data. You should then be able to open the YouTube app.

Unrooting Your NOOKcolor

From the Quick Nav Bar, tap Settings and then tap Device Info. Tap Erase &
Deregister Device. You will be warned that doing so removes all books and files,
including sideloaded content. Then you have a button to do just that. Tap Erase &
Deregister Device. Your NOOKcolor erases the data, deregisters, and reboots the
device. It is no longer rooted.

CHAPTER 11

Getting Started with Your NOOK

The most difficult part of using and setting up your NOOK is the packaging. (If you haven't opened your NOOK yet, you'll know what I'm talking about when you do.) Before getting into the details of using your NOOK, let's take a look at some of the basics: gestures, setup, and basic navigation. With these basics in place, we'll then be able to discover all the other incredible things your NOOK can do.

> NOTE: Barnes & Noble uses a lowercase *n* when it spells *NOOK* and for the NOOK's logo.

Registering Your NOOK

When you first turn on your NOOK, you see a tip informing you to use the touch-screen to get started. If the touchscreen is already lit, tap the Tap Here to Get Started link. If the touchscreen is not lit, double-tap your NOOK's Home button (the NOOK logo on the black bar above the touchscreen); then tap Tap Here to Get Started on the touchscreen.

> TIP: To wake the touchscreen when it's not lit, you can press and release the Power button at the top of your NOOK, tap the touchscreen, or use the Home button as previously described. Tapping the touchscreen doesn't always work; double-tapping the Home button works every time.

The first step in getting started with your NOOK is to register it with Barnes & Noble (simply B&N from now on). To register your NOOK, you need an account on the B&N website. If you don't have one already, go to www.NOOK.com/setup to create one. After you have an account on the B&N website, tap the Register with Your Existing Account link on your NOOK's touchscreen to register with B&N.

NOTE: B&N requires a default credit card with a valid billing address to be associated with your B&N account to register your NOOK.

NOTE: The NOOK comes in two types: 3G+Wi-Fi and Wi-Fi only. The 3G is also called B&N Fast & Free Wireless. If you have the former, you can register without setting up a Wi-FI connection. If you have the latter, you first need to set up a Wi-Fi connection (see the section "Using Wi-Fi Hotspots" to set up your Wi-Fi connection). The instructions assume you have the 3G+Wi-Fi NOOK, which is fine because all the instructions apply for the Wi-Fi-only NOOK, so long as you have set up your Wi-Fi connection.

On the Register Your NOOK screen, enter the email address and password you use to sign in to your account on the B&N website; then tap Submit on the touchscreen. To move from the email field to the password field on the registration screen, press the down arrow on the touchscreen.

Registration requires access to B&N Fast & Free Wireless or access to a Wi-Fi hotspot. If you aren't in an area with B&N Fast & Free Wireless, you can use the Wi-Fi hotspot at any B&N store or use your own Wi-Fi hotspot. If you want to use your own Wi-Fi hotspot, you need to tap Register Later on the touchscreen and register your NOOK after you connect to your Wi-Fi hotspot.

NOTE: If you live outside the United States and have trouble registering your NOOK, make sure you've upgraded to the latest firmware. As of version 1.2, B&N enables registration outside the United States.

For more information on connecting your NOOK to a Wi-Fi hotspot, **see** "Using Wi-Fi Hotspots," later in this chapter.

TIP: There's a great video walk-through showing how to register your NOOK at www.barnesandnoble.com/NOOK/video.asp?#vid1.

Do I Have to Register My NOOK?

You aren't required to register your NOOK, but if you want to purchase NOOKbooks from the B&N store, lend and borrow books using the LendMe feature, or use the special features available while in a B&N store, you need to register your NOOK.

After your NOOK has been successfully registered, you have an option to take the NOOK tour, a 10-page synopsis of NOOK features. B&N saves the NOOK tour in your library, so you can read the tour later if you'd like to skip it for now.

Using Wi-Fi Hotspots

In addition to connecting to B&N's Fast & Free Wireless, your NOOK can also connect to Wi-Fi networks. B&N offers free Wi-Fi access in all B&N stores. If you take your NOOK to a B&N store, it automatically connect a to the Wi-Fi hotspot in that store.

For more information on using your NOOK in a B&N store, **see** Chapter 17, "Shopping and Visiting B&N on Your NOOK."

To connect your NOOK to a Wi-Fi hotspot other than one in a B&N store, follow these steps:

1. If the NOOK is not currently at the Home screen, tap the NOOK logo just above the touchscreen until the Home screen is displayed.

2. Tap the Wi-Fi button on the touchscreen. You may have to scroll to the right on the touchscreen to see the Wi-Fi button.

3. Tap Wi-Fi hotspot.

4. Tap the Wi-Fi hotspot you want to use. (Your NOOK displays the SSID for all Wi-Fi hotspots in range.)

5. Tap Connect and enter the password for your Wi-Fi hotspot.

6. Tap Submit.

Your NOOK should now show that you are connected to your Wi-Fi hotspot on the reading screen. You should also see the Wi-Fi signal indicator at the top of the screen next to the battery indicator.

> NOTE: When a configured Wi-Fi hotspot is available, the NOOK connects to the Wi-Fi hotspot rather than Fast & Free Wireless.

If your Wi-Fi hotspot isn't listed after you tap Wi-Fi hotspot, tap Other hotspot. You can then enter the service set identifier (SSID), select the type of security (if the Wi-Fi is secured), and enter the password for your Wi-Fi hotspot if necessary. If you don't know this information, ask the person who set up the Wi-Fi network.

Your NOOK can connect to a Wi-Fi hotspot that requires you to browse to a web page to authenticate yourself. For example, many hotel Wi-Fi hotspots require you to enter a room number or other information to connect. Because B&N added a web browser in version 1.3 of the NOOK's firmware, you can connect to a Wi-Fi hotspot that has this requirement by launching the web browser from the Home screen after you join the Wi-Fi network.

Does My NOOK's Battery Drain Faster with Wi-Fi Connected?

I tested my NOOK's battery life using both Fast & Free Wireless and Wi-Fi hotspots. In my testing, the battery life was quite a bit shorter when using Wi-Fi than it was when using Fast & Free Wireless. However, Wi-Fi affects battery life only when your NOOK is actually connected to a Wi-Fi hotspot. Simply having Wi-Fi turned on doesn't affect battery life.

Battery life is significantly improved by switching on Airplane Mode, thereby turning off all radios on your NOOK.

For more information on using Airplane Mode, **see** "Configuring Your NOOK's Settings" in Chapter 12, "Customizing and Configuring Your NOOK."

Disconnecting from a Wi-Fi Hotspot

If you have configured a Wi-Fi connection for your NOOK, that connection will be preferred over the Fast & Free Wireless connection. If you want to stop using a Wi-Fi hotspot and use Fast & Free Wireless instead, you need to disconnect your NOOK from the Wi-Fi hotspot. To do that, follow these steps:

1. If the NOOK is not currently at the Home screen, tap the NOOK logo just above the touchscreen until the Home screen displays.

2. Tap the Wi-Fi button on the touchscreen.

3. Tap Wi-Fi hotspot.

4. Tap the name of the Wi-Fi hotspot you use. ("Connected" displays next to the name of the Wi-Fi hotspot.)

5. Tap Forget to disconnect from the Wi-Fi hotspot.

After disconnecting from the Wi-Fi hotspot, your NOOK uses Fast & Free Wireless when a network connection is required.

TIP: Disconnecting from your Wi-Fi hotspot doesn't actually turn off the Wi-Fi card in your NOOK. Your NOOK's Wi-Fi card is always on so that it can connect automatically to the Wi-Fi hotspot if you are in a B&N store.

For more information on configuring the settings in your NOOK (including turning off the Wi-Fi card), **see** "Configuring Your NOOK's Settings" in Chapter 12.

Caring for Your NOOK's Battery

Your NOOK uses a high-tech battery called a lithium polymer battery. Unlike older rechargeable batteries, your NOOK's battery doesn't suffer from a charge "memory." However, you should still follow some basic rules to maximize the life of your battery:

▶ Try to avoid fully discharging your battery. Recharge it when it gets down to about 20% or so. Although charging it repeatedly is not necessarily a bad thing, the battery seems to function optimally if you charge it only when it drops down toward that 20% area.

▶ Airplane Mode to download your new books, subscription content, and read the Daily. By not having your NOOK search for and maintain a Wi-Fi or Fast and Free Wireless Connection, you can significantly extend the life of the battery between charges.

▶ Avoid high heat. Reading in sunlight is fine, but avoid storing your NOOK near a heat source.

▶ If storing your NOOK for a long period (a week or more), charge the battery to about 50% rather than giving it a full charge.

By following these steps, your NOOK's battery should last years. However, if you ever need a new battery, you can purchase one from B&N and replace it yourself. To find out how to replace your NOOK's battery, see the video at www.barnesandnoble.com/NOOK/video.asp?#vid3.

TIP: For your new NOOK, if you let its battery drain to about 20% of battery life, recharge it, and repeat this process several times, you should actually see an increase in battery life.

Charging Your NOOK's Battery

You can charge your NOOK's battery either by plugging your NOOK into your computer's USB port or by plugging your NOOK into a wall outlet using the supplied AC adapter. Plugging your NOOK into a wall outlet is preferred because it charges the NOOK much more quickly.

Should I Plug My NOOK into a Surge Suppressor?

Just like any electronic device, your NOOK is susceptible to power spikes and other electrical anomalies. If you want to ensure that your NOOK is protected from electrical problems, plug it into a surge suppressor.

Why Does My Battery Indicator Sometimes Have a Question Mark on It?

When you first wake your NOOK or first turn it on, it can take several seconds for your NOOK to determine the current charge of the battery. While your NOOK is calculating the charge state of the battery, a question mark displays on the battery charge indicator at the top of the screen.

When You Are Not Reading

When you finish reading, let your NOOK go to sleep instead of turning it off. I realize that it's not intuitive to leave electronic devices turned on, but because your NOOK uses almost no power unless you do something that requires it to refresh the E Ink display, you can leave it turned on without draining your battery.

By leaving your NOOK on, it occasionally downloads content from B&N such as subscription content (assuming you have Airplane Mode turned off), updated information for The Daily (articles of interest to NOOKies), and any books that you purchase from the B&N website. When you're ready to start reading again, simply press and release the power switch at the top of your NOOK to wake it up.

NOTE: If you don't believe that your NOOK's display requires no power to maintain the current screen, remove the back cover of your NOOK and remove the battery while the screen displays a page. Even with the battery removed, the page still displays.

Your NOOK's Controls

Before you get into enjoying content on your NOOK, review the controls on your NOOK.

The Power Button

The Power button is a silver bar at the top of your NOOK. In addition to powering your NOOK on and off, the Power button can wake your NOOK when it's sleeping or put it to sleep when you finish reading.

To put your NOOK to sleep or wake it using the Power button, press and release the Power button quickly. To turn off your NOOK, press and hold the Power button for 5 seconds. To turn on your NOOK again, press and release the Power button quickly.

> TIP: When turning on your NOOK, it might seem unresponsive for several seconds. That's completely normal. Wait a few seconds, and your NOOK will display a message letting you know that it's starting.

The Home Button

The Home button is identified by the NOOK logo and is located in the center of the black bar along the top of the touchscreen display. Like the Power button, the Home button performs more than one function.

If your touchscreen is not illuminated, you can wake it up by double-tapping the Home button. If the touchscreen is already illuminated, tapping the Home button takes you back to your NOOK's Home screen.

> TIP: As mentioned earlier, the NOOK user guide instructs you to tap the Home button once to activate the touchscreen. However, tapping the Home button once often takes you to the Home screen instead of just waking up your touchscreen. Double-tapping the Home button to wake the touchscreen always works.

Page Turn Buttons

Along the left and right edges of your NOOK are the page Turn buttons. The top page Turn button moves back one page with each press, and the bottom page Turn button moves forward one page with each press. You probably already know that, but what you might not know is that you can quickly press a page Turn button multiple times to turn more than one page. For example, if you press the next Page button three times quickly, your NOOK will turn three pages.

Color Touchscreen

Your NOOK's color touchscreen is a feature that is unique to the NOOK. The touchscreen's functionality changes depending on what you do. For example, when you are on the Home screen, the touchscreen displays nine large buttons to access various functions of your NOOK. When reading, the touchscreen displays functions for interacting with reading content. When user input is required, the touchscreen displays a full keyboard.

As you progress through the rest of this book, you learn how to use the touchscreen to interact with your NOOK.

How Should I Clean My NOOK's Touchscreen?

Your NOOK's touchscreen is going to get dirty and covered in fingerprints. The best way to clean it is to use a dry, microfiber cloth like the one you would use to clean eyeglasses. If you must use a cleaning fluid, spray it lightly on the cloth and then wipe the touchscreen. Use only cleaning sprays designed for cleaning LCD displays.

Your NOOK's Operating System

The operating system (OS) your ebook reader runs is usually not important, but your NOOK is unique in that it runs an OS developed by Google. It's called Android, and B&N's choice to use the Android OS means that it's easy to extend the capabilities of your NOOK. If you properly prepare your NOOK using a technique called *rooting*, you can install many third-party applications on your NOOK, including a powerful book launching and management application.

This capability is such an exciting feature that an entire section of this book is dedicated to it.

For more information on extending your NOOK, **see** Chapter 19, "Rooting Your NOOK."

Now that you're familiar with the controls on your NOOK, you can discover some of the ways to customize and personalize your NOOK.

CHAPTER 12

Customizing and Configuring Your NOOK

Your NOOK has many features that enable you to easily customize it and make it your own, and many settings control how your NOOK operates. In this chapter, you examine how to customize and configure your NOOK.

Using Custom Wallpaper and Screensavers

You can customize your NOOK by using custom wallpaper images and screensaver images. Wallpaper appears on the reading screen when you are on the Home screen. Your NOOK displays screensaver images on the Reading screen when it is sleeping. Even though your NOOK's Reading screen isn't a color screen, it can display 16 levels of gray, making it ideal for displaying black-and-white versions of your favorite pictures.

Creating Wallpaper and Screensaver Images

Before you use a picture as wallpaper or a screensaver on your NOOK, you need to resize it to fit the dimensions of your NOOK's Reading screen. Wallpaper images should be 760 pixels high and 600 pixels wide, and screensaver images should be 800 pixels high and 600 pixels wide. (Wallpaper images are 40 pixels shorter to provide room for the status bar at the top of the page.) For information about creating wallpapers and screensavers, **see** Appendix D, "Using Picasa to Create Wallpapers and Screensavers."

Copying Wallpaper Images to Your NOOK

Before you can use your custom images as wallpaper on your NOOK, you need to copy them from your computer to the My Wallpapers folder on your NOOK. However, you first need to rename the images so that you can easily identify them.

TIP: If you installed a microSD card in your NOOK and want to store your wallpaper images on that card, simply create a folder called My Wallpapers on your microSD card. Then copy your images to that folder instead of the My Wallpapers folder on your NOOK's internal memory.

If you want to use an image you took with a digital camera, the filename of the image is likely something such as IMG_0743.JPG. Your NOOK uses the filename (without the file extension) for the wallpaper name, so you need to rename this image to something recognizable before you copy it to your NOOK. For example, if you copy an image of a snow-covered tree, you might want to change the name to Tree with Snow.JPG. Your NOOK can then identify the image as Tree with Snow.

Should I Use a Specific File Format for Images?

Your NOOK supports JPEG (.JPG), GIF, and PNG files. For images, using either JPEG or PNG is your best option. GIF isn't a good option for photographs, but if your image is a line art or text, GIF can work fine. If you're unsure, stick with JPEG. That's what Picasa uses by default.

After you rename your images, copy them to your NOOK using these steps:

1. Connect your NOOK to your computer with the USB cable. When you do, your NOOK appears on your computer as a new drive called *NOOK*.

2. If your computer doesn't automatically display the folders on your NOOK, open your NOOK via My Computer on Windows or the Finder on the Mac. You should see the My Wallpapers folder. (Mac users can also double-click the NOOK icon on the desktop.)

3. Open the My Wallpapers folder.

4. Copy your renamed images from your computer to the My Wallpapers folder on your NOOK.

Copying Screensaver Images to Your NOOK

Screensavers on your NOOK consist of a series of images. Each time your NOOK sleeps, it displays the next image in the series on the reading screen. Unlike wallpaper images, the image names for screensaver images aren't important. Instead, your NOOK identifies screensavers by folder name.

Copy screensaver images to your NOOK by following these steps:

1. Connect your NOOK to your computer with the USB cable. When you do, your NOOK appears in your computer as a new drive called NOOK.

2. If your computer doesn't automatically display the folders on your NOOK, open your NOOK via My Computer on Windows or the Finder on the Mac. You should see the My Screensavers folder.

3. Open the My Screensavers folder.

4. Create a new folder for your screensaver. The new folder's name is the name of your screensaver on your NOOK.

5. Copy the image files for your screensaver into the folder you created in step 4.

For example, if you have a series of images of a winter snowfall, you might want to create a new folder in the My Screensavers folder called Winter Snow and copy your images into that folder. You can then use the images in that folder as your screensaver by selecting Winter Snow as your screensaver.

> TIP: Just as with wallpaper, screensavers can be stored on a microSD card by simply creating a My Screensavers folder on the microSD card and copying your screensaver folder into that folder.

Now that you've copied your custom images to your NOOK, look at how you can change the settings on your NOOK to use the new images as your wallpaper or screensaver.

Choosing a Custom Wallpaper or Screensaver

Your NOOK's Settings menu enables you to change the wallpaper or screensaver on your NOOK. Here's how:

1. Make sure your NOOK is at the Home screen.

2. Tap the Settings button on the touchscreen.

3. Tap Display in the Settings menu.

4. To change the screensaver, tap Screensaver on the Display menu, and select your screensaver. To change the wallpaper, tap Wallpaper on the Display menu, and select your wallpaper.

Notice that your NOOK displays the image filename for wallpaper and the folder name for screensavers.

Wallpaper and Screensavers from Other Sources

You can use several online sources for NOOK wallpaper and screensavers. One of the best is NOOK-Look (www.NOOK-look.com). NOOK-Look provides a wide assortment of quality wallpaper and screensavers for your NOOK.

Another way you can locate wallpaper for your NOOK is by using the image search feature on your favorite search engine. A search for "NOOK wallpaper" in Google turns up plenty of images presized for your NOOK. The same search on Bing is less helpful, but by clicking the Images of NOOK Wallpaper link on the left of the page, clicking the Images tab, and selecting Tall on the Layout menu, plenty of images are available in the correct size for your NOOK.

One Step Further—Decals

If you want to take the ultimate step to customize your NOOK, a DecalGirl skin (www.decalgirl.com) is the perfect addition. DecalGirl skins are vinyl skins with adhesive backing that you can easily apply. Many skins also include matching NOOK wallpaper that provides a truly unique look.

Your NOOK's Settings

Your NOOK offers configurable settings for controlling many of its features. Tap Settings on the Home screen to access the Settings menu. When you do, the Reading screen displays the Summary pages for your NOOK. The Summary pages contain information about your NOOK and its settings separated into several sections.

Your NOOK displays the following information in the Summary pages.

Profile

The Profile section displays personal information about you. Your name and your NOOK's name are both contained in the profile stored on your NOOK. Your email address is part of your B&N profile that you created when you registered your NOOK.

To name your NOOK, tap Device on the touchscreen, and then tap Edit Your Profile on the Device menu. Enter your name and the name you'd like for your NOOK; then tap Submit.

Is There Any Advantage to Naming My NOOK?

There isn't any benefit to naming your NOOK, but naming it can make it more personal. You'll likely find that after reading a book or two on your NOOK, it might mean more to you than a typical electronic device. Naming your NOOK is one way to give it some personality.

Software

The Software section displays the version of software (called *firmware*) currently installed on your NOOK. B&N releases periodic updates to the NOOK to improve performance and fix known issues. As long as your NOOK has a connection to B&N's Fast & Free Wireless or a Wi-Fi connection, your NOOK automatically downloads any updates that B&N releases.

Not all NOOK owners receive new firmware updates at the same time. B&N rolls out new firmware over a period of about a week. If you would like to update your NOOK manually, you can visit www.barnesandnoble.com/NOOK/support where B&N typically provides instructions for manually updating your NOOK to the latest firmware.

If I Don't Like Changes Made by a Firmware Update, Can I Go Back to an Older Version?

On some sites you can download older versions of NOOK firmware (www.NOOKdevs.com), but because your NOOK automatically installs firmware updates when B&N makes one available, your NOOK will always install the latest update unless you keep Wi-Fi and Fast & Free Wireless turned off.

Available Memory

The Available Memory section shows you how much memory is available and how much has been used. If you have a microSD card installed in your NOOK, memory statistics are included for it as well. Reading this might be confusing, so here's a description of what the memory means. For each memory item, you have a number, a slash, and a percentage. For example, Internal Memory 1.18 GB / 1.28 GB (92%). This means that you have available 1.18 GB of memory out of a total of 1.28 GB; thus, your internal memory care is 92% free.

For more information on adding a microSD card to your NOOK, **see** "Adding a microSD Card to Your NOOK."

Battery and Wi-Fi

The Battery and Wi-Fi section displays the current percentage of battery charge remaining and the current Wi-Fi status.

If your NOOK is connected to a Wi-Fi hotspot, it displays the name of the Wi-Fi hotspot. Otherwise, it displays Disconnected.

Device Information

The Device Information is on page 2 of the Summary pages. It displays your NOOK's serial number along with several ID numbers related to its cellular modem. You can also find your NOOK's MAC address—the hardware address of the Wi-Fi modem.

Configuring Your NOOK's Settings

You've already seen how you can configure some of the settings on your NOOK. This section covers the rest of the settings available on the Settings menu.

> NOTE: Your NOOK displays the Settings menu on the touchscreen after you tap the Settings button.

Airplane Mode

When traveling on a commercial airline, it is not legal to use the cellular modem inside your NOOK. To turn off all radios in your NOOK quickly, turn on Airplane Mode: Tap Airplane Mode on the Settings menu, and then tap On.

> TIP: If you travel on a flight that offers Wi-Fi service and you want to use the hotspot with your NOOK, leave Airplane Mode off. If your NOOK is connected to a Wi-Fi hotspot, the cellular modem won't be activated. However, check with the flight crew first to avoid any problems.

When you activate Airplane Mode, an Airplane icon appears to the left of the battery indicator on your NOOK's status bar. To turn off Airplane Mode, tap Airplane Mode on the Settings menu and then tap Off. The Wi-Fi and cellular radios return to the state they were prior to activating Airplane Mode.

> TIP: You can also turn on and off Airplane mode by tapping Wi-Fi on the Home screen.

Wi-Fi Menu

The Wi-Fi menu provides options to turn the Wi-Fi modem on or off and to connect to Wi-Fi hotspots.

To turn the Wi-Fi radio on or off, tap Wi-Fi on the Settings menu; then tap Wi-Fi on the Wi-Fi menu. A check mark appears next to the current setting. Tap the desired setting to turn the Wi-Fi radio on or off.

> TIP: You'll likely find it easier to access Wi-Fi settings by tapping the Wi-Fi button on your NOOK's Home screen.

For more information on connecting to Wi-Fi hotspots, **see** "Using Wi-Fi Hotspots" in Chapter 11, "Getting Started with Your NOOK."

Display Menu

The Display menu contains several options for configuring your NOOK's display. You already learned how to change its wallpaper and screensaver using the Display menu. Now look at the other display options available on this menu.

> TIP: The Display menu contains more items than can be displayed on the touchscreen. To view all the menu items, you need to scroll down. The easiest way to scroll using the touchscreen is to tap and hold for a second and then move your finger up and down to scroll the display.

Sleep Timer

This controls the time interval after which your NOOK puts itself to sleep. This timer is set to 10 minutes by default. To change the interval, tap Sleep Timer, and then tap the desired time interval.

> TIP: If you set the sleep timer to a time interval shorter than the amount of time it takes you to read a page on the reading screen, your NOOK goes into sleep mode while you are reading. So be sure you set the interval appropriately for your reading speed.
>
> Because your NOOK uses almost no battery power when you read, 10 minutes is likely a suitable interval for most people.

Auto Adjust Brightness

Your NOOK contains a light sensor that adjusts the brightness of the touchscreen based on the ambient light level. Because the touchscreen uses less power when the brightness is reduced, it's recommended that you leave this setting turned on. However, if you want to turn off the automatic adjustment, tap Auto Adjust Brightness and then tap Off.

If auto-adjust brightness is turned off, the Touchscreen Brightness setting (described next) controls your NOOK's touchscreen brightness.

Touchscreen Brightness

This setting controls the maximum brightness of the touchscreen. To adjust the brightness, tap Touchscreen Brightness; then drag your finger to adjust the slider. When you are happy with the setting, tap the X to return to the menu.

Touchscreen Timer

This adjusts the time interval after which the touchscreen turns itself off. You can choose 10 seconds, 30 seconds, or 60 seconds.

Clock

These settings enable you to select your current local time zone, whether you want Daylight Savings Time on or off, and select a 12-hour or 24-hour clock format. Your NOOK normally gets the current time using Fast & Free Wireless if you have the 3G/Wi-Fi NOOK. However, if wireless service isn't available, the NOOK can still display the current time, provided you have configured your time zone.

If you travel to another time zone and a Fast & Free Wireless connection is available, your NOOK automatically sets the time zone for your current location. Otherwise, you need to set the time zone manually.

Device Menu

The Device menu provides device settings for your NOOK. You already explored the Edit Your Profile option. Also provided are options to unregister your NOOK (to remove the connection between your NOOK and your B&N account), to reset it to factory defaults, to require a passcode to use your NOOK, and to require the entry of your B&N password to purchase NOOKbooks, magazines, and newspapers on your NOOK. Think of the passcode protection as a PIN for your NOOK so that another person cannot just pick it up and start reading for free.

NOTE: You must unregister your NOOK prior to resetting to factory defaults.

CAUTION: Resetting your NOOK to factory defaults removes all content from its internal memory. Content stored on a microSD card is not removed. Before you reset it to factory defaults, make sure you have backups of any personal documents stored in your NOOK's internal memory.

When Should I Reset My NOOK to Factory Defaults?

If you are going to give your NOOK to someone else, you should unregister it and reset it to factory defaults. B&N technical support might also ask you to reset your NOOK during troubleshooting. However, outside of those reasons, you likely won't ever need to reset it.

Contacts Menu

One of the unique features of your NOOK is the ability to lend some NOOKbooks to your friends and family members. To lend a NOOKbook to someone else, you need to provide an email address. To make lending easier, your NOOK enables you to store email addresses so that you can easily lend a book by selecting someone from your contact list.

For more information on lending books on your NOOK, **see** Chapter 14, "Lending and Borrowing Books on Your NOOK Using LendMe."

To view your list of contacts, tap Settings and then tap Contacts. To add a new contact, tap Add a New Contact, enter the name and email address for the contact, and tap Submit.

To edit an existing contact, tap the contact and then tap Edit. Enter the new information for the contact and tap Submit. To delete a contact, tap the contact and then tap Delete.

Can I Import Contacts from My Mail Application or from Another Source into My NOOK?

Unfortunately, you can't. Your NOOK doesn't store contacts in a file that you can directly edit, so all contacts have to be manually entered.

Adding a microSD Card to Your NOOK

Your NOOK has approximately 1.3 GB of built-in usable memory. That's enough memory for an enormous library of books. However, it might not be enough memory if you add pictures, music, and audiobooks to your NOOK. Therefore, your NOOK's memory is expandable using a microSD card.

> TIP: A microSD card is not the same as an SD memory card like the kind typically used in digital cameras. A microSD card is approximately the size of your fingernail.

To install a microSD card, you need to first remove the back cover on your NOOK. Removing the back cover is easy when you know how to do it.

To install a microSD card, follow these steps:

1. Locate the small tab under the micro USB plug on the bottom of your NOOK.

2. Gently pull the back cover away from your NOOK using the tab.

3. When the bottom of the back cover begins to come off, slide your fingernail along the left and right edges between the cover and your NOOK to pull the remainder of the cover off.

4. Locate the microSD slot on your NOOK. It's located next to the battery.

5. Gently slide the metal cover for the slot toward the top of your NOOK to unlock it. You should feel and hear a snap sound. If the cover won't slide, it might already be in the unlocked position.

6. Lift the metal cover, which is hinged at the top. To open it, lift the bottom of the cover.

7. Place the microSD card into the slot so that the metal contacts in the slot contact the metal contacts on the microSD card.

8. Close the metal cover, and slide it toward the bottom of your NOOK to lock it into place.

9. Snap the back cover onto your NOOK.

When you connect your NOOK to your computer, you now see your microSD card in addition to your NOOK's built-in memory. You also see memory statistics for your microSD card listed in the Summary page in your NOOK's settings.

Can I Use a High-Capacity microSD Card in My NOOK?

Yes. Many people have reported using microSD HC cards up to 16 GB.

CHAPTER 13

Reading on Your NOOK and Beyond

Although your NOOK has many unique features and capabilities, when it comes right down to it, its primary purpose is for reading books and other content. One of the benefits of owning a NOOK is that you can carry a complete library with you everywhere you go. If you don't happen to have your NOOK with you, you can also read your ebooks on your PC, Mac, iPhone, iPad, iPod touch, Android phone, and Blackberry.

Various forms of content are available to read on your NOOK, such as NOOKbooks, secure eReader books from Fictionwise, PDFs, and other EPUB. Appendix A, "Understanding ebook Formats," explains more about the details of ebook formats.

Can I Read Word Documents or TXT Files on My NOOK?

If you want to read Word documents or TXT files on your NOOK, you need to first convert them into a format compatible with your NOOK.

Calibre can convert TXT files to the EPUB format for your NOOK. If you want to read a Word document, you should save the file as a PDF file. (Recent versions of Word provide this functionality.) If you cannot save the Word document as a PDF, first save it as an HTML file, and then use Calibre to convert it for your NOOK.

For more information on using Calibre to convert ebooks, **see** Chapter 21, "Managing Your ebooks with Calibre."

Browsing Your Library

There are two main places for content on your NOOK: The Daily and My Library.

The Daily

The Daily includes information automatically delivered to your NOOK. You can find a collection of short articles of interest to NOOKies (called *feeds*), notifications of software updates, lending offers, special offers from B&N, and notifications of new subscription content such as magazines and newspapers.

> TIP: Some notifications such as new subscription content and LendMe offers show up as balloon tips on your NOOK's Home screen. You can access more details on these notifications by visiting The Daily.

By default, The Daily displays feeds, notifications, and subscriptions. If you prefer to see only one of these categories in The Daily, tap Show on the touchscreen, and select the category you want to display. You can also sort entries in The Daily by tapping Sort and choosing Most Recent, Type, or Author. The default is to sort by type.

Because content in The Daily changes often, it's a good idea to check from time to time to see what's new. B&N not only offers interesting information about your NOOK and about ebooks and other content, but it also occasionally provides special offers to NOOK owners.

Can I Remove an Item from The Daily?

The visible items in The Daily are controlled by B&N. There isn't currently a way to manually remove an item. You can, however, filter on just the item types you want to see using the Show option on the touchscreen.

Your NOOK divides My Library into two areas: My B&N Library and My Documents. There are a few differences between these two areas, so now look at each one separately.

My B&N Library

My B&N Library contains all the content you purchase from B&N. This includes not only books you purchase, but also magazine and newspaper subscriptions, sample books, and free books downloaded from B&N.

Items in My B&N Library are in one of three categories:

▶ **Items on your NOOK**: Items on your NOOK are available for reading immediately by selecting the item. They are stored in your NOOK's memory or on a microSD card if one is installed.

▶ **Archived items**: These are items in My NOOK Library on bn.com and that have been downloaded to your NOOK at one point but that have since been removed from your NOOK. These items appear as light-colored text (grayed out) in My B&N Library.

▶ **Items in your online digital library and not your NOOK**: Items that have been added to My NOOK Library on bn.com but have never been downloaded to your NOOK display a Download option when selected. After you download one of these items to your NOOK, you can archive it to remove it.

For more information on using My NOOK Library on bn.com, **see** Chapter 22, "Using My NOOK Library."

If you purchase a book using the Shop on your NOOK, that book is automatically downloaded to your NOOK within a few minutes. If you purchase an NOOKbook from B&N using your computer, the NOOKbook is added to My NOOK Library on bn.com, but it isn't downloaded to your NOOK automatically.

CAUTION: If you plan to be away from Wi-Fi hotspots and Fast & Free Wireless, you should make sure that the items that appear in My B&N Library have actually been downloaded to your NOOK. Unfortunately, there isn't a visual indicator to show you this. The only way to tell if an item has actually been downloaded to your NOOK is to select the item to see if a Download option is on the touchscreen menu. If there is, the item hasn't yet been downloaded to your NOOK.

Some items in My B&N Library might have an Indicator icon immediately to the right of the title. This icon indicates special properties of the item (such as the ability to lend the item to a friend using the LendMe feature), or it might indicate that an item has been lent to someone or is borrowed from someone.

For more information on the LendMe feature, **see** Chapter 14, "Lending and Borrowing Books on Your NOOK Using LendMe."

The following icons might be displayed for an item:

▶ **LendMe**: Indicates that the item can be lent to a friend using the LendMe feature.

▶ **On Loan**: Indicates that the item has been lent to a friend. You cannot read this item for a period of 14 days from the lend date.

▶ **Borrowed**: Indicates that the item has been borrowed from a friend. The item will be available to you for 14 days.

▶ **From a Friend**: Indicates that the item is one that a friend has offered to lend to you. After you accept the offer, the item shows a Borrowed icon.

▶ **Sample**: Indicates that the item is a sample ebook from B&N.

▶ **New**: Indicates that the item was downloaded to your NOOK within the past 48 hours and that you haven't yet read the item.

To browse the items in My B&N Library, use the up and down arrows on the touch-screen to highlight an item. The following menu options are available for interacting with a selected item.

View Item Details & Options

When you tap View Item Details & Options, the reading screen displays the title and author (or publisher for newspaper and magazines) and any overview information provided by the publisher.

After selecting this item, the touchscreen provides a menu of options available for the selected content. The options available on the touchscreen menu differ depending on the content you select:

▶ **Download**: Displayed only when the content has not already been down-loaded to your NOOK. Tapping Download transfers it using either Fast & Free Wireless or Wi-Fi.

▶ **Read**: Displayed only when the content has been downloaded to your NOOK. Tapping Read opens the content on the reading screen.

▶ **Lend**: Displayed only when the publisher has enabled the LendMe feature. This menu item enables you to lend the content to a friend.

▶ **Rating**: A series of stars is available so that you can rate your content. Tap the stars, and five large stars display. Touch the star that corresponds to your rating.

> TIP: If you want to remove your rating, tap the leftmost star, and drag your finger toward the left away from the stars.

▶ **View**: By default, your NOOK displays an overview of the selected content, including a synopsis paragraph if available. To switch to a detailed view that includes the publisher, publication date, and other information about the content, tap View and then tap Details.

▶ **Archive**: Removes the selected content from your NOOK's storage. The item is still visible in My B&N Library, but if you want to read the content, you need to unarchive it first.

> NOTE: There isn't a way to delete content from your library from the NOOK. To delete content (including sample books), you need to use My NOOK Library at the B&N website.

For more information on using My NOOK Library, **see** Chapter 22.

Show Covers

In addition to selecting content from My B&N Library by scrolling, you can view covers for your content by tapping Show Covers. Covers display in full color on the touchscreen; by swiping your finger left and right, you can browse through them. When you find something you want to read, simply tap the cover. If you've already downloaded the item to your NOOK, it opens in the reading pane. Otherwise, you are taken to the overview for the item, where you can tap Download to copy the content to your NOOK. Tap the X in the upper right to close the gallery of covers.

Change View

You have several ways to view your library. The options in this menu enable you to determine this. You can choose to Show Shelves or Hide Shelves. If you have added shelves (for example, Fiction, European History, and so on), with Show Shelves you see books on their shelves sorted in alphabetical order. With Hide Shelves selected, your books are ordered according to what you have chosen in the Sort By option: Most Recent, Title, or Author.

The Show option enables you to narrow the type of content you see: All, eBooks, Magazines, or Newspapers.

Finally, you can choose either Hide Archived Items or Show Archived Items. If you have Show Archived Items turned on, you can then select the title in your library and unarchive it.

> NOTE: The shelves for My B&N Library and My Documents cannot be viewed together. In other words, one set of shelves exists for both sets of ebooks, but while in My B&N Library, the My Documents ebooks on the same shelf do not appear, and vice versa.

Shelves

You can organize your ebooks into shelves, aligning them into whatever categories you want for easier access to similar ebooks. You can go directly to a shelf of books by tapping Go to Shelf and then tapping the particular shelf you want to go to.

If you have shelves you created and you want to place ebooks onto those shelves, this is the option you want. Tap Place On or Remove from Shelf. You see a list of shelves in the touchscreen with up and down navigation arrows. Use those arrows to navigate from book to book. After a book is selected, tap the shelf you want it on. You can add an ebook to more than one shelf. A check mark appears next to the shelves that an ebook is on. To remove the ebook from a shelf, tap that shelf and the check mark disappears.

If you want to set the order your shelves appear in, tap Reorder Shelves. The reading screen shows your shelves. Use the up and down keys to select the shelf; then tap Move This Shelf Up or Move This Shelf Down. The reading screen refreshes showing you the new order.

To create a new shelf, tap Create a New Shelf. Type the name of the shelf and tap Submit. To remove a shelf, tap Remove a Shelf, tap the shelf you want to delete, and tap OK.

To rename a shelf, tap Rename a Shelf, tap the shelf you want to rename, update the name, and tap Submit.

Check for New B&N Content

You can check for new B&N content by tapping Check for New B&N Content. This is useful in cases where you've purchased a book from the B&N website and you want to download the book to your NOOK.

This menu option is also used to check for books a friend has lent you using the LendMe feature.

> TIP: You can continue to browse My B&N Library while your NOOK checks for new content.

Search

This menu option searches My B&N Library for all the search terms entered. This feature doesn't search inside your content. It searches only the *metadata* for your content. Metadata includes the title, author, publisher, contributors, and subject.

Sort By

You can sort My B&N Library by date (Most Recent), title, or author. The default is by date with the most recent at the top of the list.

Archiving My B&N Library Items

As mentioned earlier, you can archive an item by tapping View Item Details and Options and then tapping Archive. Archiving is a means to remove an item you purchased from B&N from your NOOK. Archived items still display in My B&N Library, but they are displayed using faded text.

> TIP: If you archive an item and it isn't displayed in faded text in My B&N Library, tap Check for New B&N Content to refresh your library; it should properly reflect the archival status. This should happen automatically after archiving an item, but the library sometimes does not refresh correctly.

When an item is archived, you can still view details on the item, rate the item, and lend the item to a friend using the LendMe feature. However, to read the item, you must unarchive it.

To unarchive an item, select it in My B&N Library; then tap Unarchive on the touchscreen. Your NOOK asks you to confirm that you want to unarchive the item. Tap OK, and you be return to My B&N Library. The item you unarchived might still be displayed in faded text, but your NOOK automatically checks for new B&N content and updates My Library shortly.

> TIP: You can manage your ebook library (including archiving and unarchiving items) using My NOOK Library at bn.com. My NOOK Library is covered in detail in Chapter 22.

After you unarchive an item, your NOOK automatically downloads it to your NOOK for reading. However, it can take a few minutes before the item downloads. If you want to start reading the item immediately, you can select it and then tap Download to download the item and read it.

> NOTE: Items often start downloading automatically after you select them. When this happens, you see a progress indicator next to the Download item on the touchscreen.

My Documents

My Documents contains content you manually copy to your NOOK from other sources. B&N calls the process of manually copying books and other content to your NOOK *sideloading*, and any reading content you sideload onto your NOOK appears in the My Documents portion of My Library.

> TIP: If you view My B&N Library, you can switch to My Documents by tapping View My Documents on the touchscreen.

Just as with My B&N Library, you can browse items in My Documents using the up and down arrows on the touchscreen. You might notice that some of the options available for items in My B&N Library are not available in My Documents. For example, you cannot browse covers for items in My Documents.

> NOTE: If a cover is available for an item in My Documents, you see the cover on the touchscreen while reading the item. The cover will not be visible otherwise.

After you select an item in My Documents, you see the following menu options on the touchscreen.

View Item Details & Options

When you tap this option, you see the details for the selected item. Details include the publisher, publication date, and so on. You also see the file path for the selected item.

> TIP: The file path begins with NOOK if the selected item is stored in your NOOK's internal memory. If the item is stored in a microSD card, it begins with external sdcard.

After you tap View Item Details & Options, the only menu option available for side-loaded content is Read.

> **How Can I Delete Sideloaded Content Because There Isn't a Menu Option to Remove It?**
>
> Sideloaded content must be deleted by connecting your NOOK to your computer and removing the content. The easiest way to manage your sideloaded content is to use Calibre, a free ebook management application. **See** Chapter 21.

Check for New Content

After you sideload content onto your NOOK's internal memory or a microSD card, you need to tap Check for New Content to add that content to My Documents. You also need to tap this option for your NOOK to reflect any content you deleted.

> TIP: If you have sideloaded a lot of content onto a microSD card, your NOOK may not recognize that content for several minutes after a reboot. If you reboot your NOOK and it looks like your sideloaded content is missing, be patient and it should appear within a few minutes.

You can think of the Check for New Content option as a refresh option for My Documents. If you add or remove any content, you need to refresh your NOOK's view of My Documents by tapping this option.

Can I Sideload Books into My B&N Library So That I Can Browse Them by Their Covers?

No. Content for My B&N Library is stored in the My B&N Downloads folder on your NOOK. You can sideload non-B&N content into this folder, but your NOOK won't recognize it and won't display it in My B&N Library.

Reading Books on Your NOOK

After you select an item to read, you are taken to the starting point that the publisher has chosen for that item. This might or might not be the first page. For example, some ebooks open on the first page of Chapter 1. Other ebooks open on the cover or title page. The publisher of the book decides which page is visible when you first open an ebook.

As you're reading, use the Next Page and Previous Page buttons along the edge of your NOOK to turn the page. When you turn the page, you notice a slight delay and a flashing on the reading screen. This is normal and is a result of the E Ink technology used in your NOOK. The flashing of the display is actually a result of your NOOK first clearing the screen and then displaying the new page. If your NOOK didn't first clear the display, you'd see remnants of the previous page each time you turned the page. By charging the entire screen before displaying the next page, your NOOK ensures that you see a fresh and crisp image of the new page.

TIP: As long as the touchscreen is not illuminated, you can also swipe it to turn pages. Swipe right to left to move to the next page and left to right to move to the previous page.

NOTE: B&N has released incremental software updates to the NOOK since its release, and each of these updates has made page-turning faster. You might see additional improvements in this area, but there's no way for B&N to eliminate the delay completely when turning pages because of limitations in the current E Ink technology.

If you want to quickly navigate to another part of the book, tap Go To on the touch-screen. You can navigate to the cover of the book by tapping Go To and then Cover. You can also navigate directly to a particular chapter by tapping Go To, Chapter, and then the chapter name. If your book has not automatically synced with another NOOK reading device, you can force it by tapping Last Page Saved on BN.com. Your NOOK can look up the page information and then jump to that page location.

Changing the Text Font and Text Size

Your NOOK enables you to easily change the text font and text size while reading. To change the font or the text size, tap Preferences; then tap Text Font or Text Size on the touchscreen while reading.

Your NOOK supports six text sizes, from Extra Small to Extra Extra Large. To change the text size, tap Preferences, tap Text Size, and then tap the desired text size. It takes a few seconds for your NOOK to resize the text.

To change the text font, tap Preferences, tap Text Font, and select one of the available fonts. Your NOOK offers a choice of Amasis, Helvetica Neue, and Light Classic. Amasis and Light Classic are both serif fonts, and Helvetica Neue is a sans-serif font.

> NOTE: Font settings affect all content, not just the content you are currently reading. In other words, if you select a text size of Extra Small, all content with sizable text appears as Extra Small.

Although you can modify the text size and text font for most content, you can't change these settings for all content:

- ▶ Light Classic is not available when reading content in eReader format.

- ▶ You cannot change the text font if the publisher created the content with a specific font embedded in it.

- ▶ You cannot change the text font for PDF files. If the creator of the PDF file embedded a particular font, your NOOK uses that font. Otherwise, it uses the Light Classic font.

- ▶ Some ebooks consist of pages scanned as images, usually as PDF files. You cannot change the text font for these ebooks.

> TIP: Depending on the format used for an ebook, text sizes can vary from book to book.

You can find out the ebook format of sideloaded content using the View Item Details & Options menu item. The file path includes the filename, and the file extension reflects the format of the ebook. However, you cannot easily tell whether B&N content is in EPUB or eReader format.

Autosaving Page Location on BN.com

In the Preferences menu, you can tap Auto Save Page on BN.com. Assuming you have the Fast & Free Wireless or a Wi-Fi connection active, this option sends the page location information to My NOOK Library on bn.com. When you open one of the NOOKapps, a NOOKcolor, or NOOKstudy registered to your account, the page information is communicated to that device. In other words, page location for NOOKbooks is now synced across devices.

> NOTE: The B&N eReader for the Mac and the B&N eReader app for Blackberry do not support syncing.

> NOTE: Notes, bookmarks, and highlights are *not* synced from the NOOK to any of the NOOK apps or NOOKcolor. Only the page location is synced.

Looking Up Words in the Dictionary

One of the most convenient features of your NOOK is to quickly look up the definitions of words you don't know. If you're reading a book and encounter a word you don't know, tap Look Up Word on the touchscreen and your NOOK displays a four-way control enabling you to highlight the word. Pressing the up or down arrow on the touchscreen moves the selection up or down a line. Pressing the left or right arrow moves the selection to the next or previous word.

> NOTE: Looking up words is not supported for subscription content on your NOOK. However, you can look up words for subscription content when reading in the NOOK for PC app application on your computer.

Highlight the word you want to look up and tap Look Up to retrieve the definition. Your NOOK displays the definition in a shaded box. After you've read the definition, tap OK and your NOOK returns to the page you were reading.

> TIP: At times, you might find that pressing down on the control skips a line of text. This happens because of the way text reflows when the text size is applied on your NOOK. If your NOOK skips a line when you press down and you want to highlight a word on the previous line, simply press the left arrow on the touchscreen to move to the last word on the previous line.

Looking up a word that is far down on a page can be frustrating because doing so requires you to tap the down arrow repeatedly. B&N could greatly improve upon this feature by enabling you to tap the up arrow when you are on the top line of a page to move to the bottom line of the same page. It would also be more convenient to hold down an arrow button to move the highlight repeatedly. Hopefully you'll see improvements in a future software upgrade for the NOOK.

Reading Subscription Content

In addition to books, B&N provides magazine and newspaper subscriptions for your NOOK. B&N automatically delivers subscription content to your NOOK as long as either a Wi-Fi or Fast & Free Wireless connection is available.

For more information on subscribing to content on your NOOK, **see** Chapter 17, "Shopping and Visiting B&N on Your NOOK."

Unlike books, subscription content isn't presented in a linear format. Content is often presented as article headlines followed by a small synopsis of each article. To read the specific article, use the up and down arrows on the touchscreen to highlight the article headline; then tap the select button on the touchscreen to open the article. After an article is open, you can use the Next Page and Previous Page buttons to navigate between pages just as you do when reading a book.

Many magazines and newspapers enable you to skip between sections using the Go To menu option on the touchscreen. Tap Go To and then tap Section to see a list of available sections. Tap the desired section to immediately go to it.

> NOTE: Some subscription content doesn't provide helpful sections for navigation. For example, I subscribe to *PC Magazine* on my NOOK, and when I tap Go To, Section, the only options are Front Cover and PC Magazine. That doesn't help much when I want to navigate to parts of the magazine.

Subscription content often contains links that make navigating the content easier. For example, when reading *The Wall Street Journal*, you can move to the next section by using the down arrow on the touchpad to highlight Next Section at the top of the reading screen and tapping select on the touchscreen.

You can search the text of subscription content by tapping Find on the touchscreen, entering your search term, and tapping Search. Tap Find Next to locate the next occurrence of your search term and Find Previous to find the previous occurrence.

For more information on subscription content, including when your NOOK automatically deletes subscription content, **see** Chapter 17.

This chapter covered a lot of information on reading content on your NOOK. However, your NOOK is only one device of many that provides access to your My NOOK Library. You can also read content on your computer, your iPhone, and other devices as well, which the next chapter covers.

CHAPTER 14

Lending and Borrowing Books on Your NOOK Using LendMe

To keep readers from sharing ebooks with all their friends, publishers usually protect ebooks with digital rights management (DRM), which ties an ebook to an individual, and unless that individual can prove that he is an authorized reader, the ebook will not open.

DRM is one of the reasons some people don't like ebooks. After all, when readers find a good read, they like to pass it on to friends and family. The number of people with whom you can share a physical book is fairly limited, but because ebooks are digital copies of a book, they can literally be shared with millions of people quite easily via email, Facebook, and any number of other methods.

One of the unique features that B&N added to your NOOK is the ability to lend some ebooks to other readers using the LendMe feature. Although there are some serious restrictions when lending and borrowing books, the LendMe feature is a step in the right direction.

Lending Books with LendMe

To lend a book to someone, the book must support LendMe. Not all books do. If a book does support lending, you see the LendMe logo on the book's page on bn.com, as shown in Figure 14.1. You also see the LendMe logo next to the book's title in My Library on your NOOK and in the NOOK app.

LendMe™   This NOOKbook is Lendable How it works

FIGURE 14.1   The LendMe logo appears on a book's page at bn.com if the book is lendable.

NOTE: When shopping for ebooks on your NOOK, the LendMe logo is not displayed on lendable ebooks. However, a LendMe Books category is available on the Home page after tapping Shop; that category displays the most popular ebooks that support LendMe.

To lend a book to someone using LendMe, follow these steps:

1. Browse to the book on your NOOK, and select View Item Details & Options on the touchscreen.

2. Tap Lend.

3. Select a contact or select Add a New Contact to add someone not currently in your contact list.

4. Type a message to send with the lend invitation. (The message is optional.)

5. Tap Submit.

Your NOOK asks you to confirm that you want to lend the book. Tap Confirm to complete the process. Your NOOK then displays a message that it's taking care of your LendMe request. When that message disappears, you're taken back to My Library. If you tap Cancel before your NOOK returns to My Library, the LendMe process will be canceled.

What Happens If I Lend My Friend a Book She Already Owns?

If you attempt to lend a book to a friend who already owns the book you're lending, a lending error occurs. On your NOOK, you simply see a message that says, "Sorry, Your LendMe Request Was Not Possible." On the NOOK for PC app, you see an error that says, "Lending Error." Unfortunately, B&N doesn't provide any useful information about why the failure occurred, so you're left to wonder if it's because your friend already owns the book or if something else went wrong.

If you see a lending error when attempting to lend a friend a book, check with your friend to see whether she owns the book already. If she does not yet own the book, contact B&N for information on why the LendMe attempt failed.

Choose carefully when lending a book because after you lend a book, you can never lend that particular book to anyone again. However, a book is considered to be on loan only if your friend accepts the LendMe offer. If your friend rejects the offer or if she allows the offer to expire without accepting it, you can lend the book again after it's returned to My Library.

I Want to Lend a Book to One of My Friends. Does My Friend Have to Own a NOOK for Me to Lend Her a Book?

No. Your friend can read an ebook you've lent to her using a NOOK app for PC, iPod Touch, iPhone, or iPad; NOOKstudy; or eReader for Mac or Blackberry. However, your friend cannot read the book unless the email address you used to send the LendMe offer is associated with her B&N account.

The person to whom you've loaned the ebook has 7 days to accept the loan offer. If she doesn't accept within 7 days, the book is returned to your library. The loan offer can also be rejected, in which case the book is returned to your library immediately.

You see notifications in The Daily about your loaned ebook if your friend accepts the loan offer or rejects the loan offer and when the loaned book has been automatically returned to your library. Loan offers and notifications are visible in The Daily on both your NOOK and the NOOK app.

While an ebook is loaned, On Loan appears next to the title in My Library and you cannot read the book. When you loan a book, you also loan your DRM rights to the book. Only one person can possess the DRM rights to a book at any one time, so you need to wait until the book is returned to your library before you can read the book again.

If My Friend Finishes a Loaned Book Before 14 Days Have Elapsed, Can She Return the Book to Me Immediately?

Yes. Your friend can click the Return It link that appears in the book's listing in the NOOK app. However, you cannot manually return a book using your NOOK.

There are many reports of LendMe emails not ever being received. In my use of the LendMe feature, I have experienced this on two occasions. In these situations, your friend might use the NOOK for PC app or My NOOK Library on bn.com to accept or reject the offer. In some cases, however, the offer doesn't appear in the NOOK app or My NOOK Library. B&N's answer to this problem is to wait for 7 days when the loan offer expires and then lend the book again. There isn't a way to force a re-send of the offer email, and there's no way to cancel the offer.

Borrowing Books

When a friend lends you a book, you get a loan offer in the From a Friend section of The Daily on both your NOOK and in the NOOK for PC app. You have 7 days to either accept the offer or reject it. You can accept or reject the loan offer from your NOOK or NOOK app. eReader for the Mac and Blackberry do not currently support the LendMe feature.

If you accept a loan offer from your NOOK, that book is also available for the loan period in the NOOK app, and vice versa. However, if you accept the offer from the NOOK app and then try to read the book on your NOOK, your NOOK might not realize that you've accepted the offer and might ask you to accept the offer again. When you do, the LendMe request will fail, and you'll see a message telling you that the LendMe request was not successful. When this happens, simply tap Check for New B&N Content from My Library, and your NOOK synchronizes with the loan offer you accepted in the NOOK app. You can then read the book you were loaned without any problems.

You can determine how much time is left on your loan period by selecting the lent book in My Library and tapping View Item Details & Options. You see the email address of the friend who lent you the book and an indicator telling you how many days are left in the loan period. If you don't finish the book within the loan period, you can buy the book by tapping Buy on the touchscreen. When you buy a book that was lent to you, the lent copy is immediately returned to your friend.

CHAPTER 15

Using Highlights, Bookmarks, and Annotations

Take a look at one of your favorite books, and you can likely find notes in the margins and perhaps dog-eared pages. Jotting down notes about passages that impact you or marking pages you want to come back and visit later is how you can make a book a personalized possession. Fortunately, you don't have to forgo these things when it comes to ebooks because your NOOK lets you easily highlight passages and add bookmarks and notes to pages.

> NOTE: Your NOOK and B&N eReader for Mac and Blackberry support adding highlights and notes. However, notes and highlights are not shared among these items. If you add a note or highlight on one device, that note or highlight will not be available on another device.

Some books don't support notes and highlights. If you add a note or highlight and the book doesn't save it between page turns or when you exit and open the book again, that book doesn't support the highlighting and notes features.

When I asked B&N about this problem, it indicated that it is by design that some books do not support notes and highlights. They also told me that there is no way to tell whether a book does or doesn't support the features. You simply have to try to add a highlight or a note to see if it works for that particular book.

Using Highlights, Notes, and Bookmarks on Your NOOK

When you think of highlighting something in a book, you typically think of using a yellow highlighter marker to draw attention to portions of the text. Highlighting on your NOOK is similar to that, but because the E Ink screen is in black and white, your highlights show up as dark gray shading.

> TIP: Highlighting and notes are not supported for subscription content. You can add highlights and notes only in ebooks that support them.

A note in an ebook is simply a highlighted area with a message attached. Therefore, the steps necessary to add, view, edit, and delete notes are the same as the steps for using highlights.

Adding a Highlight or a Note

To highlight text or add a note in an ebook, follow these steps:

1. Tap Highlights and Notes on the touchscreen.

2. Tap Add Highlight or Note.

3. Use the arrow buttons to move the selection to the first word you want to highlight.

4. Tap Start Selection.

5. Use the arrow buttons to navigate to the last word you want in your highlighted section. If you make a mistake, tap Clear and start your selection again.

6. After the desired section is highlighted, tap Add Highlight or Note.

7. Enter the text for your note if you want to add a note.

8. Tap Submit.

> NOTE: In some cases, the Clear button doesn't clear your selection. In those cases, tap Cancel and start again from step 2.

Viewing Highlights and Notes

After you complete your highlight or note, you might be surprised that you don't actually see it on the page. That's because highlights are not visible by default. To show highlights, tap Highlights and Notes and then tap Show Highlights. To hide highlights again, tap Hide Highlights. In some books, after you add a highlight or note, you are returned to the Highlights and Notes menu, so you can simply tap Show Highlights to see your newly added highlight. Other books return you to the main menu on the touchscreen; you therefore have to tap Highlights and Notes and then tap Show Highlights to see your highlight.

TIP: Even though you can't see highlighted text by default, your NOOK displays a small unfilled arrow in the left margin at the point where a highlight or note appears. If you see this indicator while reading, tap Highlights and Notes and then tap Show Highlights to see the highlighted section.

If more than one highlight or note is on a page, another way to view them is to tap Highlights and Notes and then tap View Notes on This Page. When you use this method, you see a Next Highlight and Previous Highlight button on the touchscreen, which you can use to easily navigate between highlights and notes on the page.

Using the View Notes on This Page option doesn't work the same way in all books. Some books display a small snippet of your highlight overlaid on top of the page's text along with the note associated with that highlight. Other books simply toggle the shading of highlights as you tap Next Highlight and Previous Highlight. If the book you're reading doesn't display the note superimposed over the text, you can view the note associated with a highlight by selecting the highlight and then tapping View/Edit Note.

TIP: If a book toggles the shading of highlights, you might notice that not all highlights are visible after you exit the View Notes for This Page menu. In such cases, tapping Hide Highlights and Show Highlights corrects the problem.

Editing Notes

To edit notes you've added to a page, select the highlight associated with the note. If the note displays superimposed over the page's text, tap Edit Note to edit the note. Enter the new text for the note, and tap Submit. If you want to delete the note but keep the highlight, simply backspace over the text for the note, and tap Submit.

If you select a highlight and the note is not superimposed over the page's text, tap View/Edit Note to edit the note. If you want to remove the note but keep the highlight, backspace over the text for the note and tap Submit.

CAUTION: Books that don't display a superimposed note also have a Delete Note menu option after you select a highlight. If you choose this option to delete a note, it also deletes the highlight.

Deleting Highlights

To delete a highlight, navigate to the page containing the highlight, and tap Highlights and Notes. Then tap View Notes for This Page. You see one of two things when you tap this option, and based on what you see, you can take different steps to delete a highlight.

If you see a snippet of your highlight superimposed over a faded page from the book, tap Next Highlight if necessary to move to the highlight you want to delete; then tap Delete Highlight. When you finish deleting the highlights you want to delete, tap the back arrow to return to reading.

If you see your page with each highlight visible, tap Next Highlight and Previous Highlight repeatedly until you notice that your NOOK has begun cycling through the page's highlights. (You might need to tap Next Highlight and Previous Highlight several times before your NOOK begins to cycle through highlights.) After your NOOK begins to cycle through your highlights, tap Next Highlight or Previous Highlight to move to the highlight you want to delete; then tap Delete Note.

Using Bookmarks

Bookmarks enable you to easily return to a particular page. Unlike notes, bookmarks do not have any text associated with them. Unlike notes and highlights, bookmarks work in all your ebooks. Bookmarks are not supported in subscription content.

To add a bookmark on the page you're reading, tap Bookmarks, and then tap Add Bookmark. A bookmark indicator displays in the upper-right corner of the page.

To return to a bookmark, tap Bookmarks and then tap Go to Bookmark. A list of pages containing bookmarks displays on the touchscreen. Tap the bookmark you want to go to; your NOOK immediately takes you to that page.

> TIP: Bookmarks on your NOOK are associated with a page number. Because a single page number can span several page turns on your NOOK, adding a bookmark might cause the bookmark to be added to multiple reading screens on your NOOK.
>
> When you navigate to a bookmark, your NOOK navigates to the first screen for that page.

To remove a bookmark, navigate to the bookmark, and then tap Bookmarks, Remove Bookmark. You can also remove all bookmarks for a book by tapping Bookmarks, Remove All Bookmarks.

CHAPTER 16

Playing Music, Audiobooks, and Podcasts

For people who love to read, almost nothing stirs up as much nostalgia as the thought of listening to some nice music while reading a good book and maybe sipping a nice glass of wine. Your NOOK can't make wine, but it can provide the other two ingredients to this nostalgic scene.

Adding Audio Files to Your NOOK

You can use two folders on your NOOK specifically for audio files: My Audiobooks and My Music. When you add audio files to one of these folders, your NOOK recognizes the files and enables you to play the audio using its built-in audio player.

> NOTE: Your NOOK supports only MP3 audio files.

Playing Audio on Your NOOK

To play audio on your NOOK, you first need to copy the MP3 files to its memory or to a microSD card in your NOOK. Audio files should be copied into the My Music or My Audiobooks folder. If your microSD card does not have a My Music or My Audiobooks folder, create one before copying audio files to it.

> TIP: Your NOOK uses lowercase folder names, but it actually doesn't matter which case you use when you create audio folders. In other words, your NOOK doesn't care if you use "My Music" instead of "my music."

After you copy your audio files to the My Music or My Audiobooks folder, you can play them using the audio player on your NOOK. To launch the audio player, tap Open Audio Player on the touchscreen from any menu.

> TIP: After you add audio files to your NOOK, it needs to be indexed before it can appear in the audio player. If your audio files don't appear immediately, be patient and they should appear after they are indexed.

Using the Audio Player

The audio player on your NOOK is a bare-bones, basic audio player. So if you're expecting an iPod on your NOOK, you'll be disappointed. However, for playing background music while reading and for listening to audiobooks and podcasts, your NOOK's audio player is a great feature.

When the audio player is launched, the first thing it does is collect all the audio files in both the My Music folder and the My Audiobooks folder. It then creates a playlist of all those audio files. To start playing the playlist, tap the Play button on the touch-screen.

The following buttons are available in the audio player, from left to right:

- ▶ **Previous**: Moves to the beginning of the audio files currently playing. If you tap it a second time, it moves to the beginning of the previous audio file in the playlist.

- ▶ **Play/Pause**: If the audio player is playing audio, tapping this button pauses the audio. Otherwise, it resumes playing the audio. If audio is paused and the audio player is closed, audio picks up at the same point when the audio player is reopened unless you copied new audio content to your NOOK.

- ▶ **Next**: Moves to the next track in the playlist.

- ▶ **Volume**: Tapping this button opens the volume control. Move the slider to the right to increase the volume and to the left to decrease it. Tap the X button to close the volume slider.

> TIP: The speakers on your NOOK don't produce much volume. You can hear better audio if you use headphones or ear buds plugged into the mini-jack at the bottom of your NOOK.

- ▶ **Scrubber**: Press this button to open the scrubber. The scrubber enables you to change the position in the current audio file quickly. Drag your finger on the scrubber to change the position. When you lift your finger from the touchscreen, the scrubber closes automatically. To close it manually, tap the X button.

- ▶ **Shuffle**: Toggles Shuffle mode on or off. Each time shuffle is toggled on, a new random order is created for the playlist. You can also shuffle the playlist by tapping Shuffle Playlist when the playlist is displayed.

- ▶ **Playlist**: Tapping this button displays the current playlist. You can tap an audio file in the playlist to immediately begin playing that file.

While playing audio, you can tap the X button in the audio player to close the audio player interface. Your audio will continue playing, but you can interact with other menus on your NOOK. To stop the audio from playing, tap the Pause button prior to closing the audio player.

Controlling the Order Files Are Played

As I mentioned earlier, your NOOK creates a playlist of all your audio files sorted alphabetically by title. In some cases, that might be fine, but in other cases, you might want audio files to play in a particular order. For example, classical music CDs should always be played in the correct track order, but if you copy one to your NOOK, it essentially shuffles all the tracks.

To control the order in which audio files are played on your NOOK, you can edit the title of each track and put a numerical value in front of the title. So, you can add a 1 to the title of the first file you want to play, a 2 to the file you want to play second, and so on. However, you can't just change the name of the file to make this work. You have to change the title embedded in the audio file.

You can use any application that manages MP3 audio files to change the title. That includes iTunes, Microsoft Zune, Media Monkey, or any other similar software. All these applications enable you to change information such as the title, artist, genre, and so forth.

Playing Podcasts and Audiobooks on Your NOOK

In addition to listening to music, you can also use the audio player on your NOOK to play podcasts and audiobooks.

Podcasts

Podcasts are audio programs released on a regular schedule. You can subscribe to a podcast using any number of software applications, and when a new episode is released, it's automatically downloaded to your computer.

Podcasts are available that cover just about every topic of interest that you can think of. For example, some podcasts can help you use your computer or help you take better pictures. Some podcasts can deliver the news daily or weekly and other podcasts cover entertainment gossip. There are also podcasts that enable you to listen to your favorite radio shows on demand whenever you want.

If you own an iPhone, iPad, or iPod, you almost certainly have iTunes on your computer. iTunes enables you to easily subscribe to podcasts. You can search or browse for podcasts in the iTunes store. If you own a Microsoft Zune, you can subscribe to podcasts using the Zune Marketplace. If you don't have an application that you can use to subscribe to podcasts, you can download Juice, a free podcast receiver that makes finding and subscribing to podcasts easy. Juice is available from http://juicereceiver.sourceforge.net.

When you subscribe to a podcast, each time you launch your podcast application (whether that's iTunes, Zune, Juice, or some other application), it checks for new episodes. If it finds a new episode, it downloads it automatically to your computer. You can then copy that episode to your NOOK. You need to check the documentation and options for the software you use to determine where it stores podcasts it downloads.

> TIP: Be sure that you subscribe to podcasts that are in MP3 format. Some podcasts offer an MP3 version and versions in other formats. Only MP3 podcasts work on your NOOK.

Podcasts should be copied to either the My Audiobooks or My Music folder on your NOOK. I typically copy mine to the My Audiobooks folder because I like to keep my music separated from other audio files. However, because your NOOK combines the audio files in My Music and My Audiobooks when it creates its playlist, it doesn't matter which one you choose.

Audiobooks

Audiobooks are recordings of someone reading a book out loud. They are the digital version of books on tape. The most popular source of audiobooks is Audible.com, but your NOOK is not compatible with Audible audiobooks. However, you can enjoy plenty of sources of MP3 audiobooks on your NOOK.

Following are sources of MP3 audiobooks you can use on your NOOK:

▶ **Audiobooks.org**: Free audiobook versions of some classic books. There aren't many books here, but the ones it offers are of good quality.

▶ **Simply Audiobooks (www.simplyaudiobooks.com/downloads)**: For a few dollars per month, you can download as many audiobooks as you want. Simply Audiobooks offers both MP3 and WMA audiobooks, so be sure you choose the MP3 versions for your NOOK.

▶ **B&N Audiobooks (www.barnesandnoble.com/subjects/audio)**: B&N offers a wide assortment of audiobooks. If you're a B&N member, you can get some great deals for your NOOK.

▶ **Google Product Search**: Google Product Search (www.google.com/prdhp) is an excellent way to locate MP3 audiobooks. Simply search for "mp3 audiobook," and you can find a vast assortment from many merchants.

After you download an audiobook, copy it to the My Audiobooks folder on your NOOK. You can then play it by selecting the file from the audio player playlist.

Playing Chess and Soduko on Your NOOK

Since the original release of NOOK, B&N has added two games: Sodoku and Chess. You access the games by tapping Games on the touchscreen and tapping either Soduko or Chess.

Sudoku

When you first start Soduku, you need to select the difficulty level. The E Ink screen displays the entire puzzle while the touchscreen displays a scrollable version of that puzzle. Tap an empty cell in the touchscreen. You are given some options:

▶ **Numbers**: Tap the number button that you want to fill the cell with. If you enter an incorrect option, the number appears in red in the touchscreen.

▶ **Clear**: Clears the selected cell.

▶ **Notes**: Turns on or off notes. Notes in Sudoku are a way to indicate possible options to fill the cell without filling the cell. The numbers you type appear in a small version in the cell. Tap Notes to use this feature. The Notes button and the Number buttons turn blue. Tap Notes to turn off this feature and enter a number to fill that cell.

▶ **Hint**: If you are stuck, tapping this fills in the cell with the correct number.

Chess

Feel like playing a game of chess? Well, your opponent is just a tap away. When you tap Chess, the game opens with the board displayed. Tap Settings to set your color (White, Black, or Random). White moves first. In Settings you can also set the difficulty (Easy, Normal, or Hard). You can also set the amount of time allowed to win. On this latter setting, you can set it so that only you or the NOOKcolor or both have a designated amount of time to win the game.

> NOTE: The time allowed is used up only when it is that player's turn. In other words, if you give yourself 5 minutes to win the game, your clock counts down only when it's your turn to move.

If you set Save Game Before Exit to Yes, when you exit the game, it is saved for you to return to at a later time. If you set Resume Prior Game on Startup, the next time you tap Games and then tap Chess, the game you were playing last starts.

Tap Play Against NOOK to start a game using the settings. The game appears in the E Ink and touchscreens. If you tap the Options button in the top-left corner, you can start a new game, resign, see your past moves, and save the game. To move a piece, tap the piece on the touchscreen, and tap the location you want it to move to. Tap Undo to move the pieces back to the previous positions.

CHAPTER 17

Shopping and Visiting B&N on Your NOOK

One of the greatest features of your NOOK is the capability to sample and buy content from B&N directly from the device. As long as you have a Wi-Fi or Fast & Free Wireless connection, you can get new content for your NOOK no matter where you are. However, you can also use the B&N website to sample and purchase content for your NOOK.

> NOTE: Only customers with billing addresses in the Unites States, Canada, or a U.S. territory can order content from the B&N NOOKstore. Citizens of U.S. territories cannot preorder items.

Shopping on Your NOOK

To shop on your NOOK, tap the Shop button from the touchscreen's main screen. Your NOOK establishes a network connection using either Wi-Fi or Fast & Free Wireless and displays the NOOKstore Home screen, what B&N calls the *shopfront*.

Browsing the NOOKstore

The majority of the shopfront shows collections you can browse on your NOOK. Tap the up and down arrows on the touchscreen to highlight a collection, and then tap the Select button to see items in that category. In addition to collections such as NOOKbooks, Magazines, and Newspapers, you also see special collections such as NOOKbooks Under $5 and LendMe NOOKbooks.

> TIP: If you prefer, you can select one of the collections shown on the Home screen by tapping Collections on the touchscreen and then tapping the desired collection.

You can also browse for ebooks, magazines, or newspapers by tapping Browse on the touchscreen and then tapping eBooks, Magazines, or Newspapers. Doing so gives you the option to tap Browse Subjects on the touchscreen to filter content by subject. You can also browse by covers by tapping Show Covers.

At the bottom of the shopfront is a section displaying special deals and other offers from B&N. B&N calls this area the *merchandising area*. The merchandising area often spans multiple pages, and you can navigate through the pages using the Next Page and Previous Page buttons on your NOOK. A series of dots indicates which page of the merchandising area you are viewing.

Searching for Content

If you want to find a particular item in the NOOKstore, tap Search on the touchscreen, and enter your search terms. Your NOOK displays the results of your search after several seconds. The results show all the items in which your search terms appear in one or more of the following:

- ► Title
- ► Author
- ► Publisher
- ► Subject
- ► Contributors

When your search results appear, you can tap Show Covers to browse the covers of your search results.

TIP: A Search option appears on many menus in the NOOKstore. No matter where you are in the NOOKstore, when a search is performed, the entire NOOKstore is searched for your search terms. In other words, if you tap Search while search results are displayed, you are still searching the entire NOOKstore and not just searching your search results.

Sampling and Buying Content

After you locate and select an item you're interested in, you see an overview page that describes the item and shows the rating of the item from other B&N readers. To see more information about an item, tap View on the touchscreen. You then see the following options:

▶ **Overview**: Displays the default view when you select an item.

▶ **Editorial Reviews**: Displays editorial reviews for the item. This view often shows details from the publisher along with critic reviews of the item. It can span multiple pages.

▶ **Reader Reviews**: Displays reviews from other B&N customers. This view often spans multiple pages. Note that the number of reviews presented is likely to be smaller than the number of ratings.

▶ **Product Details**: Displays details on the item, such as the publisher, publication date, sales rank, and so forth.

If you like what you see, you can download a sample to your NOOK by tapping Get Free Sample. (Sampling is only valid with NOOKbooks.) Samples typically consist of the first chapter of an ebook. However, it's up to the publisher to decide what to provide as a sample. In some cases, samples might contain just a few pages. In other cases, samples consist primarily of front matter, such as the title page, table of contents, dedication, and so on. One sample I downloaded contained nine pages of front matter and two pages of actual manuscript—hardly enough to actually get a feel for the book.

> NOTE: Samples never expire. You can keep a sample for as long as you want.

If you decide to buy a book after reading the sample, tap Buy on the touchscreen; the book is then added to your library. Because samples and full ebooks are completely separate products, a purchased book does not open at the point where the sample ended. You need to manually navigate to the point where you stopped reading the sample.

> NOTE: If a B&N gift card is associated with your account, the cost for items purchased from the B&N NOOKstore are applied against that gift card. If there is not enough credit left on the card, B&N charges the remaining balance to your credit card on file.

If you'd like to remove a sample from your NOOK, you have to visit My NOOK Library at bn.com from your computer. There is currently no way to remove a sample from your NOOK without using your computer to do so. If you delete a sample unintentionally, you can download it again.

For more information on using My NOOK Library, **see** Chapter 22, "Using My NOOK Library."

Is It Possible to Accidentally Purchase a Book I Previously Purchased from B&N's NOOKstore?

Your NOOK does not even present the option to purchase a book you already own. If you select a book in the NOOKstore that you already own, you are shown an option to download or read the book, depending upon whether the book is already on your NOOK. However, you will not be shown an option to buy the book.

Some classic titles are released by multiple publishers. Two books of the same title from two different publishers are not considered the same title, so in these cases, you can purchase the same book twice.

Subscription content also enables you to sample prior to purchasing, but it works a bit differently than it does with ebooks. When you subscribe to a newspaper or magazine, you receive a 14-day free trial. If you cancel your subscription within that 14-day period, you will not be charged. If you cancel after the 14-day trial period, you will be refunded a prorated amount based on when you cancel.

You can use a trial subscription only once for any particular item. For example, if you subscribe to *The Wall Street Journal* and cancel your subscription within the 14-day trial period, you will be charged beginning immediately if you were to subscribe to *The Wall Street Journal* again because you have already taken advantage of a trial subscription.

NOTE: Subscriptions can be canceled only using My NOOK Library at bn.com. You cannot cancel a subscription using your NOOK.

Your NOOK automatically downloads subscription content when it's available. In addition to seeing the new content in My B&N Library, you'll also receive notifications in The Daily for any new subscription content your NOOK downloads.

Using Your NOOK in a B&N Store

As mentioned earlier, B&N stores have a Wi-Fi hotspot, so your NOOK can access free Wi-Fi while in the store. B&N uses this hotspot to offer you special promotions called More in Store while in the store. Your NOOK can automatically connect to a B&N hotspot when in the store, but you do need to ensure that Wi-Fi is turned on. (It's on by default.)

After your NOOK connects to the B&N hotspot, tap Shop on the touchscreen to see the More in Store offers in the merchandising area of the shopfront. The banner on the shopfront shows an overview of what's available. To see all the offerings for More in Store, tap the down arrow, and select Select to See All in More-in-Store link.

> TIP: Your NOOK displays the B&N logo on the top status bar while you are connected to the B&N hotspot.

The typical More in Store offerings consist of several articles B&N feels might be interesting. You are likely to find some interesting and others that don't interest you at all. If you'd like to get a sneak preview of what's available before you drive down to your local B&N, you can browse to http://www.barnesandnoble.com/NOOK/moreinstore/ to see a list of all the More in Store offerings.

> NOTE: You need to connect to the B&N hotspot to download and read the More in Store offerings.

B&N sometimes offers shopping specials for NOOK owners. You might see a coupon for 10% off of a CD or for a free coffee at the coffee shop. To take advantage of these coupons, you have to show the coupon on your NOOK upon checkout.

When you're connected to a B&N hotspot in a B&N store, you have can read any ebook in the B&N store for up to 1 hour, and according to B&N, you'll soon be able to read newspapers and magazines for up to 20 minutes.

There's no doubt that B&N has a unique opportunity because of its brick-and-mortar presence. No other ebook reader has the capability of being paired with a retail outlet, and there's every indication that B&N intends to beef up this feature in the future. It's certainly one of the more unique capabilities of the NOOK, and NOOK owners should be excited about what More in Store might offer in the future.

CHAPTER 18

Browsing the Web on Your NOOK

When B&N released version 1.3 of the NOOK firmware, it added a web browser so that you can browse the Web on your NOOK. Arguably, the most useful reason to have a web browser on your NOOK is so that you can join Wi-Fi hotspots that require you to authenticate via a browser (such as those often found in hotels), but you can also use the browser to access any web page, provided you connect to a Wi-Fi hotspot.

> NOTE: The web browser on your NOOK will not work when using Fast & Free Wireless. To access web pages, you must connect to a Wi-Fi hotspot.

An Overview of Browsing on Your NOOK

B&N has used a unique method of implementing browsing on the NOOK. Because web pages are designed to be navigated by scrolling and clicking links, the page Turn buttons on your NOOK are used to pan your view of the web page you're visiting. The page Turn buttons on the left side of the reading screen pan up and down on the page, and the buttons on the right side pan left and right. Using this method, you can view any portion of a web page on the reading screen.

> TIP: If you prefer, you can slide your finger on the touchscreen to pan around the page.

In addition to the reading screen, you can also view web pages on the touchscreen. As you pan around a page, a rectangle (the Panning Indicator) highlights the portion of the page shown on the touchscreen.

To follow a link on a page, simply tap the link on the touchscreen. To enter information into a form, tap the form field, and your NOOK displays the keyboard on the touchscreen.

Now look at how you can use the browser to navigate the Web.

Using the Web Browser Toolbar

The Browser toolbar provides buttons for navigating and controlling the browser. To access the toolbar, tap the Show Tool Bar button in the upper-left corner of the touchscreen.

The following buttons are available on the toolbar from left to right.

▶ **Refresh**: Tap to refresh the current page. While a page is loading, the arrows spin. Tapping the button while a page is loading stops the loading of the page.

▶ **Go To**: Tap Go To to navigate to a page in your browser. You can go to a web page, your home page, a search page (Google search), a favorite, or see your browsing history.

▶ **Favorites**: The Star button takes you to your favorites. You can add a favorite for the page you are currently viewing by tapping Add Favorite, or you can navigate to an existing favorite by tapping the Favorite icon.

▶ **Back**: Tap to navigate back to the previous page.

▶ **Forward**: Tap to navigate forward after tapping Back.

▶ **Zoom**: Tap the magnifying glass to zoom in or out on a page. When you zoom in, text appears larger so that it's easier to read.

▶ **Settings**: Tap to access the browser settings.

Configuring Web Browser Settings

As mentioned previously, tap the Settings button to access browser settings. The following settings are available.

▶ **Hide Tool Bar Automatically**: By default, the tool bar disappears after a few seconds, and you need to tap the Show Tool Bar button to show it. You can control whether the tool bar hides itself by changing this setting to Off.

▶ **Hide Panning Indicator**: The panning indicator is visible by default. To hide it, change this setting to On.

▶ **Home Page**: To change your browser's home page, tap this setting and enter a URL into the URL textbox.

▶ **Clear Cookies**: Tap to clear your browser's cookies.

▶ **Clear History**: Tap to clear your browsing history.

B&N labeled the web browser as a beta application, meaning it is testing it and it's likely not yet in a final state. In my experience, browsing on the NOOK is awkward because of the small size of the touchscreen. I also found that many web pages displayed incorrectly, and some (including Google) had overlapping page elements that made them almost impossible to read. Hopefully, B&N will continue to improve this feature of the NOOK.

CHAPTER 19

Rooting Your NOOK

At the beginning this book, I mentioned that B&N used Google's Android operating system in your NOOK. Choosing Android makes business sense because it's an open-source operating system, and B&N didn't have to pay a small fortune to use it. However, the most exciting thing about Android for you is that it lets you easily root the NOOK and add new and exciting features.

> NOTE: To complete the steps in this chapter, you must have at least a 128 MB microSD card installed in your NOOK.

> CAUTION: B&N released later versions of the NOOK that altered the hardware configuration. If your NOOK has a serial number 10030 and above (tap Settings, Device, and go to the second page for Device Information to see the serial number for your NOOK), rooting your NOOK could brick it—that is, make it as useful as a brick for reading books, and so on.
>
> The people at nookdevs.com, who figured out the softrooting method described next, may have a potential workaround (nookdevs.com/Rooting_New_Hardware), but beware because this is for advanced users and extreme caution should be taken. If you have a NOOK with a serial number less than 10030, softrooting as described in this chapter is not an issue.

> NOTE: Rooting is another term for hacking, though without the illicit connotation of hacking.

An Introduction to Rooting Your NOOK

B&N locked down Android on your NOOK to prevent you from accessing some of Android's capabilities. However, by following a process called *rooting* your NOOK, you can open up these capabilities to make your NOOK more powerful and useful.

NOTE: In the Android OS, *root* is the superuser who has access to everything in the OS. By rooting your NOOK, you can become the superuser on your NOOK.

Following are just a few of the things you can do after you root your NOOK:

- ▶ Use a new program to browse and launch your ebooks.

- ▶ Use Trook to read news stories, browse ebook libraries, download ebooks, and access your own Calibre library via Wi-Fi.

- ▶ Add Crossword and Minesweeper games.

- ▶ Use alternative browsers, PDF readers, and media players.

- ▶ Add calculator and note-taking apps.

- ▶ Listen to music using Pandora.

These are just a few examples of the power unleashed by rooting your NOOK.

Is It Risky to Root My NOOK, and Does It Void My Warranty?

When instructions for rooting the NOOK first appeared, they involved taking the NOOK apart and messing with the actual hardware. It wasn't for the squeamish. However, you can now root your NOOK using a process called *softrooting*, which involves installing a special software update for your NOOK. Therefore, rooting your NOOK is no more risky than installing a software update, and it's a completely reversible process.

With that said, rooting your NOOK is not sanctioned by B&N and doing so likely does void your warranty. (When I asked B&N about this, it wouldn't specifically tell me whether it would void the warranty.) Rooting is one of those things you must do at your own risk, but in my opinion, the benefits far outweigh the downfalls.

How to Root Your NOOK

The experts on rooting your NOOK all hang out at nookdevs.com. Everything you need to know about rooting your NOOK, installing applications, and hacking the NOOK in general is available on this site. All the files required to root your NOOK are freely downloadable from nookdevs.

TIP: Because you obviously can't root your NOOK while reading your NOOK, use a NOOK app on another device to read, and follow the instructions in this chapter.

After you decide to experience the new functionality of your NOOK by rooting it, the steps required are quite easy:

1. Downgrade your NOOK to the factory fresh 1.0 software.

2. Install a rooted version of the 1.4 software.

3. Install any additional applications you want on your NOOK.

Now look at each of these steps in detail.

> TIP: The steps I walk you through are documented at http://nookdevs.com/ Softroot. However, there are a few points of possible confusion on that page, so although you can use it as a reference, follow my steps here for a successful rooting experience.

Downgrading to Factory Fresh NOOK 1.0

> CAUTION: When you install the 1.0 software onto your NOOK, all the files on your NOOK will be erased. Before you begin this process, be sure you back up any files you want to keep. After they are erased, you cannot get them back.

You can't root your NOOK unless you have the original 1.0 software installed. You can download the original 1.0 NOOK software from nookdevs by browsing to www.multiupload.com/10EOGCL46N. When you get there, click Download File, as shown in Figure 19.1.

| *RAPIDSHARE* | http://www.multiupload.com/RS_10EOGCL46N | **Download file** |

FIGURE 19.1 The Download File button lets you download the 1.0 version of your NOOK's software.

The file you download for the 1.0 software is `signed_bravo_update.dat`. When your NOOK starts up, it looks for a file called `signed_bravo_update.dat`. If it finds one, it recognizes it as a software update and begins installing it. If the filename is not exactly right, your NOOK won't install it. So don't change the filename from `signed_bravo_update.dat`.

CAUTION: Before you proceed any further, make sure that your NOOK has at least a 50% battery charge. You don't want your NOOK to shut down during an update because it can cause problems.

After you rename the downloaded file, connect your NOOK to your computer using the USB cable. Open the NOOK drive that appears on your computer. (The NOOK drive is your NOOK's main memory.) Copy the `signed_bravo_update.dat` file from your computer to the root of your NOOK's main memory. In other words, copy it to the drive, but don't put it in any of the folders on the drive.

After the file finishes copying itself to you NOOK, eject your NOOK from your computer, and unplug the USB cable. When you do, you should see a message in the lower-right corner of the reading screen that says Preparing Update. This message indicates that your NOOK is installing the 1.0 software.

Installing the 1.0 software can take a few minutes. Be sure that you don't mess with your NOOK or turn it off while the update is installing. When the update finishes installing, your NOOK reboots. You're now ready to move to the next step.

I Copied the 1.0 Software to My NOOK, but the Update Never Installed. What's Wrong?

First, make sure that the file you are copying to your NOOK is named `signed_bravo_update.dat`. The filename must be *exactly* as shown here; otherwise, your NOOK won't recognize it as an update.

Second, be sure you copy the file to the root of your NOOK's main memory. You can't put it inside of a folder because it won't work otherwise.

If you've checked both of these and it still won't work, it's possible that you've unintentionally copied the file to the root of the microSD card installed in your NOOK. If your computer shows two drives for your NOOK, copy the file to the root of the other drive and try that.

Install a Rooted Version of the 1.4 Software

To root your NOOK, you must install a special version of the NOOK software. As of this writing, the latest version of NOOK root software is 1.4.

NOTE: If B&N releases a new version of software for your NOOK (for example, 1.5), nookdevs will probably follow with a similar rooted release to use third-party applications on your NOOK. At the time of this writing, the rooted version for 1.5 was not available; however, I successfully softrooted, installed, and used the softroot version 1.4. I had 1.5 of the B&N NOOK software running alongside the nookdevs 1.4 version—I let the 1.5 version install *after* completing the following softroot process.

To download the rooted 1.4 software, browse to www.multiupload.com/ 3XA0O6849N. Click the Direct Download button to download the `bravo_update.dat` file.

After you download the 1.4 update, connect your NOOK to your computer with the USB cable. Copy the `bravo_update.dat` file to the root of the microSD card on your NOOK. This is not the same drive to which you copied the 1.0 update. The 1.4 update must be on the root of the microSD card and not your NOOK's main memory.

When the file finishes copying to your NOOK, eject your NOOK from your computer and unplug the USB cable. You are now ready to install the 1.4 update. To do so, follow these steps:

1. Turn off your NOOK by pressing the Power button and holding it until the display turns off.

2. Press and hold the Previous Page button on the right side of your NOOK. This is the button with the < arrow on it.

3. While still holding down the Previous Page button, press the Power button to turn on your NOOK.

4. After your NOOK's reading screen displays a message that says Installing Software Update, immediately release the Previous Page button.

5. Wait for the update to complete. Your NOOK reboots itself after the update finishes.

That's it! You have now successfully rooted your NOOK.

Using mynook.ru Launcher

One of the applications contained in the rooted 1.4 update you just installed is mynook.ru Launcher, which can replace the Home screen on your NOOK's touchscreen; it lets you customize the touchscreen by rearranging buttons, removing buttons, and adding buttons for new applications. To add icons, press and hold one of the icons. Tap the + button and then scroll through to the icon you want. Tap to add it. Some of these icons are NOOKlets (HTML and Javascript applets for the NOOK); others offer quick access to features. For example, rather than tapping Games and then tapping Chess, mynook.ru Launcher offers a Chess icon. Tap that icon and Chess starts.

To remove icons, press and hold the icon you want to delete. Tap the Trash Can button. (The icon to be deleted will be highlighted.) You can tap another icon to delete and so on.

To reorder the icons, press and hold the icon you want to move. The icon appears highlighted. Tap the appropriate arrow button to move it left or right.

> TIP: To get back to the "normal" B&N NOOK Home screen icon, tap the B&N Home icon.
>
> To switch back and forth between the two Home screen, press the Home button. The touchscreen shows two buttons: Home and Launcher. Home is the "normal" B&N Home screen. Launcher is the mynook.ru Launcher.

This is just the start of rooting your NOOK though. To do more, you need to install ADB over USB. The bad news: This is a lengthy series of steps for most casual users of smartphones, computers, and such. The good news: You have to do this only once, and then adding apps becomes so much easier. Now I know when you look at the following procedure, you'll think, "All this to install some apps?" Yes, but to make the installation of apps easier, it is necessary. So a bit of patience and careful following of the steps, and you'll be on your way to have Pandora, Minesweeper, Crosswords, and more on your NOOK.

Installing ADB over USB

The following instructions are for Windows XP and are based on the hard work of the guys at nookdevs.com. The first thing you need to do is download the Android SDK. Browse to developer.android.com/sdk and download the SDK for Windows. After you download it, extract all the files to any directory of your choice.

> NOTE: You can still softroot your NOOK if you have a Mac or Linux machine. nookdevs.com/ADB_Over_USB has instructions for these other versions along with the Windows version. However, the Windows installation is more complex and is now out of date (in a couple of areas), so follow the next instructions.

1. After you download the SDK, unzip it and place it at c:\androidsdk.

2. Download the driver from here www.multiupload.com/OI0V0DB96Q by clicking the Direct Download button. After it has downloaded, unzip it to c:\nookadbdriver.

3. Go to c:\androidsdk and double-click SDK Manager.exe. The program starts and wants to downloaded and install a bunch of items. Click Accept All and then click Install. (This took some time on my machine.)

4. When it asks to restart the ADB Server, let it.

5. Click Settings and check Force https://…Sources to Be Fetched Using http://.

6. Click Available Packages. If SDK Platform Android 1.5 is an option, click the check box. (If you do not see that option, the SDK Platform Android 1.5 is already installed.) Click Install Selected and click Accept; it then downloads and installs the 1.5 SDK platform. You can close the setup when completed.

7. Now, from your Windows Start menu, click Control Panel. System, Advanced System Settings, Environment Variables.

8. Click Path in the System Variables list. Click Edit. Add and do not delete anything ;C:\androidsdk\tools to the end of the text there. Click OK. Click Enable.

8. Click Start, Run Command. In the window that appears, type adb shell.

9. Back on your NOOK, from the mynook.ru Launcher, tap Wi-Fi Locker. Make sure it says Start ADB at the bottom.

You've now completed the most difficult portion of softrooting your NOOK.

Installing Applications on Your Rooted NOOK

Now that you have your NOOK rooted, you want to install applications, right? Well, it is super easy. Install two apps first: FileSelector and NookMarket:

1. On your computer's browser, go to www.nookdevs.com/NookMarket. In the Links section on the right, click the Download link. Save the nookMarket.apk file to your desktop.

2. On your computer's browser, go to www.nookdevs.com/FileSelector. In the Links section on the right, click the Download link. Save the FileSelector.apk file to your desktop.

3. Plug your NOOK in via the USB cable.

4. Transfer the two files from steps 1 and 2 to your NOOK's main memory or microSD card.

5. Disconnect your NOOK from your computer.

6. From the mynook.ru Launcher, tap File Manager. (If this icon is not available, add it.) Navigate to the file location for nookMarket.apk. Tap the Android icon. The touchscreen changes to show the Android icon and Cut, Copy, Delete, and Rename options. Tap the Android icon. Tap Install. Nook Market installs. Tap Done.

7. Follow step 6 but for FileSelector.apk.

8. Add these icons to your mynook.ru Launcher interface.

Simple, right? Well, now it gets even simpler. From the mynook.ru Launcher interface, tap Nook Market. Here you see a list of apps (most of the listed here: wwwnookdevs.com/Application_Directory). From now on, if you want to install an app, tap the icon in Nook Market. Tap Install. And it installs. It's that simple.

> NOTE: Some of the apps you can install are actually NOOKlets and appear as options under that app: Hangman, Currency Converter.

> NOTE: If you don't want to add icon after icon to mynook.ru Launcher, the AppManager that installs with the softrooting process is a great app to run to install apps as well while minimizing icons.

Using Trook

Trook is one of the most useful applications you can install on your NOOK (called Trook craftycoder 1.4 in Nook Market). Trook enables you to easily access news, ebook libraries, and much more via *feeds*. It comes configured with the following feeds:

- **Lexcycle Online Catalog**: An online catalog of free ebooks that you can browse and download to your NOOK right from within Trook.

- **New York Times**: Top news stories from *The New York Times*.

- **Wikipedia**: Featured articles and facts of the day from the world's largest online encyclopedia.

- **USA Today**: Top news stories from *USA Today*.

- **Nookdevs**: Information from Nookdevs about hacking your NOOK, installing applications to your NOOK, and so forth.

To access a feed in Trook, tap the Trook button on the touchscreen, and select the feed you want to view. Trook's menus are hierarchical. In other words, if you tap Lexcycle Online Catalog, you see a new menu that includes all the feeds available in the Lexcycle Online Catalog. Tapping one of those feeds displays another series of feeds, and so on.

As you drill down into the information you want, you can move back up a level by clicking the tab at the top of the touchscreen. This tab is always labeled using the name of the previous feed. For example, if you tap Lexcycle Online Catalog, the tab at the top of the touchscreen is labeled Trook and tapping it takes you back to the Trook Home screen. If you then tap Feedbooks, the tab at the top of the touchscreen is labeled Lexcycle and tapping it takes you up one level to the Lexcycle Online Catalog.

Downloading Books with Trook

If you drill down into the Lexcycle Online Catalog, you eventually see a list of books you can download with Trook. To download a book, tap the icon for the book. Trook displays a message that says Starting download in the background. Trook then downloads the ebook and saves it in My Documents.

To view books you've downloaded, tap My Library from your NOOK's Home screen and view My Documents. If your book hasn't finished downloading, it won't be visible. To refresh your view, tap Check for New Content.

Reading News with Trook

Reading news with Trook is a little different from downloading books. To read news, tap an article on the touchscreen. Trook opens the content of the article directly on the E Ink screen. You can then navigate the content using the Next Page and Previous Page buttons.

When you're reading news with Trook, you're actually using your NOOK as a web browser. Therefore, formatting might be a little off at times. You also cannot change the font or the font size while reading news in Trook.

Accessing Your Calibre Library with Trook

In addition to the feeds that come preconfigured in Trook, you can also add your own feeds. One of the most convenient uses of this feature is to add your Calibre library as a feed and download your ebooks directly to your NOOK without connecting it to your computer.

> NOTE: For more information about using Calibre to manage your ebook library, **see** Chapter 21, "Managing Your ebooks with Calibre."

To access your Calibre library, you need to enable the content server in Calibre. To do that, follow these steps:

1. Start Calibre.

2. Click the Preferences button on the toolbar.

3. Click Sharing over the Net.

4. Click the Start Server button to start the content server.

> TIP: If you want the content server to start automatically every time you run Calibre, check the Run Server Automatically on Startup check box.

5. Click the Test Server button to test the operation of the server. A browser opens. If you click All Books, your books should appear in the browser. The content server is working! Close the browser.

6. Click OK in the Sharing over the Net dialog box.

To access your Calibre library in Trook, follow these steps:

1. Start Trook.

2. Tap the button in the upper-right corner that looks like a gear. Tap Open. You should see your NOOK's keyboard and see Open feed URL in the reading screen.

3. Enter the following URL for the feed URL. Replace YOUR_COM-PUTER_NAME with the name or IP address of your computer:

```
http://YOUR_COMPUTER_NAME:8080/stanza
```

Trook loads your Calibre library feed, and you should see icons on the touchscreen that let you browse your library. If you drill down to an ebook and tap the icon for the ebook, it downloads the ebook to My Documents.

Adding Calibre to Your Feeds

You'll likely want to add your Calibre library as a custom icon in Trook so that you can access it anytime you want. To do that, open your Calibre library in Trook. When your Calibre library is open in Trook, tap and hold the button that looks like a gear until you see a menu of options on the touchscreen. Tap Bookmark to My Feeds to add your Calibre library to your bookmarked feeds.

You can now easily open your Calibre library in Trook by tapping My Feeds from the top-level Trook menu and tapping Calibre Library.

TIP: Trook actually just uses *RSS feeds* for content. Many websites have an RSS feed you can use with Trook. Just look for a link for RSS or look for the orange RSS icon (the same one you see on the feeds in Trook) while browsing a site. You can then use the RSS URL in Trook.

More Hacking

What this chapter covered scratches only the surface of what you can do with your NOOK after you softroot it. Nookdevs offer several applications you can install onto your NOOK using the steps you learned in this chapter.

For more information about hacking your NOOK, check out nookdevs.com/Main_Page. You can find tips and tricks, information on hacking your NOOK and changing all kinds of settings you normally have no access to, and a list of applications you can install onto your NOOK.

Unrooting Your NOOK

Want to get rid of all those apps and just get back to the NOOK itself? The easiest and cleanest way is to place the `signed_bravo_update.dat` file in the main memory of your NOOK. Then remove the `bravo_update.dat` file from the microSD card.

This resets your NOOK to version 1.0 of the NOOK software.

CHAPTER 20

Reading Beyond Your NOOK

If you don't have your NOOK handy, you can read items from your ebook library using the B&N NOOK apps. B&N provides a version of the NOOK application for your PC, iPhone, iPad, iPod Touch, and Android device.

> NOTE: Technically, no Mac or Blackberry version of the NOOK app exists. The B&N eReader app, however, exists for both. This is basically an older version of the NOOK app with significantly fewer features.
>
> If you want to have full functionality for a NOOK app on the Mac, you can use NOOKStudy for the Mac. Although it's intended for textbooks, it is a fully functioning and feature-rich Mac ebook reading platform that is much better than the B&N eReader for the Mac and free. The NOOKStudy is covered in "Using NOOKstudy Apps on PC and Mac."

The experience the NOOK app provides varies depending on which device you use. On a PC, the experience similar to reading on your NOOKcolor. On other devices, the experience is a bit more scaled-down.

You can download the NOOK app for your PC or another device by going to http://www.barnesandnoble.com/u/free-NOOK-apps/379002321/, clicking the appropriate NOOK app device link, and clicking the download link. (For the iPad, iPhone, or iPod Touch, you can search for Barnes & Noble NOOK in the App Store or in the iTunes Store.)

> TIP: If you use a Blackberry or Android phone, B&N requires that you download the NOOK app from your device. For the Blackberry, you can do that by browsing to bn.com on your device and clicking the link to download the eReader app. For the Android version, search for NOOK in the Android Marketplace or scan the QR code on the Barnes & Noble Android NOOK app download web page.

Using the NOOK for PC App

When you launch NOOK app on your PC, you'll be asked to sign in to your B&N account. Enter your username and password, and click Sign In if you already have an account on bn.com. If you don't have an account, you can click Create an Account to create one.

> NOTE: The Mac version of Barnes & Noble eReader currently has significantly fewer features than the PC version. Therefore, many of the features mentioned in this section may not be available on the Mac.

Browsing Your B&N Online Library with the NOOK for PC App

After you sign in to your account the NOOK for PC app checks in with My NOOK Library and synchronizes samples, last pages read, etc. You then see a series of buttons along the left side that mirror the buttons you see on your NOOK's touchscreen when at the Home screen (see Figure 20.1). The only difference you notice is that the order of the Shop and Reading Now buttons is reversed on NOOK for PC app versus your NOOK.

FIGURE 20.1   The menu buttons in the NOOK for PC app mirror several of those on your NOOK.

By default, NOOK for PC app displays ebooks and subscription content. However, you can filter the view to show only ebooks, magazines, newspapers, and manually added content (what B&N calls "my stuff") by clicking the appropriate option in the My Library menu.

Along the top of the NOOK for PC app are buttons to manually refresh your library, control the views of your library, sort your library, and search your library, as shown in Figure 20.2.

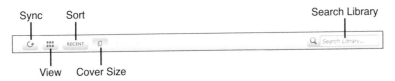

FIGURE 20.2   Function buttons at the top of NOOK for PC app enable you to control how you view your library.

Clicking the Sync button synchronizes your B&N NOOK Library with the NOOK for PC app. Use this to synchronize your notes and page location.

NOTE: When the original NOOK and NOOK apps were created, B&N had not yet created the mechanism to synchronize between devices. With the November NOOK software update and built into the NOOKcolor and NOOK apps, synchronization between these devices is now possible. No longer do you need to worry about finding your page or keeping notes across devices.

The View button (by default an image of six little boxes) controls how your ebook library appears in the NOOK for PC app. By default, the NOOK for PC app shows your library in list view. In this view, a small image of the cover of each item displays along with items such as the author, the last read date, and so on. You can switch to a grid or bookshelf view that shows only large images of each item's cover by clicking View button, as shown in Figure 20.2. When you do, the View button changes to show three parallel lines.

When you select to show your items in list view, the Cover Size button enables you to control the size of the cover image that displays. (The button shows a small rectangle.) The smallest size is slightly smaller than the size displayed when in grid view, and the largest size is approximately twice the size of the covers shown in grid view.

NOTE: Most covers provided with ebooks and other content look terrible when you select the largest available size in list view because they're not intended for display at such a large size.

You can sort your online library in the NOOK for PC app by clicking the Sort button, which defaults to Recent, but changes to Title and Author as you continue to click it.

After you've owned your NOOK for a while, you're likely to accumulate a large digital library of content. The NOOK for PC app enables you to easily find content as your NOOK library grows; you can search your library for content. When you click inside the Search Library box, you're given a choice to search for a title, an author, a publisher, or all three, as shown in Figure 20.3. Select an option, enter your search text, and either click the magnifying glass or press Enter to search your library.

FIGURE 20.3   Searching your library using the NOOK for PC app.

TIP: Searches are filtered based on how your library is filtered. For example, if you've selected eMagazines from the My Library menu, searches show only magazines that match your search terms.

If you want to view all the items in your NOOK library instead of just those that match your search terms, click the X inside the Search Library box. Doing so clears your search term and shows all the items in your online library.

Viewing the Daily in the NOOK for PC App

Clicking the Daily menu button displays the Daily. Assuming you are connected to the Internet, it updates with the latest articles. Click Read Now to read the particular article, which appears in a small box. Clicking Close hides the article from view.

Shopping for ebooks in the NOOK for PC App

Clicking the Shop button opens up your web browser at BN.com. For more information about shopping for ebooks, **see** "Shopping on Your Computer" in Chapter 9, "Shopping and Visiting B&N on Your NOOKcolor."

Reading Items in the NOOK for PC App

When you hover your mouse pointer over an item in My Library, the NOOK for PC app displays several options (see Figure 20.4).

▸ **Read Now**: Opens the item in the NOOK for PC app. If the item hasn't been downloaded to your computer, the NOOK for PC app downloads it first and then opens it.

▶ **LendMe**: Displayed only for items you can lend to friends. When clicked, it opens a dialog box for entering the email address of a friend to whom you'd like to lend the item. **See** Chapter 4, "Lending and Borrowing Books with LendMe on Your NOOKcolor," for more details about the LendMe feature.

▶ **Download**: Displayed when the item hasn't been downloaded to your computer. When clicked, the item is downloaded to your local computer and Download changes to Remove Local Copy.

▶ **Remove Local Copy**: Displayed when the item has been downloaded to your local computer. When clicked, the item is removed from your local computer. If you want to read it at a later time, you need to download it again.

▶ **Move to Archive**: Moves the item to your archive. Archived items appear in the Archive category in My Library.

▶ **Unarchive**: Displayed only for archived items. When clicked, the item is moved from the archive to your main digital library.

▶ **Details**: Displays the details for the item. Details typically consist of a larger image of the cover and a brief synopsis of the item.

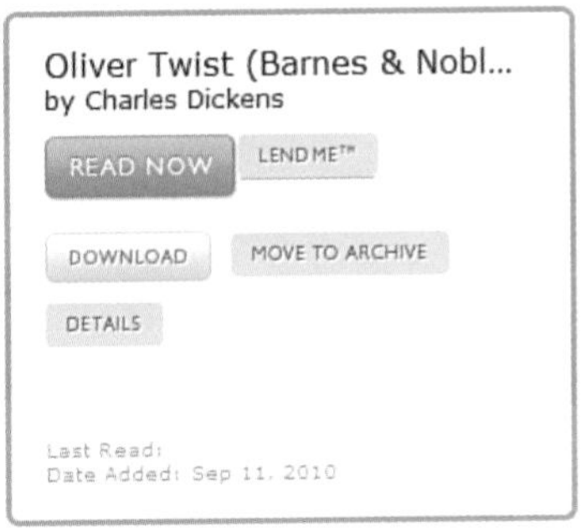

FIGURE 20.4 Available options for when you hover over a cover.

TIP: Archiving or unarchiving an item in the NOOK for PC app on your PC also archives or unarchives the item on your NOOK, NOOKColor, and other apps (except the B&N Blackberry and Mac eReader apps).

While you're reading content, the NOOK for PC app displays the Reading Now menu. Using the Reading Now menu, you can easily navigate to the last page read, access the table of contents, and access bookmarks, annotations, and highlights for the item you're reading.

NOTE: Neither annotations nor highlights are available for subscription content.

For more information on using bookmarks, highlighting, and annotations, **see** Chapter 5, "Using Highlights, Bookmarks, and Annotations."

Using Highlights, Notes, and Bookmarks in the NOOK for PC App

You can also use highlights in the NOOK for PC app. However, you cannot add highlights or notes to subscription content.

Adding Highlights and Notes

To add a highlight to an ebook in the NOOK for PC app, click your mouse on the starting point where you want your highlight. While holding the mouse button, drag your mouse to the ending point for the highlight. When you do this, the NOOK for PC app highlights the text and displays a pop-up menu (see Figure 20.5). To make the highlighted text an actual highlight, click Highlight Selection.

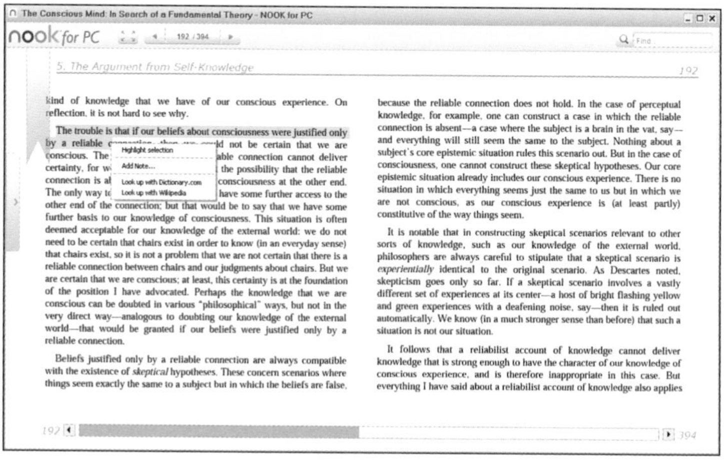

FIGURE 20.5   Adding a note in NOOK for PC app.

If you want to add a note, click Add Note from the pop-up menu. Type your note, and then click OK. If you want to add a note to text that is already defined as a highlight, highlight a portion of that text again. The pop-up menu offers a couple of extra options (see Figure 20.6). Click Add Note to add a new note to the existing highlight. Add the text for your note, and then click OK.

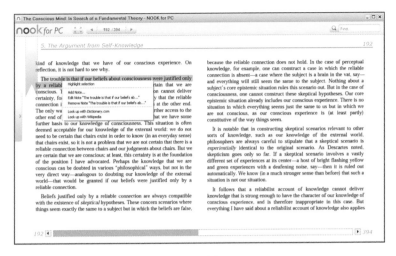

FIGURE 20.6   Editing an existing note or highlight.

Viewing Highlights and Notes

To view highlights, click Highlights under the Reading Now menu. Highlights that don't have notes associated with them can be found by clicking Highlights. If a note is associated with the highlight, click Annotations in the Reading Now menu to see the note. You can quickly jump to any note or highlight by clicking the specific note or highlight (see Figure 20.7).

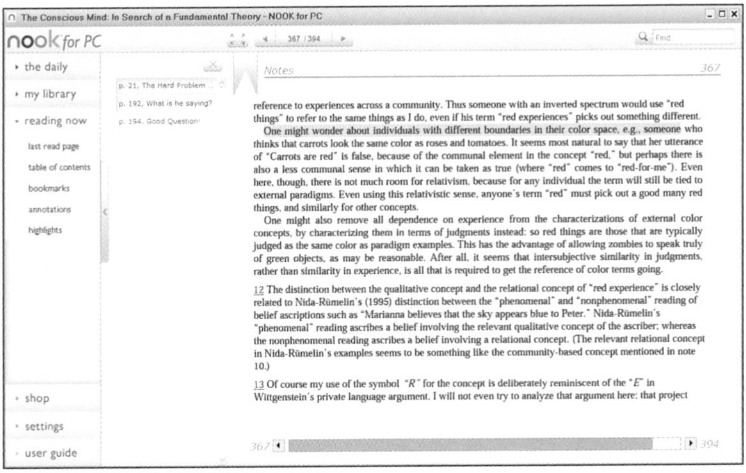

FIGURE 20.7   Jump to any highlight in a book.

> **Can I Change the Green Color the NOOK or PC App Uses for Highlights?**
> You can't change the color of highlights on the PC.

Editing and Deleting Highlights and Notes

To edit a note associated with a highlight, highlight a portion of that text that comprises the note and click Edit Note. Enter the new text for the note, and click OK. To delete the note, select Remove Note; then click Yes when asked to confirm that you want to delete the note. Follow the same steps to remove a highlight that doesn't have a note associated with it.

Using Bookmarks

To add a bookmark to a page in the NOOK for PC app, click the ribbon with pointed ends in the corner of the page. When you do, the ribbon drops down onto the page and your bookmark appears in the bookmark pane when you select Bookmarks from the Reading Now menu. To remove the bookmark, click the ribbon again.

You can easily navigate to a particular bookmark by clicking the bookmark in the bookmark pane (see Figure 20.8).

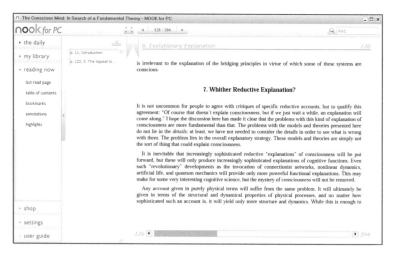

FIGURE 20.8   Jump to any bookmark in a book.

Importing Books into the NOOK for PC App

All books in your B&N online library are automatically added to the NOOK for PC app. If you want to read a book you purchased from another source, you can add it to the NOOK for PC app by clicking the My Library, clicking My Stuff menu, and then clicking the Add New Item button (see Figure 20.9).

FIGURE 20.9   Click this button to add non-B&N ebooks and content.

> NOTE: You can only import eReader format (PDB files) and EPUB format ebooks along with PDFs into the NOOK for PC app.

If the book you are importing contains DRM, you will be asked for your name and credit card information when you attempt to read the book in the NOOK for PC app. You need to supply this information only the first time you read the book.

> **Can I Read Books in Formats Other Than eReader and EPUB in the NOOK for PC App?**
>
> Kind of. To read a book in the NOOK for PC app, you must first convert the book to either eReader format or EPUB format. You can use Calibre to convert books into a format that is compatible with the NOOK for PC app, provided the book is not protected with DRM. To learn how to use Calibre, **see** Chapter 21, "Managing Your ebooks with Calibre."

Configuring the NOOK for PC App Settings

Clicking the Settings menu lets you change the appearance of content in the NOOK for PC app and change your account settings.

To change the appearance of content, click Settings and then click Reading Preferences. From this screen, you can change the font size and margin spacing used in the NOOK for PC app. Clicking the font size adjusts the sample text size to give you an idea of how it will appear when reading an actual ebook. The Margins option is controlled by clicking and dragging the Indicator icon or clicking anywhere along the bar. Toward the right increases the amount of white space on either side of the text. Toward the left decreases the amount.

> NOTE: Account Settings appears by default when you click Settings.

To change account settings, click Account Settings. You can sign in or sign out of your B&N account from this screen. You can also choose whether recent purchases are downloaded automatically. The other option you have is Autohide Navigation When Opening Reading Now. By default, this is selected, and what it means is that when you are reading an ebook, the Daily, My Library, and such, options on the left disappear. (You can get it back by clicking the left-facing arrow bar.) Otherwise, the menu is always available.

Using NOOK Apps on Your iPhone, iPod Touch, or Android Phone

The NOOK for PC application is a straightforward program. It's similar to your NOOK, and is intuitive and easy to use. The NOOK for iPhone, iPad, iPod Touch, and Android (referred to as simply the NOOK app from now on) are different from the NOOK for PC app because of the devices, but each of them still offers an easy-to-use interface.

> NOTE: As of this writing, B&N has disabled reading subscription content on the NOOK app. If you want to read content other than ebooks, you need to use either NOOK for PC app, NOOKStudy app, or your NOOK.

> NOTE: The focus of this section is on the iPhone app though the iPod Touch app is identical. The Android app is essentially identical in features and general interactivity, as well, though with the quirks of the Android phone navigation vis-à-vis the quirks of the iPhone navigation.

The NOOK app launches and syncs with your NOOK library. You have quite a few options on this small screen (see Figure 20.10).

- ► **Shop for eBooks**: Tapping this launches the Safari web browser and opens the NOOKstore.

- ► **Sync**: Tapping this synchronizes page location, notes, and so on with your NOOK Library.

▶ **View**: Tapping this switches between a list and grid view. (The default is grid view.) If you change to list view, the Shop for eBooks becomes a link at the top.

▶ **Sort**: Tapping these options sorts your list by the designated category.

▶ **Type**: Tapping this lets you see either your ebooks or archived ebooks. By default, your ebooks are sorted by most recent.

▶ **Search Library**: Tapping this allows you to search your library for a specific book.

FIGURE 20.10   Though small, the NOOK app interface has a lot of options.

Browsing My NOOK Library

Browsing your library is easy; just swipe up and down with your finger to scroll.

> CAUTION: Don't be surprised if while you scroll through your library you accidentally tap the Download icon and download the book to your device.

To read an ebook, you first need to download it to your device. You can easily tell whether a book has been downloaded. If a Download button appears, you have not downloaded it to your device. Just tap the button to do so. After the ebook has been downloaded to your device, it opens so that you can begin reading.

Reading Books in the NOOK App

To read an ebook in the NOOK app, just tap the cover image to open it in reading mode. When there, to move to the next page, swipe your finger from right to left. To move to the previous page, swipe your finger from left to right. The reading screen, however, offers more options than just reading (see Figure 20.11).

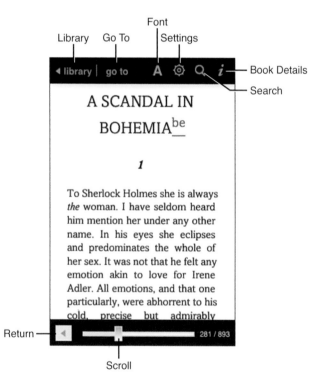

FIGURE 20.11   The NOOK app reading interface.

If you do not see the surrounding bars in the reading screen, just tap the page, and they will appear. Before discussing some of these options, take a quick tour:

▶ **Library**: Tapping this returns you to your NOOK library.

▶ **Go To**: Tapping this opens the table of contents with links to see your notes and annotations and bookmarks. You can scroll through any of these items and click the appropriate link to go quickly to that spot in the ebook.

▶ **Return**: This icon appears when you have tapped a footnote link (the blue link in Figure 20.11), going to the footnote. Tapping the Return button takes you back to the page you were originally on.

▶ **Book Details**: Tapping this brings up a page with many details related to the book.

▶ **Search**: Tapping this lets you search for specific text in this ebook.

▶ **Settings**: Tapping this lets you adjust the margin width and brightness.

▶ **Font**: Tapping this allows you to adjust the specific font, justification, colors, and font size.

Two of these screens deserve more attention: Book Details and Font. Now take a closer look at these.

Using the Book Details Screen

After tapping Book Details, you see a screen like Figure 20.12.

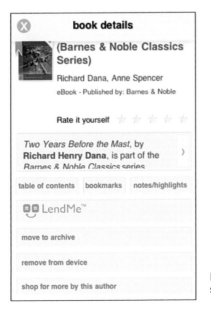

FIGURE 20.12 The NOOK app's Book Details screen.

As you can see, you have several options here. Tapping the X returns you to the reading screen. You can rate the ebook by tapping a star. (Tap the third star, and the first three are marked.)

> NOTE: If you give a star rating to an ebook, you cannot remove the star rating. You can only adjust it up or down.

In Figure 20.8, if you tap the right-pointing arrow next to the *Two Years Before the Mast* text, you are taken to a book synopsis. Clicking the X there returns you to the Book Details screen.

Tapping Table of Contents, Bookmarks, or Notes/Highlights quickly returns you to the reading screen and opens up the Go To page at the corresponding list of Contents, Notes, and so on. Clicking the X there returns you to the reading screen.

B&N has the unique LendMe feature for many NOOKbooks. Whether you can lend NOOKbooks is up to the publisher. To use this feature, just tap the LendMe icon. This takes you to another screen where you can type in the email address of the person you want to lend the NOOKbook, too. (You can also tap the blue plus sign and select an email from your contacts.)

You can also type a message to the person. Click Send to send the offer to the person. After you've done this, you will notice in your library that the sash that once read Lendable now reads Lent. You can no longer read this book (until either the recipient turns down the offer, returns the ebook to you, or the lending time runs out).

You can also archive this book by pressing the Move to Archive icon. The Remove from Device option does just that. You can always download it again to your NOOK app by tapping Download.

Finally, you can click Shop for More by This Author to open a Safari browser window displaying other NOOKbooks available from that author.

Adjusting Fonts

After tapping Fonts, you see a screen like Figure 20.13.

Again, a small screen that provides many options. The general purpose of this screen is to provide settings related to the reading experience in the NOOK app. Clicking the X closes this screen, returns you to the reading screen, and makes any changes that you have indicated.

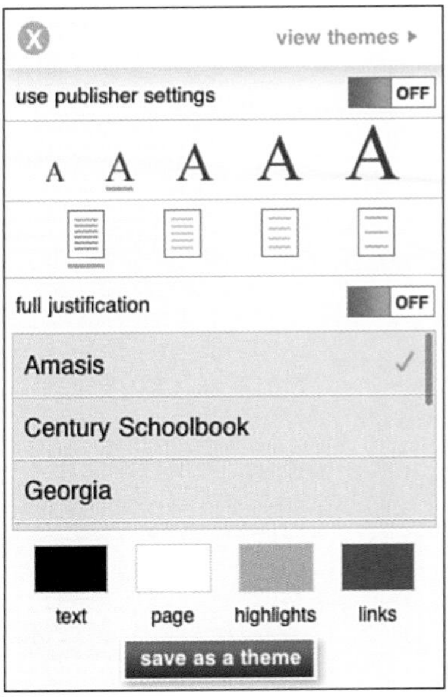

FIGURE 20.13   The NOOK app's Fonts screen.

We will come back to View Themes. You can choose Use Publisher Settings. In an ebook, the publisher often provides a series of defaults (font size, type of font, and so on). Changing this option to On sets the settings to those publisher default settings. You can change it to Off at any time you want.

Clicking the A icon adjusts the font size. The current font size has an underline beneath it.

The set of icons beneath the font size determine line spacing. Think of this like single space, double space, and so on. The current setting has a line beneath that icon.

The Full Justification setting is either On or Off (and is Off by default). I have yet to see any difference in the reading screen with this option On or Off.

Depending on what the publisher of this ebook allows, you can adjust the font. You can scroll through the available list. (A check mark appears to the right of the currently selected one.) You have options between serif and sans serif fonts. Serif is a technical term that refers to the "hanging structure" on a letter. In Figure 20.13, if you look at the A icons, notice the little base at the bottom of each leg of the A? That's a serif. Sans (French for "without") serif fonts lack these structures. In general, most people find reading serif fonts easier on the eyes. Unfortunately, the fonts in the Fonts screen don't give you a preview, so you may need to experiment a bit to find the one you like best.

> NOTE: Of the available font options Amasis, Century Schoolbook, Georgia, Joanna, and Times New Roman are serif fonts. Ascender Sans, Gill Sans, and Trebuchet MS are sans serif fonts.

The bottom part of this screen gives you options for color related to the text, high-lights, page, and links. Tap it and you end up in the reading screen color options screen. Figure 20.14 shows the basic screen for adjusting the color for all four of these items.

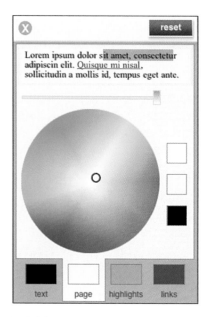

FIGURE 20.14   Altering the NOOK app's color.

Basically, you have a lot of colors to choose from. Your first task is to select the par-ticular part of the reading screen you want to change the color on: Text, Page, Highlights, or Links. The top part of the screen with the nonsense Latin "Lorem ipsum dolor…" reflects the alterations you make here. Thus, change the text to red, and the Lorem ipsum text changes to red.

The three squares next to the color wheel offer three quick ways of applying color. The black square adjusts whatever color you are changing to black. In other words, if you tap Links and then tap the black square next to the color wheel, the links appear in black. (In the Lorem ipsum text, the Quisque mi nisal link text changes from the default blue color to black.) The white square on top changes the color wheel from solid black to what you see in Figure 20.14. Tap an area of the wheel to choose that color for the item.

So what's the middle tan square for? Tap it and it changes the selected item to a neutral color (works great for the page background). Tap Reset or the X icon to save your changes.

The world of colors for your ebook reading brings us to themes. On the Fonts screen there are two theme-related buttons: View Themes and Save as a Theme. Tap Save as a Theme and a screen appears prompting you to provide a name for the theme. (You can see the default themes: The Printed Page, Night Light, and so on.) Assuming you like the color set you have, give them a name, tap Done, and tap Save Theme. If you have a theme or you want to use one of the default themes, tap View Themes and tap the theme you want. A check mark appears next to the selected them. Tap the X icon to apply the theme. If you tap Edit, you can change the name of the themes (including the default ones).

Deleting a theme is as easy as tapping View Themes, tapping Edit, tapping the circle next to the theme you want to delete, and tapping Delete Selection.

Adding Notes and Highlights in the NOOK App

Adding Notes, Highlights, and Bookmarks in the NOOK app is as easy as using your finger to select the part of the ebook to which you want to add a note or highlight. Here's how you do it:

1. Using your finger, select the text you want to add a Note or Highlight to. The text will be highlighted according to the Font settings' Highlight color. As soon as you lift your finger from the selection, the Notes & Highlights screen opens (see Figure 20.15).

2. Tap Highlight to add the highlight and nothing else.

    Tap Add Note to go to the Add Notes screen, where you can type in a note and tap Save.

If you select a single word, the Search Dictionary is an available option. Tapping it brings up a dictionary entry for the word. Tapping See More Definitions Online opens a Safari browser at Dictionary.com. Tapping the X icon takes you back to the reading screen.

Tapping Google or Wikipedia opens a Safari browser with the text you selected entered as the search criteria.

3. The note and highlights are available for easy access using the Go To menu from the reading screen.

FIGURE 20.15   The Note & Highlights screen.

Although the NOOK app saves your location in reading, you may still want to add a bookmark. In the reading screen, but without the options bars, in the bottom-right corner, you see a plus sign (see Figure 20.16). Tap it to set a bookmark. Tap it again to remove the bookmark.

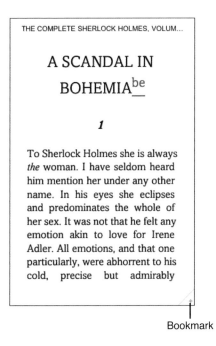

Bookmark

FIGURE 20.16 Tap the plus sign to set a bookmark.

Using the NOOK for iPad App

The NOOK for iPad app is a larger version of the NOOK for iPhone app adapted to the larger screen size of the iPad.

> NOTE: As of this writing, you can read newspaper and some magazines from B&N has on the NOOK for iPad app. Make sure to check the available apps and devices you can read a particular magazine on at BN.com prior to purchasing. You will see what apps and devices you can read that magazine on at the magazine's product page. However, even if you cannot read a magazine on the NOOK for iPad app, its cover will still appear in that library.

The NOOK app launches and syncs with your NOOK library. This default Home screen has many similarities to the NOOK for iPhone app, though adjusted for the more spacious real estate of the iPad (see Figure 20.17).

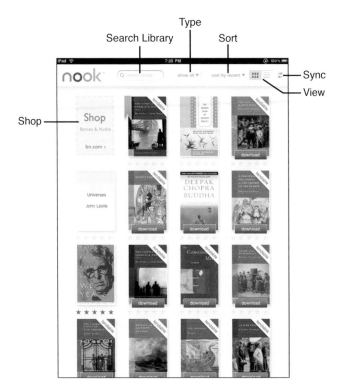

FIGURE 20.17 The NOOK app for iPad home page.

Now take a look at the options available on this screen.

▶ **Shop for eBooks**: Tapping this launches the Safari web browser and opens the B&N NOOKstore.

▶ **Sync**: Tapping this synchronizes page location, notes, and so on with your NOOK Library.

▶ **View**: Tapping one of the two options organizes this Home screen. The default is the grid view. You can switch to an individual book view by tapping the right button (the one with four lines)—see Figure 20.18. Switch back to grid view by tapping the left button (the one with six boxes). The individual book view offers a scrolling list of your library and detailed information about the current book, which is covered here in a bit.

▶ **Sort**: Tapping these options sorts your list by the designated category.

▶ **Type**: Tapping this lets you see either your ebooks or archived ebooks. By default, your ebooks are sorted by most recent.

▶ **Search Library**: Tapping this allows you to search your library for a specific book.

Move book by book.

Hide/show the scrollable list of your books.

Scrollable list of your books

FIGURE 20.18   Book-by-book view in the NOOK for iPad app.

Browsing My NOOK Library

Browsing your library is easy; just swipe up and down with your finger to scroll.

To read an ebook, you first need to download it to your device. You can easily tell whether a book has been downloaded. If a Download button appears, you have not downloaded it. Just tap the button to do so. The ebook will be downloaded to your device. After the ebook has been downloaded, it will open to begin reading.

Reading Books in the NOOK for iPad App

To read an ebook in the NOOK app, just tap the cover image to open it in reading mode. When there, to move to the next page, swipe your finger from right to left.

To move to the previous page, swipe your finger from left to right. The reading screen, however, offers more options than just reading (see Figure 20.19).

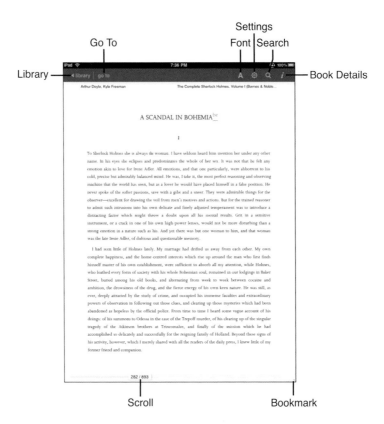

FIGURE 20.19　The NOOK for iPad app reading interface.

If you do not see the surrounding bars in the reading screen, just tap the page and they will appear. Before exploring some of these options, take a quick tour:

- ▶ **Library**: Tapping this returns you to your NOOK library.

- ▶ **Go To**: Tapping this opens the table of contents with links to see your notes and annotations and bookmarks. You can scroll through any of these items and click the appropriate link to go quickly to that spot in the ebook.

- ▶ **Bookmark**: Tapping this adds a bookmark to this page.

- ▶ **Book Details**: Tapping this brings up a page with many details related to the book.

▶ **Search**: Tapping this lets you search for specific text in this ebook.

▶ **Settings**: Tapping this lets you adjust the margin width and brightness.

▶ **Font**: Tapping this allows you to adjust the specific font, justification, colors, and font size.

Two of these screens deserve more attention: Book Details and Font. Now take a closer look at these.

Using the Book Details Screen

After tapping Book Details, you see a screen like Figure 20.20.

FIGURE 20.20   The NOOK app's Book Details screen.

In the NOOK for iPad app, two versions of this screen exist. Figure 20.20 shows the screen as it appears by tapping the Book Details button from within the reading screen. If you are in individual book view at the Home screen, you see a slightly larger version of this same page. Also, if you press and hold a cover image in grid view, a similar Book Details screen appears (refer to Figure 20.20). All the functionality between the different versions of the Book Details screen is the same.

As you can see, you have several options here. Tapping an area outside of the Book Details screen returns you to the reading screen. You can rate the ebook by tapping a star. (Tap the third star, and the first three are marked.)

> NOTE: If you give a star rating to an ebook, you cannot remove the star rating. You can only adjust it up or down.

Tapping Table of Contents, Bookmarks, or Notes/Highlights quickly returns you to the reading screen and opens the Go To page at the corresponding list of Contents, Notes, and so on. Tapping outside the Table of Contents, Bookmarks, or Notes/Highlights part of the screen, returns you to the reading screen.

B&N has the unique LendMe feature for many NOOKbooks. Whether you can lend NOOKbooks is up to the publisher. To use this feature, just tap the LendMe icon. This takes you to another screen where you can type in the email address of the person you want to lend the NOOKbook to. (You can also tap the blue plus sign and select an email from your contacts.)

You can also type a message to the person. Tap Send to send the offer to the person. After you do this, you can notice in your library that the sash that once read Lendable now reads Lent. You can no longer read this book (until either the recipient turns down the offer, returns the ebook to you, or the lending time runs out).

You can also archive this book by pressing the Move to Archive icon. The Remove from iPad option does just that. You can always download it again to your NOOK for iPad app by tapping Download.

Finally, you can click the More by This Author to open a Safari browser window displaying other NOOKbooks available from that author.

Adjusting Fonts

After tapping Fonts, you see a screen like Figure 20.21. (The Fonts screen for newspapers and magazines has fewer options, though the ones there function the same.)

The general purpose of this screen is to provide settings related to the reading experience in the NOOK app. Tapping outside the Fonts screen closes it, returns you to the reading screen, and makes any changes that you have indicated.

Now back to View Themes. You can choose Use Publisher Settings. In an ebook, the publisher often provides a series of defaults (font size, type of font, and so on). Changing this option to On sets the settings to those publisher default settings. You can change it to Off at any time you want.

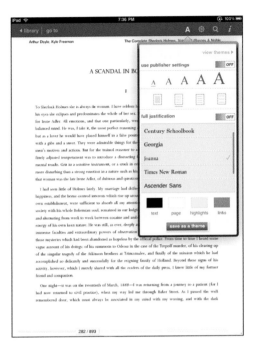

FIGURE 20.21 The NOOK for iPad app's Fonts screen.

Tapping the A icon adjusts the font size. The current font size has an underline beneath it.

The set of icons beneath the font size determines line spacing. Think of this like single space, double space, and so on. The current setting has a line beneath that icon.

The Full Justification setting is either On or Off (and is Off by default). I have yet to see any difference in the reading screen with this option On or Off.

Depending on what the publisher of this ebook allows, you can adjust the font. You can scroll through the available list. (A check mark appears to the right of the currently selected one.) You have options between serif and sans serif fonts. What is this? Serif is a technical term that refers to the "hanging structure" on a letter. In Figure 20.21, if you look at the A icons, notice the little base at the bottom of each leg of the A? That's a serif. Sans (French for "without") serif fonts lack these structures. In general, most people find reading serif fonts easier on the eyes.

> NOTE: Of the available font options, Amasis, Century Schoolbook, Georgia, Joanna, and Times New Roman are serif fonts. Ascender Sans, Gill Sans, and Trebuchet MS are sans serif fonts.

The bottom part of this screen gives you options for color related to the text, highlights, page, and links. Tap it and you end up in the reading screen color options screen. Figure 20.22 shows the basic screen for adjusting the color for all four of these items.

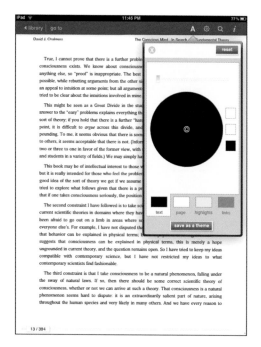

FIGURE 20.22   Altering the NOOK for iPad app's color.

Basically, you have a lot of colors to choose from. Your first task is to select the particular part of the reading screen you want to change the color on: Text, Page, Highlights, or Links.

The three squares next to the color wheel offer three quick ways to apply color. The black square adjusts whatever color you change to black. In other words, if you tap Links and then tap the black square next to the color wheel, the links appear in black. The white square on top changes the color wheel from solid black to a rainbow of colors. Tap an area of the wheel to choose that color for the item.

So what's the middle tan square for? Tap it and it changes the selected item to a neutral color (works great for the page background). Tap Reset or the X icon to save your changes.

The world of colors for your ebook reading brings us to themes. On the Fonts screen there are two theme-related buttons: View Themes and Save as a Theme. Tap Save as a Theme, and a screen appears prompting you to provide a name for the theme. (You can see the default themes: The Printed Page, Night Light, and so on.) Assuming you like the color setup you have, give them a name, tap Done, and tap Save Theme. If you have a theme or you want to use one of the default themes, tap View Themes and tap the theme you want. A check mark appears next to the selected them. Tap the X icon to apply the theme. If you tap Edit, you can change the name of the themes (including the default ones).

Deleting a theme is as easy as tapping View Themes, tapping Edit, tapping the circle next to the theme you want to delete, and tapping Delete Selection.

Adding Notes and Highlights in the NOOK for iPad App

Adding Notes, Highlights, and Bookmarks in the NOOK for iPad app is as easy as using your finger to select the part of the ebook you want to add a note or whatever to. Here's how you do it:

1. Using your finger, press and hold until you see the word your finger is on become highlighted; then select the text you want to add a Note or Highlight to. (If you just want that word, you can lift your finger.) The text will be highlighted according to the Font settings' Highlight color. As soon as you lift your finger from the selection, the Note & Highlights screen opens (see Figure 20.23).

2. Tap Highlight to add the highlight and nothing else.

   Tap Add Note to be taken to the Add Notes screen, where you can type in a note and tap Save Note.

   If you selected a single word, the Search Dictionary is an available option. Tapping it brings up a dictionary entry for the word. Tapping See More Definitions Online opens a Safari browser at Dictionary.com. Tapping outside the definition screen takes you back to the reading screen.

   Tapping Google or Wikipedia opens a Safari browser with the text you selected entered as the search criteria.

3. The note and highlights are available for easy access using the Go To menu from the reading screen.

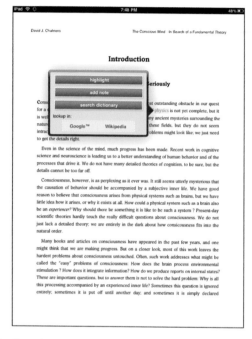

FIGURE 20.23   The Note & Highlights screen.

Using NOOKstudy Apps on PC and Mac

NOOKstudy is an app for the laptop or desktop developed by Barnes & Noble for reading and marking textbooks while at the same time prepping for tests, papers, and so on. Although intended for students, the NOOKstudy app is a useful, feature-rich program, especially for Mac users, because the B&N eReader app for Mac lacks many features. For example, the NOOKstudy app for the Mac includes syncing with your online library and reading of books that, at the Barnes & Noble store, are noted as "not readable on the Mac or Blackberry apps." For PC users, you do not need both apps, though having both doesn't cause any problems.

Following are the feature highlights. (The NOOKstudy app for both the PC and Mac are essentially identical, so the focus is on the PC version for the rest of this section.)

▶ Syncing with your online library.

▶ Viewing multiple books at once and dual-book view.

► Customizable courses, which is a fancy way to say, "You can organize your books into categories."

► Enhanced note and lookup features.

These are covered while looking at the program.

Downloading, Installing, and Setting Up the NOOKstudy App

To use this software, you need an Adobe Digital Editions (ADE) account. Go to adobe.com/products/digitaleditions/ to create one if you do not already have one.

You can find the NOOKstudy app at barnesandnoble.com/nookstudy/download/ index.asp. Download the appropriate version for your operating system. After the file has downloaded to your computer, double-click the file, and follow the instructions.

> NOTE: On the Mac, you first need to unzip the file. Then double-click the setup file.

After NOOKstudy has installed, start the program. When you first start it, you are asked to agree to the License Agreement. Click Agree. You are then asked to enter your B&N account information. (This is the same account you use to purchase books on BN.com.) You can also create an account by clicking Create Account. If you have an account, click I Have an Account, and enter the account information. Next, enter your Adobe ID and password. Finally, enter your school. That's it! You are now ready to use NOOKstudy.

> NOTE: If you are not a student and just want to use NOOKstudy (particularly for Mac users), enter a school near you. I, so far, have not been able to gauge any effect on how the school matters.

Navigating NOOKstudy

When you open NOOKstudy (see Figure 20.24), it syncs with your My NOOK Library, so if you were on page 400 of *Moby-Dick* on you NOOK for iPhone app, when you open *Moby-Dick* on NOOKstudy, it opens at page 400.

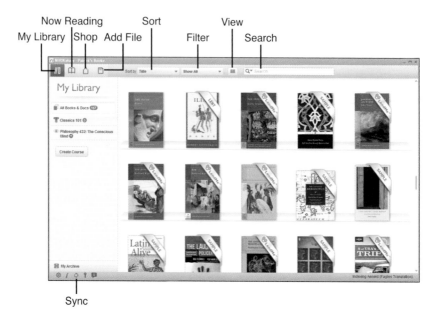

FIGURE 20.24   The My Library screen.

Unlike the NOOK app for PC, there is no My Library, Shop, and such buttons. Instead, your library is shown. At the top of the screen, you have four buttons:

▶ **Library**: Clicking this takes you to your library.

▶ **Now Reading**: Clicking this takes you to the reading pane, where all ebooks you have open appear in tabs (much like the omnipresent browser tabs).

▶ **Shop**: Clicking this takes you to a link to purchase eTextbooks.

▶ **Add File**: Clicking this enables you to add PDFs and other ebooks.

These four buttons are always present and available.

Navigating NOOKstudy's My Library View

While at the My Library screen, choose to see all your books and documents. You can also choose a particular course, which filters your viewing list to just books in that course. If you haven't yet done so, you can create a course. To create a course

1. Click Create Course. The Create a Course dialog box appears.

2. Give the course a name.

3. By default, for Course Icon, None is selected. Just click None or the drop-down arrow next to it to see a list of icons. Choose any that you like. (You'll notice these are thematic according to probable types of courses: Law, Science, Economics, Classics, and so on.)

4. Click Yes, Create Course. The course name and icon are added below the All Books & Docs option.

5. You can now select books from your library and drag them to the course to add books to that course. Note, doing this does not remove them from the All Books & Docs view.

After you finish with the course or if you need to make changes at any point in time, this is easy to do:

1. Click the course name. When you do this you see two options: Edit and Delete.

2. Click Delete to delete the course. NOOKstudy asks you to confirm that you want to delete the course. You are not deleting the books from your library, just deleting that particular course.

3. Click Edit to edit the name or icon for the course. The Edit Course Details dialog box appears.

4. This dialog box functions exactly as the Create a Course dialog box. After you have made your changes, click Proceed. Clicking Cancel dismisses the dialog box without implementing your changes.

You have a few more options on this screen. You can choose to view your Archived Books & Docs. From here, you can unarchive books or documents.

The Sync button forces a sync with My NOOK Library, which means that the existing page you were reading is sent to your library. When you next open your NOOK for iPad app or NOOKcolor, you will be taken to that same page.

For some book purchases, you will be given an access code. Open NOOKstudy, and click Redeem. Enter the access code here to get your eTextbook.

Clicking Settings enables you to modify your account information or unregister this instance of NOOKstudy, which has the effect of removing your Barnes & Noble library from visibility and use.

Notifications indicates if you have loan offers for your review.

In the view of your books, you see some features similar to the NOOK for PC app. You can choose to Sort your books by Title, Author, Last Read, Note Count, or Recently Added.

You can also choose what type of books and documents you are looking at in this view by choosing the Filter drop-down list. Your options here are Show All, eBooks, eTextbooks, eNewspapers, eMagazines, and My Stuff.

You use the Search box to search the entire contents of your NOOKstudy library. If I type **conscious**, NOOKstudy searches for that word in all titles, notes, and text (see Figure 20.25). If you click the down arrow in the Search box, you can filter the results. For example, if I turn off the checkmark next to Title, Author, ISBN, NOOKstudy does not search those items. Clicking the Matches Found next to the title displays the results in detail where the search term was found in that particular book. Click the specific result to go to that page in the book.

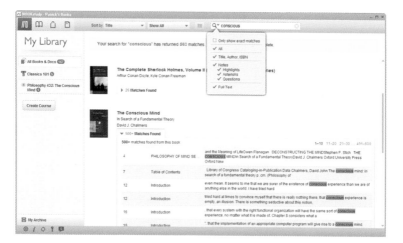

FIGURE 20.25 NOOKstudy searches not only the titles, but the notes you've added and the full text.

You can also choose to see your books in either grid or list view. In grid view, clicking the book cover opens the books for reading. If you have not downloaded the book yet, it will download first. If you hover your mouse over the cover, you can see a plus sign in the bottom-right corner of the cover. Clicking it gives you a variety of options depending on if you have downloaded the ebook or issue, added notes, etc. (see Figure 20.26). If you haven't downloaded the book yet, you are also given an option to download the book.

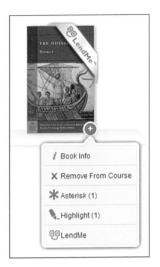

FIGURE 20.26 Click the plus sign on the cover to see available options.

Book Info is straightforward (see Figure 20.27): It takes you to a page with some information about the book along with options to Read Now, Download, Remove the Local Copy, and Archive it (or unarchive it if you have archived it). Click Go Back to go back to My Library. If you have added notes to the ebook, when you click the plus sign, you see a list of links for the type of notes you have made. Clicking one of types of notes opens the ebook with the Notes view open, which is discussed in the section "Using the Highlights, Notes, and Look Up Features of NOOKstudy."

FIGURE 20.27 The Book Info screen.

In list view, clicking the cover image opens the book for reading. The Book Info link takes you to the Book Info page that is the same as what you get from the grid view. The notes links function the same as the notes links in the grid view.

> NOTE: For subscription content, instead of Book Info, you see Subscription Info. That screen let's you download, archive, and remove specific issues.

Reading Your Books in NOOKstudy

Clicking the Now Reading button or a book cover takes you to the reading view (see Figure 20.28). Although initial impressions may be that this functions the same as the reading view in the NOOK app for PC, that impression will quickly disappear when you see the variety of options you have available.

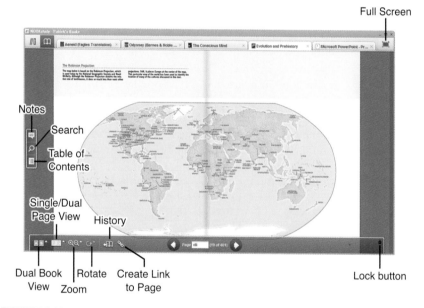

FIGURE 20.28   The Reading Screen in NOOKstudy.

First and foremost, you can have multiple books open at once and navigate between them by clicking the tabs. Beyond that you have a host of buttons and options to explore, so dive into those features:

Dual Book View

You can look at books side by side to compare. Say you wanted to compare the Latin and English versions of *The Aeneid*. Easy.

1. Open one of the books, and then click the Dual Book button. The Dual Book View screen appears (see Figure 20.29).

FIGURE 20.29   Select the other book to read in dual book view.

2. You can either click From the Same Book to view side-by-side contents of the same book. Or you can click From a Different Book.

3. Assuming the latter in the previous step, you can scroll through your books until you find the one you want to open or use the search field to narrow that list. Click the book you want to open side by side.

> NOTE: The second book you want to open cannot already be open. If it is, close it first.

4. The second book opens and you get two reading screens, both with the same options (see Figure 20.30). The book that you are *in* (that is, the one where if you press the arrow key to turn the page, the page turns) has a large green arrow in the upper-left corner of that book's reading screen.

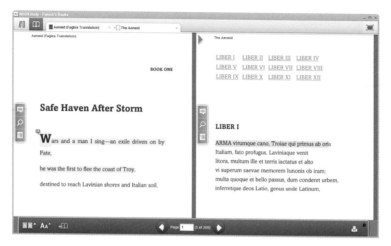

FIGURE 20.30   Reading two books side by side.

When you finish looking at the books in Dual Book view, click the Dual Book View button. You can close the left one, the right one, or split into single books. This last option changes the screen to appear as if you had opened each book individually into tabs.

Font

Click the Font button to adjust the font and font size for the book.

Page Turning

You can click the page right or page left buttons to turn the page (or use the arrow keys on your keyboard). Or you can enter the page number text box and type a specific page number.

Lock

The tiny Padlock icon on the far bottom right enables visibility of the bottom pane. Clicking it locks it so that it is always visible. Unlocking it changes the behavior so that the bottom pane drops out of view when you move the mouse cursor. To see the bottom pane, just drop the mouse cursor down.

My Notes View

Click this to open a screen on the left side of the reading screen to see the notes for this ebook (see Figure 20.31). The notes and highlights are presented in tabular format. The Type column indicates the type of note (Highlight, Asterisk, or Question). The Page column provides the page number of the note.

FIGURE 20.31 Viewing notes while in the Reading screen.

NOTE: For more about entering notes and highlights and the associated options, **see** "Using the Highlights, Notes, and Look Up Features of NOOKstudy."

TIP: For the Type, Page, Added, and Tag columns, if you click the column header, you can sort the table based on that column's information.

The Note column provides the text of the note. The Date Added column provides the date the note was added. The Tag column lists any associated tags you indicated in the note. Clicking the individual notes displays the note on the page and provides note details.

Clicking Back to Reading hides this notes screen. Click Export to export the notes out to a Word or text document. You can also search for specific content in the notes by entering search criteria.

Full Screen Mode

Click this to open the book to take up the entire screen. Press Esc to close full screen mode.

Find

Use this button to search for a word or phrase in the ebook.

Table of Contents

Clicking this displays a table of contents for quick navigation to specific parts of the ebook (see Figure 20.32).

FIGURE 20.32   Navigating the table of contents while in the Reading screen.

Using the Highlights, Notes, and Look Up Features of NOOKstudy

Adding notes and highlights to ebooks in NOOKstudy is easy, and you have a variety of options. To add a highlight, follow these steps:

1. With the ebook open, select the text you want to highlight with the cursor. A pop-up menu appears (see Figure 20.33).

2. Click Apply Markup. You can choose Highlight, Asterisk, or Question from the menu. Other than using them for three different types of highlighting, the distinction is the icon used:

> Highlight: No icon
>
> Asterisk: Asterisk icon
>
> Question: Question mark icon

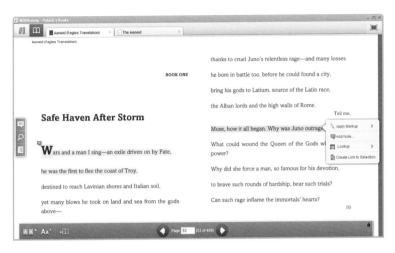

FIGURE 20.33   Text selection tools.

To add a note, follow these steps:

1. With the ebook open, select the text you want to highlight with the cursor. A pop-up menu appears.

2. Click Add Note. The Add Note dialog box appears (see Figure 20.34).

FIGURE 20.34   The Add Note dialog box.

3. Set the Markup Style to Highlight, Asterisk, or Question.

4. Enter the text of your note.

5. Add tags if you want them.

> NOTE: Tags can be useful for identifying notes with a similar type or theme. These can then come in handy if searching notes.

6. Add a hyperlink to outside research or articles. Click Add Link.

7. Click Save.

You can always edit the note by clicking the note in the reading screen.

NOOKstudy also provides some look-up features. Just like creating a note, select the text you want to perform a search on at one of five websites:

- ▶ Dictionary.com

- ▶ Google

- ▶ YouTube

- ▶ Wikipedia

- ▶ Wolfram Alpha

The final option you have after you select text is Create Link to Selection. You can paste the created link into a research paper for reference.

Zooming and Rotating Books

With eTextbooks (versus NOOKbooks), you can rotate and zoom in and out (see Figures 20.35 and 20.36). Click the Rotate and Zoom buttons respectively. The Rotate button basically gives you the option to view the book in landscape or portrait mode.

Using LendMe in NOOKstudy

With NOOKstudy you can use B&N's LendMe feature. You can access the LendMe options, assuming LendMe is available for that NOOKbook, either from the plus sign menu or the Book Info screen. Clicking LendMe in either location opens the LendMe dialog box (see Figure 20.37).

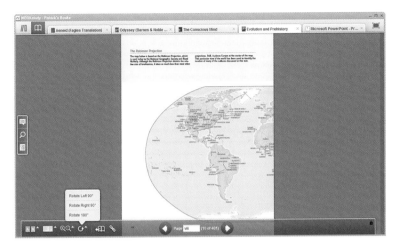

FIGURE 20.35   The Rotation options.

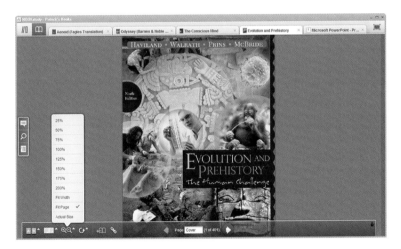

FIGURE 20.36   The Zoom options.

Enter the email address of the person you want to lend the NOOKbook to, enter a personal message if you want, and click Send.

The normal LendMe rules apply.

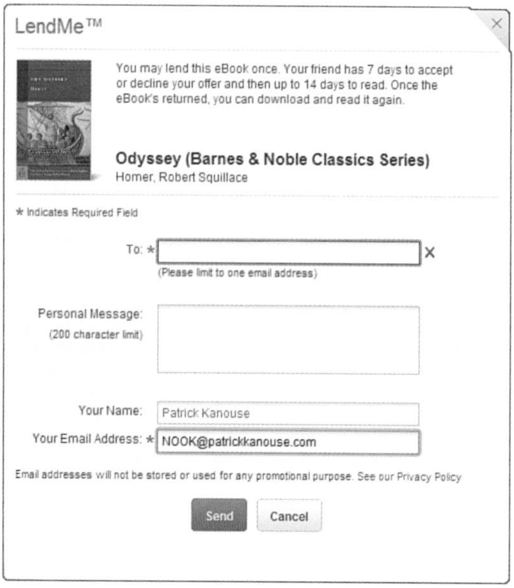

FIGURE 20.37   NOOKstudy's LendMe dialog box.

Using Print to NOOKstudy

Have a PowerPoint or Word document you want to add to your NOOKstudy library? If so, it's easy. When you installed NOOKstudy, it placed a print driver on your computer. So if you are in PowerPoint or another program and you want to add that file to your NOOKstudy library, choose File, Print. In your printer options, choose Print to NOOKstudy (see Figure 20.38). (On the Mac, choose PDF down in the bottom left and click Print to NOOKstudy from there.) Click Print. And the file is automatically placed into your NOOKstudy library.

Shopping with NOOKstudy

You can shop for eTextbooks within NOOKstudy. Click the Shop button. If you know the ISBN, you can enter that or enter keywords. When you click Search now, your browser opens at BN.com with the search results already in place.

Adding Your Own Files to NOOKstudy

If you have a PDF or ePub file you want to add to NOOKstudy click Add File, navigate to the file, and click Open. The file is added to your library and you can manipulate it like any other document.

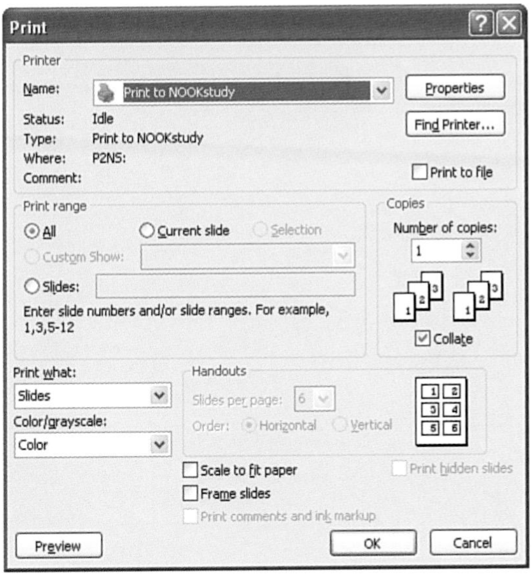

FIGURE 20.38 Printing to NOOKstudy in PowerPoint.

CHAPTER 21

Managing Your ebooks with Calibre

I have a huge library of ebooks. Because I get my ebooks from many different sources, they are spread out all over my hard drive. My ADE books are in one folder, books I've bought from Kobo are in another folder, and so on. All my files on my computer are backed up, so I'm not concerned about losing them, but it sure is easier to manage them when they are all in one location.

A while back, I discovered Calibre, a free application for managing an ebook library. Calibre is incredibly powerful, but it's also easy to use. In this chapter, you learn to use Calibre to manage your library, edit the metadata for your ebooks so they show up correctly on your NOOKcolor and NOOK, get cover art when covers are missing, and sideload books to your NOOKcolor and NOOK quickly and easily.

Configuring Calibre

You can download Calibre from calibre-ebook.com. There's a version for practically every type of computer on the market today. After you install Calibre, you need to specify a location for your Calibre library. When you add books to Calibre, it copies the ebook to your Calibre library. That way, all your ebooks are kept in one location.

To set up your Calibre library, simply launch Calibre, and it starts the Welcome Wizard. In the first step of the wizard, specify where you want Calibre to store your ebooks. You can choose any disk location you want, or you can leave it at the default setting.

Is There Any Advantage to Using a Custom Location for My Calibre Library?

In some situations, yes. For example, if you keep all your ebooks on your Windows Home Server, when you add a new ebook to your Calibre library, you may want Calibre to automatically copy the ebook to Windows Home Server, so you can specify your Calibre library on your Windows Home Server.

It might be better to say that there's no disadvantage to using a custom location for your Calibre library unless the location you specify is a network location you don't always have access to.

In the next step of the Welcome Wizard, select Barnes & Noble from the list of manufacturers and then select Nook from the list of devices. (Don't worry if you have a NOOKcolor because Calibre treats both as a generic Nook.) Calibre uses your choice here for the default conversion settings. In other words, because you are choosing a NOOK as your reading device, Calibre knows it needs to convert ebooks to EPUB format when it sideloads ebooks onto your NOOK.

In the final step of the Welcome Wizard, Calibre displays links for tutorial videos and the Calibre user's guide. The videos are an excellent way to learn all the features of Calibre, but if you just want information you need to manage your library and sideload ebooks onto your NOOKcolor or NOOK, you can skip them for now. (You can also access them at calibre-ebook.com/help.)

Adding Books to Your Calibre Library

When you first start using Calibre, your library is empty. To add books to your library, click the Add Books button on the toolbar. Select the books you want to add, and then click Open.

> TIP: You can select multiple ebooks before you click Open; all the ebooks you select are added to your Calibre library.

> **Can I Add NOOKbooks I've Purchased for My NOOKcolor or NOOK to My Calibre Library?**
>
> Absolutely! Although Calibre does not allow you to read books protected by DRM, you can manage protected books with Calibre. That includes managing the book's metadata and adding a cover graphic.

When adding ebooks protected with DRM, you need to make sure that they are in either eReader or EPUB format. However, unprotected ebooks can be in any format. When you sideload unprotected ebooks to your NOOKcolor or NOOK, Calibre automatically converts them into the correct format.

> NOTE: If you use a NOOKcolor, it cannot read eReader (PDB) formatted ebooks. Those books need to be converted to EPUB format, which you *cannot* do if they are secure eReader files.

Editing Metadata

As you add books to your library (see Figure 21.1), you might notice that some books have missing or incorrect metadata. For example, the book's title might not be formatted correctly or the listing in Calibre might be missing the author's name. You can edit the information Calibre uses for the book's listing by editing the book's metadata. You'll almost certainly want to be sure that your metadata is correct for all your ebooks because your NOOKcolor and NOOK also uses metadata to display information about the ebooks.

FIGURE 21.1   The Calibre main window.

To edit metadata for an ebook, first select the ebook in Calibre, and then click Edit Metadata on the toolbar. Calibre displays the current metadata for the book you selected (see Figure 21.2). At this point, you can manually change the metadata or let Calibre retrieve metadata from either Google or ISBNdb.com.

To let Calibre automatically retrieve metadata for your ebook, click the Fetch Metadata from the Server button at the bottom of the Edit Meta Information dialog. Calibre uses the metadata shown in the dialog box to attempt a lookup on the book. If the metadata that already exists isn't sufficient, Calibre lets you know.

> TIP: If Calibre cannot retrieve metadata for a particular book, enter the ISBN number (you can usually get it from BN.com or Amazon) for the book and try again. I've never experienced a problem when the ISBN number was entered first.

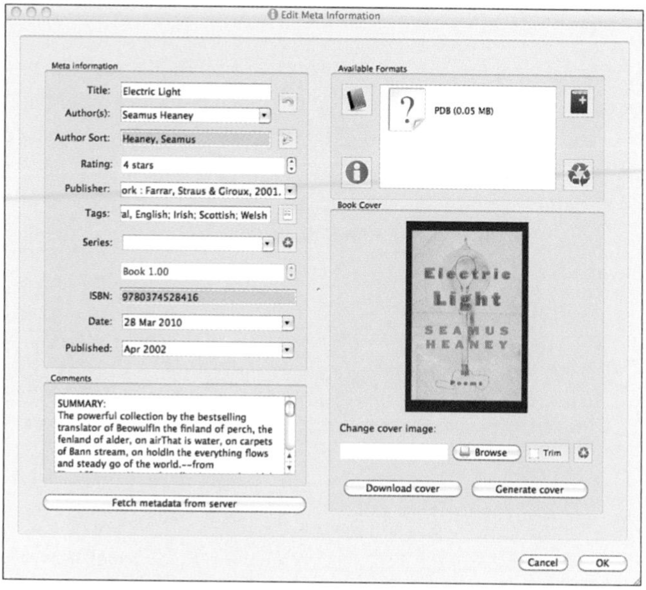

FIGURE 21.2   The Calibre Metadata Information screen.

By default, Calibre searches only Google for metadata. In most cases, Google has the metadata you need, but if it doesn't, you can also use ISBNdb.com as mentioned previously. To use ISBNdb.com, you need to sign up for a free account at ISBNdb.com/account. After you create your account, you must generate an access key that you can use in Calibre to authorize it to use ISBNdb.com. Here's how you do that:

1. Create an account at ISBNdb.com/account.

2. After you create your account, click Developer Area in the upper-left corner of the page.

3. Click the Manage Access Keys link.

4. Click Generate a New Key.

5. Enter a comment for your key. I entered "Calibre" so I know that's what this key is for.

6. Leave the Daily Use Limit blank, which sets the limit to unlimited.

7. Click the Generate New Key button to generate your key.

After you generate your key, copy it to your Clipboard. Switch over to Calibre and click the Fetch Metadata from the Server button. Enter your access key in the textbox,

and click Fetch. From then on, Calibre will look up metadata in both Google and
ISBNdb.com.

> NOTE: If it seems like too much work to create an ISBNdb.com account and
> generate a key, don't worry about it. Google almost always has complete meta-
> data for most books.

> TIP: If you need to edit the title or author of an ebook, you can double-click the
> title or author name (and other metadata as well) in the Calibre library, type the
> new information, and press Enter.

Adding Covers

Because books you sideload onto your NOOK are kept in My Documents, you can't
browse them by cover. However, you can see the cover on the touchscreen while
you're reading the book—assuming a cover image is available. Sideloaded books on
your NOOKcolor, however, do show the cover when you view them in the Library.

> NOTE: Recall that sideloaded books and content are ebooks and documents
> you have from sources other than B&N (for example, Fictionwise, Project
> Gutenberg, and so on).

Calibre can download covers for your ebooks automatically. You can even add covers
to ebooks protected with DRM from the B&N NOOKstore or from another ebook
store.

The easiest way to flip through cover images for your ebooks is to enable browsing
by covers in Calibre. Click the Browse by Covers button shown in Figure 21.3 to
enable this feature. You can then click either side of the current cover to flip to
another cover or use the arrow keys on your keyboard to flip through your covers. To
return to full library view, click the Browse by Covers button again.

> TIP: You can also browse ebooks by tags using the Browse by Tags button
> immediately to the right of the Browse by Covers button. Tags are part of the
> metadata for an ebook, so you can edit how an ebook is tagged by editing the
> metadata.

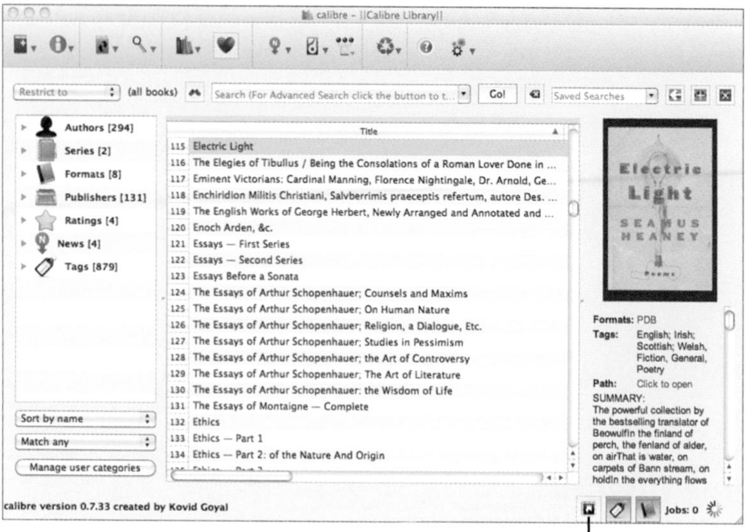

Browse by Covers

FIGURE 21.3 The Browse by Covers button makes locating missing covers much quicker.

To add (or replace) the cover image for an ebook, select the ebook and then click Edit Metadata. Click the Download Cover button at the bottom of the dialog box to add a cover image.

You can add cover images to multiple books by selecting more than one book in the Calibre library. On Windows, you can press Ctrl+A to select all your books. If you want to select multiple books that are listed contiguously, click the first book and then hold the Shift key, and click the last book. If you want to select multiple books that are not contiguous, click the first book; then hold the Ctrl key as you select the other books.

After you select all the books to which you'd like to add covers, click the down arrow to the right of the Edit Meta Information button, and select Download Only Covers from the menu. Calibre automatically downloads covers for all the books you selected.

Sideloading Books with Calibre

Sideloading books onto your NOOKcolor or NOOK with Calibre is fast and easy. After you connect your NOOK to your computer, Calibre detects it and displays an icon for it in the area directly under the toolbar. If you have a microSD card installed in your NOOKcolor or NOOK, Calibre displays an icon for both your NOOKcolor and the microSD card.

NOTE: When you connect your NOOKcolor or NOOK to a Windows computer, Windows assigns drive letters to your NOOKcolor and to the microSD card if one is installed. Calibre assumes that the first drive letter assigned to your NOOKcolor is its main memory and the second drive letter is the microSD card. However, sometimes Windows assigns the first drive letter to the microSD card; when it does that, Calibre incorrectly identifies your NOOKcolor's main memory and the memory card.

To resolve this problem, you need to explicitly assign drive letters to your NOOKcolor and its microSD card inside of Windows. For information on how to change drive letters in Windows, see www.online-tech-tips.com/computer-tips/how-to-change-the-drive-letter-in-windows-xp-for-an-external-usb-stick-or-hard-drive/.

TIP: Sometimes Calibre, if it is already open when you plug in your NOOKcolor, won't recognize the NOOKcolor as being installed. Close Calibre and restart it.

NOTE: At this point in time, Calibre treats the NOOKcolor and NOOK as the same device, so the image for your NOOKcolor in Calibre is the NOOK. This is cosmetic only, and Calibre correctly interacts with the NOOKcolor or NOOK.

To sideload one or more books onto your NOOKcolor, make sure your NOOK is connected to your computer. Select the books from your library, and click Send to Device on the toolbar. Calibre automatically converts any ebooks that are not already in a format compatible with your NOOKcolor and then transfers them to your NOOK. By default, Calibre transfers ebooks to your NOOKcolor's main memory, but you can choose to transfer them to the microSD card if you want. Simply click the down arrow next to the Send to Device button, and select Send to Storage Card A from the menu.

TIP: You can also select Set Default Send to Device Action and select Send to Storage Card A. From then on, clicking the Send to Device button automatically sideloads any selected ebooks to your NOOK's microSD card.

Depending on what action is necessary, Calibre might take a while to sideload books. Calibre indicates that it's working and how many jobs it's currently processing using the progress indicator in the lower-right corner of the main window. If you click the progress indicator, you can see details on what Calibre is doing.

If I Update Some Metadata Information for an ebook That's Already Sideloaded onto My NOOKcolor and Sideload It onto My NOOKcolor Again, Will It Overwrite the Existing Copy on My NOOKcolor?

Yes. Both Calibre and your computer use the filename of an ebook to identify it as a unique ebook. If you change metadata information (such as the title, author, and so on) of an ebook that is already on your NOOKcolor, sideloading it onto your NOOKcolor will overwrite the existing copy. Essentially, you're just updating the metadata of the copy on your NOOKcolor.

There is one exception to this. If you sideload an ebook to your NOOKcolor's main memory and the same ebook is already on its microSD card, you will have a duplicate copy of the book and it will show up twice in your library.

Can I Read My ebooks Using Calibre?

You can read an ebook on your computer using Calibre as long as the ebook isn't protected with DRM. To read an ebook with Calibre, select the ebook, and click the View button on the toolbar.

Subscribing to News Content in Calibre

Calibre also has an excellent news subscription feature that makes it easy to subscribe to various news feeds that you can then sync to your NOOKcolor. To access this feature, click the Fetch News button, select a news feed, and set the subscription options that determine how often the feed is downloaded. Keep in mind that for feeds to download, Calibre must be running.

TIP: I particularly like this feature (subscribing to news content in Calibre). I have print subscriptions to *The London Review of Books* and *The New York Review of Books*, which I paid for long before I got my NOOKcolor. Although I could subscribe again to *The New York Review of Books* at BN.com, I would be paying for two subscriptions...so I use Calibre to fetch that news (using my account information from *The New York Review of Books* website). When my print subscription runs out, I will switch to the BN.com subscription...but for now, I only pay for one.

Calibre uses a collection of properties known as a "recipe" to subscribe to a particular news feed. If you don't see a news feed that you're interested in, you can find others and submit requests for new recipes by browsing to http://bugs.calibre-ebook.com/wiki/UserRecipes.

Converting ebooks in Calibre

Calibre can convert a wide variety of formats. Although your NOOKcolor can read Word, PDF, HTML, and text documents, these are not treated as "real" ebooks by the NOOKcolor. What that means is that you cannot add notes or highlights, bookmark pages, and so on. So although you can read those formats, you may want to convert them to the EPUB format so that they get the full ebook treatment.

Calibre's conversion options are rich, and I won't go into the details here. The standard default PDF to EPUB, HTML to EPUB, and such work quite well. To convert a document, follow these steps:

1. Add the document to your Calibre library if you haven't already.

2. Select the book you want to convert.

3. Click the Convert Books button.

4. Click OK.

If you want more details about the vast number of options for conversion, go to calibre-ebook.com/user_manual/conversion.html.

> NOTE: PDFs are the most problematic documents to convert because of the way they are created. So if the results are less than satisfactory, you might tweak some of the settings to see if you can get better results.

In this chapter, you've seen how powerful Calibre is for managing your ebook library. You've also seen how easily you can edit the metadata for your ebooks, add missing covers to your ebooks, and sideload ebooks onto your NOOK.

In Chapter 19's "Accessing Your Calibre Library with Trook," you see how to take this a step further so that you can sideload ebooks onto your NOOKcolor or NOOK from anywhere with Wi-Fi or a Fast & Free Wireless connection by accessing Calibre remotely.

CHAPTER 22

Using My NOOK Library

All your B&N content is saved on the bn.com website in what B&N calls My NOOK Library. Using My NOOK Library, you can browse through your B&N content, lend and borrow books with LendMe, move items to and from your archive, and delete items from your B&N library.

Accessing My NOOK Library

You can access My NOOK Library by browsing to http://my.barnesandnoble.com/ ebooks/ebookslibrary.html. Two views are available in My NOOK Library: Full view (the default) and Reduced view. To switch between the two views, click one of the View buttons, as shown in Figure 22.1—the one that is colored green is the one not in use.

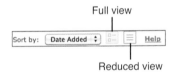

FIGURE 22.1   The View buttons enable you to choose between Full and Reduced view.

> NOTE: The only difference between Full and Reduced view is that covers display in Full view and are not in Reduced view.

By default, all items in your B&N online library that have not been archived are displayed in My NOOK Library. You can filter the view by clicking Books, Sample Books, Magazines, Newspapers, or eTextbooks on the left side of the page. You can also view any items that have been archived by clicking the Archive link.

To sort the items displayed in My NOOK Library, click the Sort By drop-down (refer to Figure 22.1) and select from one of the sorting options.

Archiving, Deleting, and Lending Books in My NOOK Library

You can easily delete or archive content in My NOOK Library. Archiving an item moves it to your archive, and you can move items from the archive back to the library by unarchiving them. On the other hand, deleted items are permanently removed from your library.

> CAUTION: Be careful about deleting items. If you delete an item from your library, it will be removed from your NOOKcolor and all other devices where you access your B&N content. The only way to get it back is to buy it again. Archiving is the safe bet.

If you have downloaded sample NOOKbooks onto your NOOKcolor or NOOK and you want to remove them, you must use My NOOK Library to do that. Locate the sample and click Delete to remove them from your library. After you removed them from your library, your NOOKcolor updates. (Or you can force it to update by tapping Library from the Quick Nav Bar and then tapping the Sync button.) On your NOOK, open My B&N Library, and tap Check for New B&N Content to update your library.

To archive an item, click the Move to Archive link in My NOOK Library. The item is moved to your archive on your NOOKcolor or NOOK as well. To move the item back to your library, click Archive on the left side of My NOOK Library; then click the Move to Library link for the item you want to move back to your library.

> TIP: Think of My NOOK Library as another way that you can view your NOOKbook library on your NOOKcolor or NOOK. When you interact with content via My NOOK Library, you also impact the content on your NOOKcolor, NOOK, NOOK apps, and NOOKstudy.

Books that can be lent to friends using the LendMe feature are marked as such in My NOOK Library. To lend a book to a friend, click the LendMe logo and enter your friend's email address (see Figure 22.2). While the book is on loan, its cover displays a Lent badge notifying you that it cannot currently be read by you.

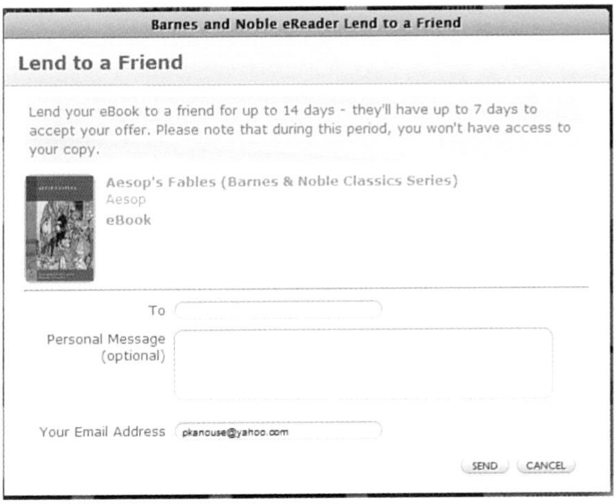

FIGURE 22.2   Lending a book from My NOOK Library.

Downloading Content from My NOOK Library

You can download NOOKbooks and subscription content from My NOOK Library for reading on your computer or for local archival purposes. You can download items to your computer and then sideload them onto your NOOKcolor or NOOK later. However, keep in mind that if you do this, the item will not show up in My B&N Library on your NOOK. Instead, it will show up in My Documents just like all other sideloaded content.

> NOTE: The only difference between Full and Reduced view is that covers display in Full view and are not in Reduced view.

When you download ebooks to your computer, you can then add them to your Calibre library. This is a convenient way to ensure that you have a backup of your B&N content in case you accidentally delete an item.

Can I Send an Item to My NOOKcolor or NOOK from My NOOK Library?

There isn't a way that you can manually send an item to your NOOKcolor or NOOK from My NOOK Library. However, because My NOOK Library is actually just another way to view your B&N online library, you should always see the same content on your NOOKcolor, NOOK, NOOK apps, or NOOKstudy.

CHAPTER 23

Using PubIt to Sell Your ebooks

PubIt is a B&N feature that enables you to submit your ebook for sale through the B&N website. PubIt books are NOOKbooks. When people visit BN.com and browse or search for ebooks, yours will be available. If they buy it, it downloads, can be lent, and can use the social features like any other NOOKbook.

Setting Up PubIt

Setting up and using PubIt is easy:

1. Go to http://pubit.barnesandnoble.com/pubit_app/bn?t=pi_reg_home.

2. Enter in your BN.com username and password and click Sign In or create one from here. The Account Setup screen appears.

3. For PubIt, B&N needs to set up a PubIt account though it uses your BN.com information. Update any information here.

4. Because you are publishing your work, provide a name and website if you want. Note: If you leave this blank, your first and last name will be used as the publisher. Click Continue. The Terms and Conditions page appears.

Important Information about PubIt Terms and Conditions

Normally you might just blindly click I Agree or Accept when you see the kind of legalese included in the PubIt Terms and Conditions, but it is important that you understand something about PubIt before you agree to this.

B&N can update the pricing and payment terms whenever it wants. At the time of this writing, you, the publisher, can set a price for your content anywhere from $.99 to $199.99. For books priced $2.99 to $9.99, the publisher receives a 65% royalty. For books priced from $.99 to $2.98 or from $10.00 to $199.99, the publisher receives 40%.

B&N also requires that the publisher comply with the Content Policy. So if B&N deems your content offensive, harmful, legally obscene, and so on, it can choose not to sell your content. It then provides some specific examples but certainly does not cover all areas.

You cannot include the following in the Product Data:

▶ Hyperlinks of any kind, including email addresses.

▶ Request for action (for example, "If you like this book, please write me a review.").

▶ Advertisements or promotional material (including author events, seminars, and so forth).

▶ Contact information for the author or publisher.

B&N will make your product available in the Read In and LendMe programs. Additionally, 5% of the book's content will be provided as a sample for people to download to their NOOKColor, and such, to try before they buy.

A whole lot of other information is in this agreement (covering such things as withdrawing a book from the Publt program, book rejection and reformatting, and so on), so I highly recommend reading through all the legalese before agreeing. This is your content, so treat this document as what it is: a contract.

5. If you agree with these terms, click I agree and Continue. The Payment Information screen appears.

6. Enter Bank Account, Tax Information, and Credit Card Information and click Submit. A page appears indicating that your account is being set up.

Putting Content into Publt

Now that your account is set up, load up your first title:

1. Click Add a Title (see Figure 23.1) and enter the required fields (see Figure 23.2).

2. To upload your ebook click Browse, navigate to it, click it. Click Upload & Preview. If the file you chose is not an EPUB file, B&N converts it to an EPUB file. Either way, you then see a virtual Nook with your text in it. Flip through pages to make sure you are satisfied with the appearance. If you need to tweak it, do so on the source file and then re-upload it.

3. Upload a cover in JPEG format between 750 and 2,000 pixels in length.

4. Enter the metadata info. Accurate and thorough metadata about the content, genre, and so on is important when visitors to BN.com search for a title. If your book is a spy eco-thriller taking place on the remote island of Tonga, you want to give potential buyers the best chance to find it.

FIGURE 23.1 The My Titles screen on PubIt.

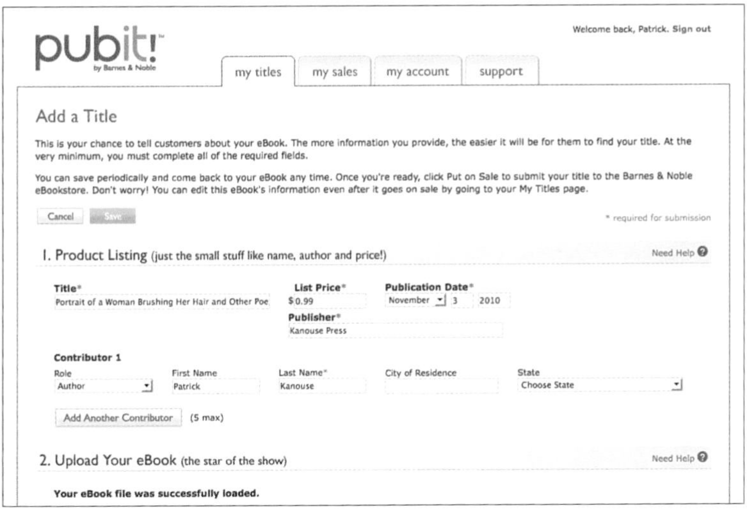

FIGURE 23.2 Setting up a new title to sell.

5. Click the I Confirm box, and then click Put on Sale. A window appears indicating a 24–72 hour timeframe for it be done (see Figure 23.3).

If you later want to adjust any of the information, from My Titles, click Actions, Edit. You can then modify the price, title, metadata, cover, and upload newer versions of the content.

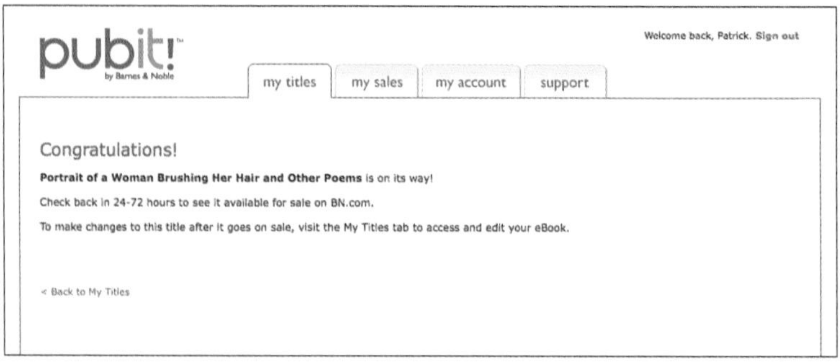

FIGURE 23.3   Soon your ebook will be for sale!

NOTE: The first time you upload a document, it can take 48–72 hours for the item to be on sale. Subsequent updates tend to update much faster, usually within 4–8 hours.

If I Update My Book with a New File, Does It Automatically Get Sent to Customers Who Purchased My ebook?

If you update your ebook after it has gone on sale with a new version of the content, customers who have purchased the original version do *not* automatically receive the new version. However, if they delete the local copy on the device, when they redownload it, they receive the latest version available.

With the other tabs in the PubIt interface, you can watch your sales (including any royalties coming your way), adjust your account information, and get support.

TIP: If your child has a kids book idea, check out B&N Tikatok books at http://www.barnesandnoble.com/u/kids-activities-publish-a-childrens-book/379002382. Here, kids can create their own books that can be made into hardcover, softcover, or PDF.

Understanding ebook Formats

An Overview of ebook Formats

You can use the following types of ebooks on your NOOKcolor:

- ▶ EPUB (including Adobe Digital Editions)
- ▶ PDF

> NOTE: That's right. If you purchased secure eReader (PDB) files from Fictionwise or eReader.com, your NOOKcolor will not read those files. It is rumored that a future NOOKextra app will enable you to read PDB files from Fictionwise or eReader.com.

You can use the following types of ebooks on your NOOK:

- ▶ EPUB (including Adobe Digital Editions)
- ▶ eReader (PDB) from B&N and non-DRM eReader from third parties

Can I Read Word Documents or TXT Files on My NOOKcolor or NOOK?

If you want to read Word documents or TXT files on your NOOKcolor and treat them as ebooks versus Word documents, you need to first convert them into EPUB files.

Calibre can convert TXT files to the EPUB format for your NOOKcolor. If you want to read a Word document, it's best to save the file as a PDF file. (Recent versions of Word provide this functionality.) If you cannot save the Word document as a PDF, first save it as an HTML file, and then use Calibre to convert it for your NOOKcolor.

For more information on using Calibre to convert ebooks, **see** Chapter 21, "Managing Your ebooks with Calibre."

EPUB Format

EPUB (electronic publication) is an open-source format for ebooks. That means the format isn't owned by any single entity, making it an ideal format for electronic books. EPUB ebooks have a file extension of `.epub`, but EPUB files are actually Zip files (a compressed collection of files) that contain content files for the book along with other supporting files that specify the formatting.

> NOTE: The EPUB format was created to replace the Open eBook format, a format that was widely used in the first ebook readers.

EPUB ebooks are actually just HTML files—just like the files used for web pages. The same technologies used in displaying web pages are used to display EPUB ebooks. If you rename an EPUB book and give it a `.zip` file extension, you can open the file and see all the files contained in the EPUB archive.

EPUB ebooks can be protected with *digital rights management* (*DRM*), which is designed to prevent unauthorized users from accessing digital content such as ebooks. When you purchase a book on your NOOKcolor or from bn.com, that content is tied to your bn.com account using DRM. B&N uses its own DRM mechanism for books purchased from B&N, but your NOOKcolor also supports Adobe Digital Editions DRM.

eReader Format

ebooks in the eReader format have a `.pdb` file extension. The eReader format was originally used for reading books on Palm PDAs. However, other ebook readers adopted the format as well.

> NOTE: The Stanza application for the iPhone, iPad, and iPod touch uses the eReader format.

The eReader format enables DRM using the purchaser's name and credit card number. Your NOOKcolor can read DRM eReader files—but only those that you purchase from B&N, Fictionwise.com, or eReader.com. If you want to read eReader files from third parties, you need to ensure that they do not contain DRM.

> TIP: Both Fictionwise.com and eReader.com are B&N companies, so the DRM they use for eReader ebooks is compatible with your NOOK.

For more information on sideloading content on your NOOKcolor, **see** "Sideloading Books with Calibre" in Chapter 21.

Using Adobe Digital Editions

Adobe Digital Editions (ADE) is software that manages ebooks that use ADE DRM. Your NOOKcolor and NOOK are compatible with ADE DRM and can be configured as an authorized device in the ADE software.

> NOTE: You can download ADE software free from adobe.com/products/digitaleditions/.

To authorize your NOOKcolor or NOOK for ADE DRM, connect your NOOKcolor or NOOK to your computer while ADE is running. When you do, you see a dialog box informing you that your NOOKcolor or NOOK was detected and needs to be authorized (see Figure A.1). Click the Authorize Device button to authorize your NOOKcolor or NOOK.

FIGURE A.1   Authorize your NOOKcolor to use ADE ebooks.

> NOTE: Sometimes I have to connect the NOOKcolor or NOOK first before starting ADE.

After your NOOK is authorized, ADE displays an icon for your NOOKcolor or
NOOK in the bookshelf on the left side of the main window. If you click that icon,
you see all the content on your NOOKcolor that is compatible with ADE. Any content in EPUB or PDF format is available for reading directly in ADE.

NOTE: ADE does not yet distinguish between the NOOKcolor or NOOK. It simply
refers to it as NOOK.

TIP: I have a few ADE books I have purchased that I could not read on my
iPhone or iPad because apps such as Stanza, eReader, and others did not support ADE books. However, the Bluefire eReader app does support ADE, so
check it out.

Sources for ebooks Other than B&N

EPUB Sources

You can buy EPUB books or download free EPUB books that you can read on your NOOKcolor from numerous places. Here are just a few:

▶ Gutenberg.org

▶ Fictionwise (www.fictionwise.com)

▶ Feedbooks.com

▶ eBooks.com

▶ Smashwords (www.smashwords.com)

▶ BooksOnBoard (www.booksonboard.com)

▶ Kobo Books (www.kobobooks.com)

▶ Diesel eBook Store (www.diesel-ebooks.com)

▶ Powells.com

▶ Baen (www.baen.com)

Some of these sites offer ebooks in several formats, so be sure you select carefully and get the EPUB version.

Perhaps one of the greatest benefits to having an ebook reader that supports the EPUB format is that you can read ebooks from many public libraries. Check with your local library to see if it offers the capability of checking out EPUB ebooks. If it doesn't, you might still be able to get a library card from a nearby library. Check out the Overdrive website at www.overdrive.com. You can enter your ZIP code and it will give you a list of libraries in your area that support Overdrive for checking out EPUB books.

eReader Sources for Your NOOK

Following are a few sources for free, non-DRM eReader ebooks:

▶ Manybooks.net

▶ eReader.com

▶ Fictionwise.com

> TIP: Inkmesh.com and Ebooks.addall.com are ebook price comparison sites. Enter a title or author and see what Amazon, B&N, Fictionwise, Kobo, and others are charging for that ebook.

Libraries and eBooks

Many libraries offer selections of ebooks that you can read on your NOOKcolor or NOOK. A popular ebook lending service for libraries is Overdrive. If you are curious if your library offers ebook lending services, go to http://www.overdrive.com/ and enter your ZIP code. A list of libraries appears. Select the link to your library to see what they have available.

To check out library ebooks, you first need to have a valid library card from that particular lending library. The specifics can be found at that library. Using the library's website, select the title you want. Most offerings from libraries are either PDF or EPUB, both of which you can read on your NOOKcolor or NOOK.

Download the file as instructed by the library. Most of the time, you need to open the file using Adobe Digital Editions (see Appendix A's section, "Using Adobe Digital Editions," for information about using that software). You can then sideload the book to your NOOKcolor or NOOK.

> NOTE: Libraries have their own policies, guidelines, and requirements, so be sure to check all the available information on the library's website to understand the options related to ebook lending. You can also contact the library directly and speak to a librarian to get answers.

Sideloading Adobe Digital Editions

To sideload ADE content to your NOOKcolor or NOOK (referenced as NOOKcolor from here on), connect your NOOKcolor to your computer, and launch ADE if it's not already running. Drag the ebook from your ADE library to the NOOK icon in the bookshelf.

ADE supports both protected PDF files and protected EPUB files.

> TIP: One of the most popular ebook stores for ADE books is ebooks.com.

When ADE books are copied to your NOOKcolor, ADE creates a folder called Digital Editions, and the books are copied to this folder. Unlike protected books from eReader.com and Fictionwise, ADE ebooks don't require you to enter any information to open them. As long as your NOOKcolor is an authorized device, you can open ADE EPUB books.

> TIP: When you sideload content onto your NOOK, you find the items in My Documents. You need to tap Check for New Content before the new item is visible in My Documents.

> NOTE: ADE does not yet distinguish between the NOOKcolor or NOOK. It simply refers to it as NOOK.

You don't need to use ADE to sideload ADE EPUB books onto your NOOKcolor. I prefer using Calibre to manage all my ebooks and use it to sideload ADE books onto my NOOKcolor. **See** Chapter 21, "Managing Your ebooks with Calibre," for more information about Calibre.

APPENDIX D

Using Picasa to Create Wallpapers and Screensavers

Creating Wallpaper and Screensaver Images

Before you use a picture as wallpaper or a screensaver on your NOOKcolor or NOOK, you need to resize it to fit the dimensions of the reading screen. For the NOOKcolor, the wallpaper image needs to be at least 600x1024. However, if you want the scrolling wallpaper (where the image shifts slightly as you flip through the home pages), the size needs to be 768x1024.

For the NOOK, wallpaper images need to be 760 pixels high and 600 pixels wide, and screensaver images need to be 800 pixels high and 600 pixels wide. (Wallpaper images are 40 pixels shorter to provide room for the status bar at the top of the page.)

> TIP: I use Google's Picasa (www.picasa.com) to resize images for my NOOKcolor and NOOK. It's a free program and is available for Windows, Macs, and Linux computers.

> TIP: Of course, on the NOOKcolor, you can use the create wallpaper features. **See** Chapter 2, "Customizing and Configuring Your NOOKcolor." So the rest of this appendix focuses on making images for the NOOK.

Many of your pictures are likely in landscape orientation. In other words, they are wider than they are tall. If you want to use a landscape-oriented picture as wallpaper or a screensaver on your NOOK, your best option is to crop the image. When you crop an image, you select part of the image to keep and discard the rest of the image.

Picasa enables you to create custom aspect ratios for use when cropping images. This feature enables you to quickly and easily crop images for use on your NOOK. To set up a custom aspect ratio in Picasa, follow these steps:

1. Locate the image you want to use, and double-click it to open it in the editor.

2. Select the Crop tool on the Basic Fixes tab in the panel on the left.

3. Click the dimension drop-down and select Add Custom Aspect Ratio.

4. In the Add Custom Aspect Ratio dialog, change the dimensions to 600 x 800.

5. Enter NOOK Screensaver in the Name textbox as shown in Figure D.1, and click OK.

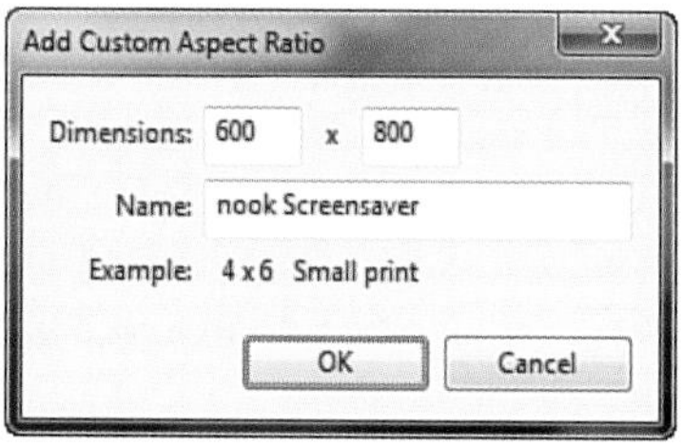

FIGURE D.1   A custom aspect ratio in Google Picasa.

Use the same steps to create a custom aspect ratio for NOOK wallpapers by using dimensions of 760 x 800 and NOOK Wallpaper for the name. After you set up these custom aspect ratios, you can simply select either NOOK Screensaver or NOOK Wallpaper from the dimension drop-down in Picasa to easily crop your image to the appropriate dimensions.

> TIP: When cropping your image, make sure that the cropped portion is taller than it is wide. If the cropped area looks almost square, move your mouse pointer left or right toward the center of the crop area; Picasa flips it to the taller orientation necessary for your NOOK.

Now consider a couple of important things about cropping in Picasa. First, you don't need to worry about ruining an important picture because Picasa performs all editing operations on a copy of the original image. Therefore, when you crop an image in Picasa, the original image remains unchanged.

Second, when you crop an image using one of your custom aspect ratios, Picasa doesn't actually resize the image to the dimensions necessary for your NOOK. Instead, it crops out an area that is the correct aspect ratio for your NOOK. To actually resize the image for your NOOK, you need to export the image. If you're still using the crop tool, apply your crop or click cancel first. After you do that, you can export the image for use on your NOOK by following these steps:

1. Select the image(s) you want to export for use on your NOOK. (If you're viewing a single image in the editor, you need to click Back to Library to select multiple images.)

2. Click the Export button at the bottom of the Picasa interface.

3. Choose a location for your exported images. Remember where you are exporting the images so that you can find them. (I find it easiest to export to my desktop.)

4. Select the Resize To option button, and enter 800 for screensaver images and 760 for wallpaper images.

5. Click the Export button to export the image(s).

When you enter the size in step 4, you are actually specifying the height for the exported image. Picasa automatically adjusts the width to match the aspect ratio. If you cropped the image using the correct custom aspect ratio earlier, the final dimensions of the image will be perfect for your NOOK.

Can I Use Images for My Wallpaper or Screensaver That Won't Properly Size to the Necessary Dimensions for My NOOK?

Yes. Your NOOK isn't picky about the size of the images you use. Your NOOK can resize images automatically to fit on its reading screen. However, if the aspect ratio of the image isn't correct, you see black bars at the top and bottom or left and right of the screen.

Remember that your images take up memory on your NOOK, so you should try to use the smallest file size possible. By resizing your images to the appropriate size, you can substantially reduce the size of the image file. That means less memory used on images and more free memory for your books!

The steps to get your exported images onto your NOOK differ depending on whether you use the images for wallpaper or a screensaver. Therefore, look at each process separately.

APPENDIX E

Can I Read This Here?

With all the devices available for reading NOOKbooks, the following should help you distinguish which formats can be read on each device.

	NOOK color	NOOK	NOOK for PC App	NOOK for iPhone and Android	NOOK for iPad	B&N eReader apps	NOOK study
NOOKbooks	Yes	Yes	Yes	Yes	Yes	Yes	Yes
NOOKbooks for Kids with Read to Me	Yes	No	No	No	No	No	No
eTextbooks	No	No	No	No	No	No	Yes
Newspapers	Yes	Yes	Yes	No	Yes	No	Yes
Magazines	Yes	No	No	No	Yes[1]	No	No
Supports LendMe	Yes	Yes	Yes	Yes	Yes	Yes[2]	Yes

[1] Some magazines are readable—check the magazine's product page at BN.com to verify.

[2] You must first download the file from My NOOK Library at BN.com.

Frequently Asked Questions

Questions Often Asked by NOOKies

Throughout this book, numerous questions are highlighted that I've seen from NOOKies. This appendix includes a list of all these questions and the page within the book where each question is answered.

1. Do I have to register my NOOK? p. 154

2. Does my NOOKcolor's/NOOK's battery drain faster with Wi-Fi connected? p. 5, 156

3. Should I plug my NOOK into a surge suppressor? p. 158

4. Why does my battery indicator sometimes have a question mark on it? p. 158

5. How should I clean my NOOKcolor's/NOOK's touchscreen? p. 8, 160

6. Can I use images for my wallpaper or screensaver that won't properly size to the necessary dimensions for my NOOK? p. 295

7. Should I use a specific file format for images? p. 16, 162

8. Is there any advantage to naming my NOOK? p. 165

9. If I don't like changes made by a firmware update, can I go back to an older version? p. 165

10. Can I use a high-capacity microSD card in my NOOK? p. 171

11. When should I reset my NOOK to factory defaults? p. 169

12. Can I import contacts from my mail application or from another source into my NOOK? p. 169

13. Can I read Word documents or TXT files on my NOOK? p. 173

14. How can I delete sideloaded content because there isn't a menu option for removing it? p. 46, 180

15. Can I sideload books into My B&N Library so that I can browse them by their covers? p. 181

16. Can I remove an item from The Daily? p. 174

17. Can I read books in formats other than eReader and EPUB in the NOOK for PC app? p. 231

18. I want to lend a book to one of my friends. Does my friend have to own a NOOKcolor/NOOK for me to lend her a book? p. 71, 189

19. If my friend finishes a loaned book before 14 days have elapsed, can she return the book to me immediately? p. 189

20. Can I change the green color the NOOK or PC app uses for highlights? p. 230

21. What happens if I lend my friend a book that she already owns? p. 188

22. Is it possible to accidentally purchase a book that I've already purchased from B&N's NOOKstore? p. 134, 204

23. Is it risky to root my NOOKcolor/NOOK? p. 142, 212

24. Is there any advantage to using a custom location for my Calibre library? p. 267

25. Can I add NOOKbooks I've purchased for my NOOKcolor or NOOK to my Calibre library? p. 268

26. If I update some meta information for an ebook that's already sideloaded onto my NOOKcolor and sideload it onto my NOOKcolor again, will it overwrite the existing copy on my NOOKcolor? p. 274

27. Can I read my ebooks using Calibre? p. 274

28. Can I send an item to my NOOKcolor or NOOK from My NOOK Library? p. 279

29. I copied the 1.0 software to my NOOK, but the update never installed. What's wrong? p. 214

30. If I update my PubIt book with a new file, does it automatically get sent to customers who purchased my ebook? p. 284

You're now a NOOK expert. I hope you take all you've learned and use it to get the most out of this extraordinary device. Happy reading!

Index

G–H

OWN OTHER GEEKY DEVICES? CHECK OUT THE MY... BOOK SERIES.

ISBN 13: 9780789747198   ISBN 13: 9780789742858   ISBN 13: 9780789744715   ISBN 13: 9780789747143

Full-Color, Step-by-Step Guides

The "My..." series is a visually rich, task-based series to help you get up and running with your new device and technology and tap into some of the hidden, or less obvious features. The organized, task-based format allows you to quickly and easily find exactly the task you want to accomplish, and then shows you how to achieve it with minimal text and plenty of visual cues.

**Visit quepublishing.com/mybooks to learn more
about the My... book series from Que.**

quepublishing.com